Turkey's Transformation
and American Policy

With contributions by

Morton Abramowitz

Cengiz Çandar

Heath W. Lowry

Alan Makovsky

Ziya Öniş

Philip Robins

M. James Wilkinson

Turkey's Transformation and American Policy

Morton Abramowitz, Editor

A Century Foundation Book

2000 ◆ The Century Foundation Press ◆ New York

The Century Foundation, formerly the Twentieth Century Fund, sponsors and supervises timely analyses of economic policy, foreign affairs, and domestic political issues. Not-for-profit and nonpartisan, it was founded in 1919 and endowed by Edward A. Filene.

LIBRARY OF CONGRESS CATALOGING-IN-PUBLICATION DATA
Turkey's transformation and American Policy / edited by Morton Abramowitz.
    p. cm.
    Includes bibliographical references and index.
    ISBN 0-87078-453-6 (hardcover: alk. paper) — ISBN 0-87078-454-4 (pbk.: alk. paper)
    1. United States—Foreign relations—Turkey. 2. Turkey—Foreign relations—United States. 3. United States—Foreign relations—1989–. 4. Turkey—Politics and government—1980– I. Abramowitz, Morton, 1933–
    E183.8.T8 T69 2000
    327.561073—dc21

00-009976

FOREWORD

Despite all the talk about globalization, most of the time the average American voter is simply not very interested in foreign policy. Our national spending on foreign policy activities, excluding defense, is a crude, but roughly accurate, reflection of that political reality. In fact, even in this era of historic federal budget surpluses, as a nation we are remarkably parsimonious—currently devoting only about 1 percent of the federal budget to this category.

America's inattention to other nations, however, may be more a matter of out of sight out of mind. We have seen how quickly the climate can change, bringing a sudden and intense surge of interest and activity in some part of the world that was all but ignored before something dramatic, usually heartrending or hazardous to U.S. interests, took place. In such circumstances, our attention swiftly becomes riveted on places such as Kuwait, Bosnia, or Somalia, or, with a little prompting from the media, on the ultimate home of one small boy from Castro's Cuba.

What these episodes reveal, of course, is that U.S. interests and concerns, when sparked by events, can be exceptionally broad. Sometimes, they also turn out to be deep enough to justify direct action and involvement in a wide range of states. All this presents a paradox for policymakers and scholars: The research and analysis about other nations that they undertake is seen as merely academic or even esoteric—until public attention focuses on the area they study. Then, and usually only then, their work becomes very important.

With this in mind, The Century Foundation is developing and supporting a series of studies of potential areas of renewed foreign policy activity involving issues and individual nations that, even if they are not currently in the headlines, have the potential to become the center of American attention. Our goal is to provide solid information in a form that will be useful to a broad audience if and when that happens.

This work, in some cases, will take the form of country studies that can enrich the understanding and potentially sharpen the thinking of policy-makers, journalists, and the interested public. We feel confident that Turkey, one of our most reliable cold war allies, deserves a place high on such a list.

In the years after World War II, Turkish troops fought with exceptional valor at America's side in Korea and Turkey proved a firm barrier to potential Soviet expansion during the cold war. While the U.S.-Turkish relationship always has been complicated by the domestic political implications of the long-time enmity between Greece and Turkey, as a key member of NATO Turkey was usually seen as a source of support and strength for U.S. policy, not as a problem. While this remains true today, the absence of the Soviet threat and America's continuing intervention in Iraq, Turkey's neighbor, inevitably have led to a more complex and nuanced set of issues between the two nations.

As we have learned since the end of the cold war and as this group of essays makes clear, what happens in Turkey has implications for American interests far beyond those of Soviet containment. Now, with Turkey at what may well be a crossroads in terms of its economy, its relations with Europe, its Kurdish minority, and its domestic Muslim political movement, the direction of its policies and politics have critical implications for the Middle East, Russia, Central Asia, the Caucasus, the Balkans, and, of course, Greece.

Given the importance and complexity of the relationship between the United States and Turkey, we were fortunate that Morton Abramowitz, former president of the Carnegie Endowment for World Peace and former U.S. ambassador to Turkey, offered to organize and edit a volume on this topic. Ambassador Abramowitz, who, among other things, is currently a senior fellow at The Century Foundation, assembled a diverse group of experts with backgrounds in government, journalism, and scholarship to write the essays in this volume. In his own essays, he explains that while the deeper causes of continuing strain remain unresolved, sustained diplomatic support for Turkey over the past decade has significantly improved bilateral relations. But he also stresses that managing policy in this part of the world remains difficult and uncertain.

These essays, while not meant to be a comprehensive study of all aspects of U.S.-Turkish relations, go well beyond a mere survey or set of highlights. For example, the authors consider, in addition to regular foreign policy analysis, the domestic aspects of questions affecting the foreign policy of both nations. They explore such issues as human rights and democracy that affect the perceptions of American policy-makers, and they also discuss the effect of these internal issues on Turkey's aspirations to join the EU, which would require difficult changes in domestic policy, including greater democratization and a reduced role for the military in Turkish political life. They also point to the possible changes in U.S.-Turkish relations that could ensue from the process of EU accession.

The authors do not speak with one voice, nor even provide a single view of the policy problems that they discuss. But their efforts, taken together, offer an insightful and important explanation of American interests, Turkey's domestic problems, and a likely future agenda of bilateral relations. This volume is a welcome addition to the long list of foreign policy studies, both broad examinations of international relations and specific country studies, published by The Century Foundation.

We thank Ambassador Abramowitz for his leadership in editing this volume and the authors for their valuable contributions to our understanding of this critical relationship for the United States.

RICHARD C. LEONE, *President*
The Century Foundation
July 2000

CONTENTS

Acknowledgments

The authors want to express their gratitude and appreciation to the vast number of friends, colleagues, and associates from the United States, Turkey, Greece, and the United Kingdom who have contributed to the shaping of these essays. We also want to thank The Century Foundation for the latitude and encouragement provided the authors, the outstanding support which enabled the authors to get together periodically in the writing of these essays, and the excellent assistance in preparing the manuscripts for publication. Finally a word of appreciation to the Council on Foreign Relations for helping launch this enterprise.

CHAPTER ONE

INTRODUCTION AND OVERVIEW

MORTON ABRAMOWITZ

This book was conceived and started in one era in Turkey and finished at the beginning of another. The sharpest dividing point was the earthquake of August 1999, which not only produced terrible destruction and loss of life, but also sent tremors through the Turkish psyche and body politic and in a small way (though no less traumatic to the authors) through this book. Indeed, the year 1999 was a watershed for Turkey, producing surprising, even remarkable, developments that are hastening what may turn out with all its twists and turns to be a Turkish revolution. Certainly the country may not be the same again. For the observer it has become harder to sort out what seemed to be relatively permanent in the Turkish political scene and what may be becoming more or less peripheral or rapidly changing. These chapters, which were completed in early May 2000, look a little different from where they started.

A PIVOTAL YEAR

Entering 1999 one saw political stasis in Turkey, weak and ineffective governments, and not much chance of overcoming the deep-seated internal problems that have held back sustained economic growth and

1

the development of civil society and democracy. Turkey, many Turks as well as outsiders believed, would one day "make it"—but no one seemed to know quite how and when. However, by the end of 1999 a unique confluence of events had taken place, opening up new and more optimistic vistas for Turkey. For the moment at least the stars seemed to be in better alignment.

First was the capture in February—with American help—of the most wanted and most hated man in Turkey, the only leader of the PKK (Kurdistan Workers' Party), Abdullah Öcalan. His arrest was a stunning blow to the PKK and its supporters; it created turmoil within the organization and a rapid decline in its military insurgency in southeast Turkey. It was a windfall to the political prospects of Bülent Ecevit, who happened to be heading a caretaker government until the April parliamentary elections; his party doubled the percentage of its vote in those elections and became Turkey's leading party. The Öcalan affair also very publicly revealed Greek government support for the PKK and led to the political demise of Foreign Minister Theodore Pangalos, a publicly vociferous critic of Turkey and its leaders, and his replacement by George Papandreou, who immediately started to pursue a more conciliatory policy.

Second, the April parliamentary elections produced surprising results. The once-leading Islamist party—*Fazilet* (Virtue), formerly *Refah* (Welfare)—suffered serious losses, and there was at least a momentary decline in the consuming political religious issue. A strange but surprisingly workable coalition government including the renascent ultranationalist Nationalist Action Party (MHP) was established, headed by Mr. Ecevit, a figure—like the recently departed President Süleyman Demirel—out of the Turkish past, a longtime social democrat, and once the scourge of the EU. To much surprise the coalition proceeded to pass some important legislation including difficult new taxes to help pay for earthquake reconstruction and improvements in the social security system, led Turkey's effort to be accepted as a candidate for the EU, and worked out a long-sought standby agreement with the IMF, which, if implemented, could significantly change the Turkish economy. A year of success for the coalition also has created a growing sense that with the right leader coalition governments could be made to work in today's Turkey.

Third, the initial handling of the August earthquake raised some basic questions among the public about the general effectiveness and responsiveness of Turkey's government, lending support to the need and the increasing, if inchoate, public demand for internal reform. The earthquake also stimulated a sharp change in the attitudes of the Greek and Turkish peoples toward each other, heralding a new—or at least a much better—day in Greek-Turkish relations, which, along with a change in government in Germany, facilitated Turkey's candidacy for EU membership.

Fourth, President Clinton's visit in November, the third presidential trip in forty years, was an impressive success. It capitalized on and helped deepen the trends toward internal reform that were at work in Turkey, gave a lift to Turkey's EU candidacy, and added to U.S. influence in the country.

Finally, at Helsinki in December all these developments in a sense came together when the EU reversed its 1997 stance and accepted Turkey as a candidate for admission. The government was vindicated in the eyes of its public, and, at least for the moment, much of Turkey was pleased that one day Turks could belong to the European club. But now comes the hard part for Turkish governments.

If Turkey wants to enter the EU, it will be required to consider and ultimately make political and economic changes that many in its ruling elites are reluctant to make at this time—in essence to become more democratic and to reduce the role of the state and the military in Turkish life. Turkey will have to get rid of torture, end restrictions on thought and expression, abolish the death penalty, produce a fairer justice system, greatly diminish inflation, establish greater civilian control, and resolve in some better fashion the problems with its Kurdish citizens. There will be much resistance, most likely on grounds of security and the need for unity and stability in the face of Turkey's heterogeneity and its perceived internal and external enemies. How it all will be achieved politically is not apparent. Indeed, it is not clear that Turkey in the end will want to become part of the EU. Many Turks do not care much about the EU or share its common values, however deep the interest of Turkey's modern sector. Many in this highly nationalistic country will question the loss of sovereignty. Other issues, like Cyprus, can still be a hurdle, either because of Greece's frustration at a continuing failure of negotiations between the two Cypriot sides or because of how the EU handles Cyprus's accession should it come up for resolution before a negotiated settlement is reached.

Turkey's accession to the EU in any event will take a long time, particularly if Turkey's political fragmentation continues and coalition governments prove difficult to cobble together and to maintain. The stability of the present coalition depends largely on the aged Mr. Ecevit; his Party of the Democratic Left (DSP) probably cannot survive without him. Moreover, coalitions can easily stumble. As this book was completed, Prime Minister Ecevit failed to read correctly his people and his parliament. Insisting that President Demirel was key to political stability, in part to prevent his other coalition party leaders from seeking the presidency, Ecevit tried to change the constitution to permit Demirel to serve another term. In a rare show of independence, parliament prevented that. Instead of establishing political stability, he generated some uncertainty about the durability of his coalition government. He also surprisingly produced a presidential candidate whom Turks had never heard of or hardly knew—Ahmet Necdet Sezer—succeeding, however, in putting together a consensus of all parties in the parliament, including *Fazilet,* to support Sezer.

The real question more likely will turn out to be not whether Turkey persists in its quest to join the EU, but rather how long the process of internal reform will take before the EU can accept Turkey. Nor, as Turks feel still to be the case, are EU countries in any hurry to compress the timetable and digest such a huge morsel as Turkey. Some Europeans, perhaps many, do not see Turkey's admission to EU candidacy as anything more than that, fundamentally still questioning whether Turkey belongs in Europe. There is no apparent EU strategy to bring Turkey along toward membership. The Europeans will ultimately have to do much more than simply preach to the Turks.

THIS BOOK

There is much in these chapters that readers—certainly many Turkish ones—will disagree with, some perhaps vigorously. That is probably inevitable because so many issues surrounding Turkey have been contentious and arouse strong passions in Turkey and elsewhere. These are mostly, but not entirely, internal issues, ones that go to the heart of contemporary Turkey: its nature and orientation, its governance, where it belongs in the world, and where it is going—issues easy to pontificate on and less easy to comprehend. Defining these issues concretely and determining the relevant facts surrounding them can be elusive and vexing. Indeed, the subject of each of these chapters is worth at least a book. Trying to deal with big and difficult political issues in chapters of ten to twenty thousand words is itself an invitation to trouble. But Turkey's internal difficulties have a heavy impact on its foreign relations, including whether and when it enters the EU and its capacity to run an effective foreign policy and to exert greater influence abroad. These difficulties also have been a central consideration in American policy toward Turkey over the past decade and continue to be.

If Turks themselves disagree over how to fix their political system, or the dangers of political Islam or the Kurdish issue or other painful domestic problems, it is not surprising that the authors of these chapters have their own views of these issues, particularly on what needs to be done. There are some who argue that the EU accession process and the growing impact of globalization have rendered a good bit of contemporary discussion on Turkey a little stale, that serious political change in Turkey has become inevitable. This judgment may turn out to be correct, but it is premature. Views differ over how domestic political and economic reform will be affected by the EU's acceptance of Turkey as a candidate. Some see it as more hype than ultimate political reality, not the compelling driver of events that many Turks and foreigners hope for. While the individual chapters were collectively chewed over several times, the chapters express the views (and styles) solely of the individual authors.

But what is it then we sought to do in this volume? Most simply, to examine in relatively brief compass American policy toward Turkey over the past decade, the rapidly changing environment surrounding the making of policy, and some important issues in the U.S.-Turkish relationship, including possible future ones. The authors have tried to focus on the broader picture, not the compelling and often incredible daily events. If from this broad approach some useful recommendations for American policy have emerged, so much the better. But to understand policy toward Turkey we also had to take a look at Turkey itself, particularly at those questions about Turkey's internal situation and foreign policy that touch on the principal concerns and thinking of U.S. policymakers. Four of the chapters are devoted to the Turkish scene and Turkish attitudes toward the United States, and three directly to American policy. We have not tried to be comprehensive; indeed, we made somewhat arbitrary exclusions of subjects that might well have merited chapters of their own. Even so, we have not been able to remove some duplication. All the contributors had their own approach to much common material. Each chapter stands on its own.

DOMESTIC PROBLEMS AND FOREIGN POLICY

To the extent Americans debate Turkey on what are normally considered foreign policy issues, it is mostly over Greek-Turkish problems, and since 1991 over the American effort with its allies to get rid of or at least contain Saddam Hussein as well as to keep the Iraqi Kurds out of Saddam's control. For the United States, Iraq is a major foreign policy headache with domestic political overtones. For Turkey it is an enormously difficult domestic issue with important foreign policy overtones. Turkish governments have feared since the Gulf War's end that Iraq will disintegrate, and that will lead to the creation of an independent Kurdish entity in northern Iraq, seriously enhancing their problems with their own Kurdish population. While they do not particularly like Saddam Hussein, they see him as the best barrier to chaos in Iraq. That is why they do not support Iraqi opposition groups trying to get rid of Saddam. But they cannot simply dismiss their differences with the United States over Saddam and Iraq, given the importance to Turkey of political and military ties to the United States. The United States looks at Saddam's Iraq and what might happen to the Iraqi Kurds also with concern for the potential impact on Turkey's management of its own Kurdish problems.

But the biggest concerns in the United States—and in the EU—about Turkey have been frequently over what is happening inside the country, how the United States should evaluate it and respond. The U.S. debate on Turkey—such as it is—has been most vocal over Turkish human rights abuses and whether and how the American government should try to influence the Turkish government to prevent or to limit them. For the American policymaker the problem is to relate concern for Turkey's internal difficulties and a host of other policy considerations to U.S. needs and interests and come up with an appropriate balance. Some concerned Americans disagree on how Washington has balanced the considerations, tending to think it has been "soft" on the Kurdish problem and human rights abuses. Other Americans believe the U.S. government has been insufficiently concerned about Turkish domestic stability, the benefits to the United States from enhancing Turkey's strategic position, and expanding bilateral cooperation. Much, of course, depends on what you put in the equation. For example, since the beginning of the 1990s Washington has given great diplomatic support to Turkey in its quest to become a candidate for EU membership. This resulted in part from the government's belief that the EU accession effort would both anchor Turkey's position in the West and serve as a major catalyst to domestic reform, including ending human rights abuses, which Turkish governments, however well intentioned, most likely could not do politically on their own.

THE INTERNAL FACTOR

The next three chapters examine three interrelated, critical domestic questions that Turkey must better deal with to enter the EU, to enhance internal stability and achieve a better life for all its citizens, and to expand its influence across the wide swath of the still turbulent world it touches on:

♦ Can the Turkish political system produce effective, increasingly democratic governments and maintain stability?

♦ Can Turkey put an end to the PKK insurgency once and for all, diminish the hostility of many of its Kurdish citizens, and better unite its population?

♦ Can Turkey overcome its continuing economic difficulties—including its chronic high inflation—and provide sustained high rates of growth?

Turkey presents a complex kaleidoscope of First and Third World, of impressive growth and continuing poverty, of democracy and authoritarianism, of enormous potential but uneven economic performance and deep and increasing disparities of income—one-third of the population has no plumbing and one-quarter no healthy drinking water. It is a multiethnic country but always has had difficulty integrating its largest ethnic minority, the Kurds. The communications revolution has taken hold and is shaking up the country and making Turkey a livelier place. At the same time a significant portion of the population has less than four years of schooling. It is sometimes difficult to determine whether the glass is half full or half empty. Still, fueled by the EU candidacy, optimism has been growing in Turkey and outside that somehow the country will deal with its domestic problems and soon will grow more rapidly.

Whatever their optimism about the future, Turks are quick to point out the difficulties in today's political environment: the electoral decline of both the center-left and center-right political parties and the political fragmentation that inevitably leads to weird political bedfellows and weak coalition governments, such as in 1996 and 1997, when the secularist party of Tansu Çiller was wedded to the Islamist *Refah* Party of Necmettin Erbakan, with ensuing difficulties in developing and carrying out government programs and what seemed to be two, or at least one and a half, foreign policies; the almost absolute power of political party leaders, which reduces accountability, stifles talent, and produces governments led by figures who appear to have stepped out of Madame Tussaud's; the difficulty of getting the best people to go into political life; the still large, often dead hand of the state in economic life and the vast corruption that it brought during the past decade. There has been no shortage of discourse on these matters—it fills the media and much private discussion. But there has been scant effort to find politically realistic ways to change them. Professor Heath Lowry discusses these factors in Chapter Two on Turkey's political prospects, but he principally focuses on the role of the military in Turkey's political life and the growth of religious political parties—two closely related issues that roil many facets of Turkish life, from political power to education, and complicate Turkey's relations with the United States and the EU.

The Turkish military have long had a dominating role in Turkey beyond defense. To many Turks, particularly modern urbanites, they are a pillar of stability, the final barrier against the forces of Islamic fundamentalism; to others, they have an anachronistic political mindset, contribute to political instability, and hinder the growth of democracy. The military have the last word on security and some foreign policy and domestic issues, they consume some 30 percent to 40 percent of the government budget, and they see themselves as the dedicated guardians of Turkish territorial integrity, public order, and the secular state. For them political Islam is a security, not a political, issue. They remain the most respected institution in Turkey, and their public words are closely parsed. Insulting the military is still a criminal offense.

While clearly wanting to avoid taking over the Turkish government again, the military have not hesitated to make their weight felt on those public issues they believe to be of supreme importance. Their most prominent recent political intervention was the destruction in 1996 and 1997 of the coalition government led by the *Refah* Party, a feat that has been labeled a "soft coup." However great their ability to set a policy direction on some key issues, the military do not always get their way; for example, they have not yet been able to get governments to implement numerous elements of their 1997 program, approved by the National Security Council, to contain and ultimately reverse the growth of political religion. But few are prepared to criticize the military directly—only the most courageous journalists, and there are not too many of those. Islamist leaders are mostly cautious, though occasionally their anger gets the best of them and they lash out. The Islamist press can be scathing. The Turkish military draw more public negatives in EU countries, including from senior officials who openly express their distaste for "Kemalism." Keeping the military out of politics is such an article of faith in Europe that the issue is likely to complicate the EU accession process. The U.S. government is circumspect in its references to the political role of the Turkish military; it says little except to declare its support for democracy.

The military's involvement in and management of the political religion and Kurdish issues divides both Turks and interested Westerners. Secular Turks, particularly women, see the growth of religious parties this past decade as a real and dire threat to their personal freedom and Turkey's modernization. Many Turks support the military's crackdown on religious parties and religious manifestations in public life such as the wearing of headscarves in public institutions. They believe that if the Turkish military were not around, the Islamists would behave very differently. They have little confidence in the existing political parties: one normally restrained former cabinet minister often told me, usually in great agitation, that if the religious party were to lead the government once again he would get his gun. Nevertheless, the continuing involvement of the military in political life also makes even many strongly secular Turks uncomfortable.

Other Turks, more conservative and religious, see the military as preventing a substantial portion of the populace from practicing their religion freely. They now argue that the Turkish government is violating human rights and destroying the free functioning of political parties. Some Islamist political party leaders have rushed publicly to embrace democracy and beat a path to Washington's door to demonstrate their devotion to democratic practices. They also fear that the existing religious party—now renamed *Fazilet*—will eventually be banned and want to try to head that off. That is one reason why, reversing course, many Islamists have been supportive of Turkish candidacy for the EU, although secular Turks are extremely skeptical about their sincerity and their interest in turning their party into something of a "Christian Democratic" one.

Westerners also are divided in their views. Some believe the Islamist threat to Turkey is very serious and in any event should not be minimized. They consider it folly to weaken basic institutions of the state such as the military, which provide the ultimate protection against the triumph of political obscurantism. Others believe the military and Turkey's civilian secularists exaggerate the threat of fundamentalist Islam, that Turkey is vastly different from Iraq or Algeria, that the religious parties have long been a part of the Turkish political scene and are not prepared to change it radically or use violence. They emphasize the caution induced by the banning of the *Refah* Party, the difference in ideas and tactics within the Islamist movement, the weaknesses of Islamist political leaders and the growing differences among them and their supporters, culminating for the first time in 2000 in a contest for leadership of the party. They also point to the way the *Fazilet* Party has performed in the present parliament, including its joining in the political party consensus to elect a new president to succeed Demirel. Many party members also are involved in the modern economy and seem prepared to work within the general parameters of the Turkish system.

Western countries are cautious in their public handling of the political religious issue. The U.S. government continually expresses support for democracy in Turkey and does not want to see the *Fazilet* Party banned like the *Refah* Party. But it does its best to avoid actions that could be interpreted as encouraging support for the Islamists. It was relieved to see the demise of the *Refah* Party–led coalition government in 1997. So were European governments.

Lowry details the uncertainties involved in these difficult issues but believes the Turkish military must relax its rigid control efforts and do much better in distinguishing between manifestations of religious sentiment and the efforts of Islamist parties to win political power. Like many observers, he thinks the present military approach of cracking down on religious garb and limiting or proscribing Islamist political parties is unnecessary and more likely to lead to a polarization of major segments of the populace and greater militancy than to a reduction in the growth of political Islam. How far the Turkish military is prepared to reconsider their approach in light of the requirements of the EU accession process remains to be seen. So far they have shown little inclination to reduce their pressures on the Islamists, or "reactionaryism" as they call the movement. For the military the Islamists still rank as the major "security threat" to Turkey, greater since 1997 than the threat of Kurdish separatism. The next big public display of this issue will be over whether the *Fazilet* Party is also banned from political life. It is doubtful that adverse EU reaction will keep the military from seeing that party judicially proscribed if they believe the political situation is dangerous enough to warrant it.

There are some positive signs in the overall political climate, notably the widespread belief that the political system needs to be overhauled. Major elements of the Turkish elite, such as big business (through its own organization, commonly known as TUSIAD), are increasingly focusing publicly on the need to reexamine basic Turkish attitudes on such major issues as Kurds and greater democracy. Prospects for basic political reform are being facilitated by the growth of a more active civil society and the growing number of NGOs— which nonetheless have a long way to go before being able to have a serious impact on Turkish political life. A major impediment to internal reform is the relative absence of a dynamic, dedicated, independent press.

On Kurdish problems Turkey's populace, except for most of its Kurds, seems united in backing the Turkish military efforts to destroy the PKK, to make life difficult for Kurdish political parties, and to limit Kurdish cultural expression, as well as other aspects of government management of this issue. There is a sense in the country that only Turks (and not large numbers of Kurds) have been hurt by the fighting in the southeast. The southeast itself remains mostly an appendage of Turkey, rarely visited by Turks outside the area and a real blot on the country. Political parties invariably call for accelerated economic development of the southeast, where half of Turkey's Kurds live, but have never been capable of carrying out that very difficult effort when they have been in power. By and large the political parties shy away from recommending real changes in the overall government approach. Only a few hardy souls publicly dispute the basic tenets of Turkey's Kurdish policy, and they often get locked up.

A gulf developed in late 1999, both within and outside the government, over whether or not to execute PKK leader Öcalan—much favored by the Nationalist Action Party (MHP), one of the ruling-coalition members—and, with the PKK insurgency in what may well be its death throes, over whether Turkey should begin to take publicly controversial measures to deal with the non-PKK aspects of the Kurdish issue.

Prime Minister Ecevit succeeded in getting his coalition partners to put off any decision on executing Öcalan until the European Court of Human Rights had acted on Öcalan's appeal. On other aspects much will depend on whether the PKK tries to resume serious hostilities. For the short term the Turkish military have not felt it desirable or necessary to make what they regard as concessions—such as allowing TV broadcasts in Kurdish (Foreign Minister İsmail Cem publicly urged this in December 1999 but quickly quieted down)—despite a seemingly growing sense among the elite that the government cannot just stand still. It is hard to imagine that after fifteen years of fighting, numerous casualties, and apparent victory the military will accept measures they resolutely opposed during the war. In any event the Kurdish issue seems more fluid than ever before, public confidence seems greater, possible new Kurdish leaders are appearing, Kurdish politicians are using the EU card, and there is a small possibility that some surprising things could happen.

The outside world, particularly those EU countries with large, politically active and sometimes violent Kurdish populations, would like to see a change in Turkey's approach to its Kurds. Mostly this means to refrain from hanging Öcalan, to give the Kurds minority rights, to promote greater democracy and freedom of expression, and to consider greater decentralization of governmental functions. So far the Turks have not paid much attention to international advice and have done what they felt they had to do. Had they followed Western advice, many Turks believe, it would have led to internal chaos. That argument will not be resolved. Conceivably Turkey's interest in EU accession may increase its receptivity to policy change. But one basic change in the nature of the issue has already long been under way— the movement of Kurds out of the southeast—many displaced by the fighting—to the big cities of western Turkey, where they have more opportunity and are over time being better integrated into the economy. Interestingly enough, there has been little urban Kurdish terrorism during the sixteen-year-old PKK insurgency.

Philip Robins points out that the human, material, moral, and foreign policy costs from the failure to resolve or at least significantly diminish Kurdish problems over the whole history of the Turkish Republic have been enormous. He argues in Chapter Three that a window of opportunity has opened to address the Kurdish problem, the best since the intensification of the PKK insurgency in the late 1980s. He hopes the Turkish state will seize this opportunity and use the weakness of the Kurdish nationalists to settle the issue on the basis of greater cultural self-expression and economic development, and on overall improvement in democratization and human rights. He points to the attractiveness of the formation of a broad-based platform on which to work out a new deal; failing that, a unilateral approach on the part of the Turkish government offers the best prospects for improvement. External pressure from the EU and United States can help move the process along. In the absence of a clear and purposeful attempt to address the core concerns that underpin this situation, many, including Robins, believe that the Kurdish problem will persist for Turkey, regardless of the particular fortunes of the PKK and its leader Abdullah Öcalan, and will continue to roil Turkey's domestic and foreign policies.

PROSPECTS FOR GROWTH

Like the political system, the Turkish economy also may be on the brink of major change. The Ecevit government has carried out some important economic reforms and seems to have begun a serious privatization effort. With the aid of the IMF, it has mounted an attack on Turkey's chronically high inflation. But in the past the conditions of many Turkish standbys with the IMF were rarely met and the agreements eventually abandoned. The basic question remains: are Turkey's leaders prepared to open the economy much wider and abandon politically populist measures for often politically painful economic medicine?

In the twenty years since Turgut Özal took charge of the Turkish economy it has been significantly transformed—capital flows freely, the private sector has vastly expanded, and economic effort has largely turned outward. There has been significant growth, but, as Professor Ziya Öniş shows in his analysis of this transformation (Chapter Four), nothing on the order of the Asian Tigers. Sustained high rates of growth have eluded Turkey. Nor has the rate of expansion been sufficient to match population pressures and generate substantially higher levels of per capita income. The reforms of the 1980s, however important and deservedly praised, failed in some important ways to transform the economy. Even Turkey's much-vaunted private sector prospered mostly on the basis of reservoirs of cheap labor and less on innovation and new products. Indeed, the economy in the 1990s, many would argue, has grown despite, not because of, the government. The economy remains beset by stuttering growth, a bloated state-enterprise sector, poor infrastructure, a gray economy perhaps half as large as the statistical economy, a primitive tax system, and private and public corruption. Turkey also has failed to attract much foreign investment.

There is much to do to achieve macroeconomic stability and create a more vibrant economy. That will not be easy if coalition governments resume their normal ways. Whether the promising first year of the Ecevit government represents a real departure in the workings of Turkish coalitions remains to be seen.

AMERICAN–TURKISH RELATIONS AND U.S. POLICY

The four chapters in the second half of the book examine various aspects of U.S.-Turkey relations and U.S. policy toward Turkey. They conclude that both the external and internal dynamics are rapidly transforming relations, that Turkey will be a bigger factor in American foreign policy as time goes on, that the American-Turkish relationship has been given a much more solid footing by the Clinton administration, and that some of the problems that have haunted relations in the past decade are more likely to get better than to worsen. The biggest uncertainties in U.S.-Turkey relations are what happens to Saddam Hussein and the unity of Iraq; the instability in Russia, the Caucasus, and Central Asia; the possible changes in bilateral dealings generated by Turkish integration into Europe; and, above all, Turkey's handling of its internal problems.

There have been many Turkish voices deeply skeptical about the United States, distrustful of American intentions, and wary of too great a Turkish embrace of the United States. As Cengiz Çandar shows in his revealing chapter, a suspicion—even hostility—of the United States has existed in the Turkish elite from the beginning of the republic, in great part originating in the French-oriented background of Turkey's political class and political culture. Such distrust is found in all segments of the elite, but more often, perhaps, in the one that many American supporters of Turkey thought was most dedicated to the U.S.-Turkey relationship—the military.

Negative attitudes toward the United States got a huge boost with the famous—or in Turkey more accurately the *infamous*—Johnson letter of 1964, and even more by the U.S. arms embargo of 1974, which almost destroyed the close relationship created by U.S. support of Turkey at the beginning of the cold war and Turkey's entrance into

NATO. The military were incensed that a fellow NATO member could be embargoed, and by their closest ally. More recently the establishment of the security zone for Iraqi Kurds, protected by U.S. and British planes flying from Turkey, accentuated long-standing notions in some Turkish quarters—astonishing to Americans—that there were senior U.S. officials who were ready to promote the dismemberment of Turkey so that a Kurdish state could be established in Anatolia, much as the victorious allies tried to impose on a prostrate Turkey in 1919. Despite their dependence on the U.S. military and the generally good relations between the two establishments, many Turkish officers also became embittered over the annual congressional battles for approval of military assistance or military sales to Turkey and American preaching on human rights. Economic expansion, education, and the growth of civil society, and particularly the major diplomatic role the United States played in the 1990s in support of Turkey appear to have gone a long way toward diminishing Turkish elite distrust. Çandar believes that democratic change in Turkey will be facilitated by Turkey's quest for EU membership and will go further in reducing remaining elite Turkish suspicions of the United States, making cooperation easier and more sustainable. The acid test of the U.S.-Turkish relationship is likely to come in Iraq when Saddam departs the scene.

The environment of American policymaking and the factors influencing it—my topics in Chapter Six—also are changing. For the past decade, as in earlier ones, strategic factors have remained dominant in Washington's policy thinking. Some strategic factors remain the same, most important, Turkey's continuing role in NATO and the ability to use Turkish bases for a Middle East contingency like the Gulf War. Some are very different, and historically impressive, notably Turkey's increasing involvement in the Caucasus and Central Asia, our dependence on Turkey to protect the Iraqi Kurds, and the growth of Turkey's military power. All have added enormously to the bilateral agenda and made Turkey a more complex component of American foreign policy management. U.S. decisionmakers have not been able to escape the influence of American domestic ethnic politics, but they have managed, sometimes in acrimonious circumstances, to get by without much damage to U.S.-Turkish relations but also without any solution to Greek-Turkish differences. But, as has been noted, over the past decade it is Turkey's domestic difficulties and the associated human rights abuses, which also give ammunition to American ethnic lobbies, that have complicated American dealings with Turkey. The process of Turkish integration into Europe, building on the recent improvement in Greek-Turkish relations, and hopefully a Cyprus settlement, offers for the first time the possibility of reducing the ethnic political element in the U.S.-Turkey relationship.

Few people—none whom I know—would have a year ago predicted a transformation in Turkey's relations with Greece and the emergence of a real possibility of resolving Greek-Turkish differences. These differences—the longest-running sore in U.S. relations with Turkey—are discussed in detail by M. James Wilkinson in Chapter Seven. No specific problem in U.S. relations with Turkey has taken so much of the attention of policymakers over the years, even at the highest levels, and continues to do so. That is why it is the one foreign policy issue receiving its own chapter.

In examining whether the long-standing Greek-Turkish rivalry could erupt into war—a question that may now seem remote but that raised frantic American diplomatic activity as recently as 1996 from an armed incident over some pieces of rock in the Aegean—Wilkinson concludes that their own interests would most likely bring both countries back from the brink of hostilities in the future. There are, however, no guarantees, which points up the basic rationale for serious U.S. engagement. As for the standoffs in Cyprus and the Aegean, they cannot be completely divorced from their history, but in essence the quarrels are neither unique to the region nor driven by some Balkan ghosts. The broader contemporary Greek-Turkish competition—the bilateral arms buildups and the long Greek effort to limit Turkey's relations with the EU—has contributed much to tension and complicated the resolution of disputes.

Over the past two decades Turkish and Greek leaders have been unable to sustain serious initiatives to improve relations. Despite persistent efforts American envoys have not been able to achieve much, and developments in the EU by and large have made matters more difficult, not less. But an act of God in the form of a terrible earthquake revealed widespread grassroots support in both Turkey and Greece for reconciliation. The fresh look inspired by natural disaster facilitated serious if circumscribed Greek-Turkish dialogue and opened new possibilities for an improvement in relations and even some possibility of a resolution of frozen issues like Cyprus. So, of course, did the EU shift from snubbing Turkey to opening the prospect for membership. Governments along with the UN have been scrambling to find the necessary compromises before opportunity slips away. The challenge for U.S. policymakers is to help find ways to make it happen. That will not be easy and will probably require some political daring, yet the goal seems tantalizingly closer. The changes in the external aspects of the Cyprus issue in my view have made it much more likely that in the next few years we will see a settlement on Cyprus.

If better relations between countries is the standard for measuring the success of a country's foreign policy, then U.S. policy toward Turkey under the Clinton administration has been very successful. It has had to deal with eight different coalition governments—one, the Islamist *Refah* Party–led government, posed a particularly difficult problem—on thorny issues ranging from human rights to Iraqi Kurds to a possible Turkish-Greek conflict. The administration survived them all and ended the decade making a friend out of that nationalist and longtime acid critic of the United States, Prime Minister Bülent Ecevit.

Although few big issues, internal or external, have been resolved, the Clinton administration, as Alan Makovsky notes in Chapter Eight on U.S. policy toward Turkey, went to bat incessantly in support of major Turkish projects. These included Turkey's war against the PKK, its successful entrance into a customs union with the EU in 1995 and then its achievement of candidacy for EU membership in 1999, and the current efforts to realize the construction of the Baku-Ceyhan pipeline. All this has resulted in a much more solid and ramified relationship between the two countries and a rise in American influence in Turkey. And that has come at a critical time when Turkey is emerging as a regional power and prospects have increased for major internal reform and greater integration into Europe.

There are numerous areas of foreign policy where the interests of the United States and Turkey are close, and several that could very well roil relations. They range from Israel and the Middle East peace process through Iran and the EU to human rights and political Islam. Makovsky's basic approach in essence parallels that of the U.S. government: Turkey is a good friend and ally, strategically very important to the United States, and moving in the right direction domestically. The United States should seek ways to support Turkey, consult closely with the Turkish government, and work hard in developing common approaches on issues of importance to both countries.

Probably the most difficult issue between the two countries has been Iraq, particularly the sanctions on Iraq, which have hurt Turkey economically, and Turkey's hosting of Operation Northern Watch (previously Operation Provide Comfort). Turkish governments have disliked the U.S. approach toward Iraq, but Turkey's importance to that policy has ironically increased U.S. policymakers' respect for Turkish interests. Nobody knows what will happen to the unity of Iraq when Saddam Hussein disappears from the scene, but it could produce even more serious differences between Turkey and the West over Iraq's future and that of its Kurdish population. Human rights problems in Turkey will remain a principal preoccupation and domestic political concern in the United States, but realistically external influence on this issue will come more from the EU and how Turkey handles its accession process than from what the United States does. (Makovsky finds U.S. leverage on Turkey in general to be very limited.) The most unpredictable areas are the Caucasus and Central Asia, where both the United States and Turkey have become increasingly involved with weak and unstable states, raising serious questions about a much larger issue, the management of their relations with Russia.

A Few Personal Observations

In 1995 I had a conversation in Ankara with Korkut Özal, brother of President Özal and then a member of parliament, about the future of Turkey. It was, as it often has been, a time of political turmoil in Turkey. He warmed to the topic and ended our lengthy discussion with a metaphor. He compared Turkey to a very long highway. On each side of the road all the way down its length there were numerous potholes, big and small. Driving was a real hazard, and a wrong movement could be calamitous. The Turkish approach to solving the highway problem, he said, is to find a good driver who can maneuver around the holes and reach a destination. The problem is that Turkey does not have any good drivers left—no more Atatürks or Özals. It is time for Turkey to fix the road.

To be fair, the Turks have filled in plenty of the potholes. They have lengthened the road enormously. A great deal has been accomplished in integrating Turkey into the global economy in the past two decades; it has become a more open, somewhat more democratic, much more powerful country. It is essentially a constructive player in the world. I continue to remind myself that Turkey has remained sturdy through two decades of internal and external turmoil—one and a half military coups, a sixteen-year internal war, the Gulf War, the remaking of the economy, the growth of political religion, and many other difficult developments.

Nor is there any question about the hard work and dedication of Turkey's people. They are also long-suffering, putting up for years with the meaningless rhetoric and the endless populist promises but few deliveries of their political leaders. Turkey is clearly not a revolutionary country. But many Turks would probably agree with Korkut Özal's assertion that Turkey's most basic problems remain internal, that the way the country is run must be changed if Turkey is to take its rightful place in the world, which it has every reason and capability to aspire to.

This is not to say that Turkey is without serious external problems. For most of the republic's existence, the Turks have lived in a "terrible neighborhood"—next to the Soviet Union—as they are quick to tell everyone. They have needed a sizable army and still do. They badly need friends. Turkish paranoia is not simply to be dismissed. Their southern neighbors—the wonderful trio of Iran, Iraq, and Syria—have little love for the Turks and continuing serious differences such as over water and terrorism. Some may obtain weapons of mass destruction. The PKK war with Turkey would probably never have taken off or lasted for sixteen years without the support that Syria provided the insurgents and the refuge and resting place they found in Iraq. Iran mendaciously denies its support of terrorist activity in Turkey. More fundamental, Turkey's ethnic and religious heterogeneity, its tortured history, its paucity of friends, and its numerous problems with its neighbors have helped perpetuate a focus on unity and centralized control—an obsession with security, some would say—that would not leave the country prey to external and internal enemies. That is one reason many Turks are publicly loath to criticize the actions of their government and particularly the political intrusions of the Turkish military. Other reasons include a great deference to authority and a personal patronage ethos.

Can Turkey come to grips with its difficult internal problems, which at bottom will require major governmental and political reform? Or will it continue to do what it has done for the past forty years—fill in some of the potholes and hope that the dynamism of its private sector and the forces of globalization will generate enough growth to keep the country headed in the right direction and ultimately transform the political system? A prerequisite for sustained reform would be a recognition by the ruling elites in government, politics, and the military that something not only needs to be corrected but also that concerted effort is necessary. On that score, despite the increasing democratic rhetoric, one cannot take too much comfort.

Turkey is one of the least transparent democratic countries in the world. The government reigns supreme. Corruption is extensive. Illegal or unpleasant state activities have been simply buried, usually on grounds of national security. The major Susurluk scandal of 1996 died without public knowledge of what really happened and who was involved, much to the skepticism of most everyone in Turkey. Strong government action is promised, time passes, the public clamor surrounding such episodes is allowed to dissipate, and the media and public quickly turn to another scandal. Indeed, most of the media cooperate when the government or the military call and tell them to knock off their criticism, in part because their owners are often in one way or another in bed with the government and as in many countries bend their media properties to serve their economic needs. There is much freewheeling public discussion in all media but not on neuralgic issues like Kurds.

It is hard to believe that torture would not be further reduced if the government were adamant in doing so, even if it may be difficult to convince elements of the police who believe, not without reason, that torture usually works. Differential and politically influenced justice remains pervasive in Turkey. And the state not only intrudes significantly in the lives of individuals, it also remains a major force in the economy beyond monetary and fiscal policy.

How these basic governmental problems will be resolved over time—let alone the major issues of Kurds and political religion—is still unclear. Certainly economic growth, greater mobility, increasing integration into the world, and a new political generation will lead to positive change. These will take time, although a new generation of politicians is in the offing. The political system has not shown much capability to shake things up, and no widespread, nongovernmental national political reform movement has ever started. Most hopes are now focused on some new faces, like the new president, and on the EU and the need to enact the political and economic reforms required for Turkish entry. Those reforms and that accession may take place; change seems inevitable but it is hard to predict when. Too much can still get in the way, no matter how salutary that integration would be for Turkey and the world.

As for the United States, it has business of all sorts with Turkey, and that is likely to increase as Turkey grows and its influence expands. Even if all the potholes do not get filled in, or it takes longer than everyone would like, Turkey remains a significant force in the world. For a long time to come Turkey will continue to look to the United States as the best external guarantee of its security. What the United States says and does in Turkey is important for this and many other reasons.

U.S.-Turkish relations will continue to encompass an enormous range of interests from northern Iraq to the EU to the Caucasus, to the privatization of state enterprises and the building of power plants to help satisfy Turkey's major energy needs. If there is a Cyprus solution, it will likely have to be brokered by the United States. If Turkey is to clean up the terrible blot on the country that is the southeast, the United States and its allies will constantly have to prod and help Turkish governments. America's higher education system continues to be of great interest and importance to Turks. So increasingly will be America's nongovernmental actors. But the basic American interest, whatever the current specific foreign policy concerns, remains what it has been for a long time, almost a mantra: that Turkey should be a politically stable, secular, economically dynamic, increasingly democratic country integrated into the West. That is reasonably secure, but it should not be taken for granted.

CHAPTER TWO

BETWIXT AND BETWEEN
TURKEY'S POLITICAL STRUCTURE ON THE
CUSP OF THE TWENTY-FIRST CENTURY

HEATH W. LOWRY

INTRODUCTION

To the Western political analyst schooled in the idea that success in elections determines longevity in politics, Turkey and its political leaders are an enigma. Süleyman Demirel, the nation's recent president, became prime minister for the first time in 1965. In the ensuing three and a half decades he has been the subject of a coup d'état by the Turkish military on two occasions, banned from political activity following the military intervention of September 12, 1980 (a ban repealed by national referendum in 1987), and has served as prime minister of no less than seven different governments. With the exception of his 1965 election debut (where he obtained 52.9 percent of the vote), he has only twice exceeded 30 percent of the popular vote (in 1969 with 46.5 percent and in 1977 with 36.9 percent) in any election. The others were all lower: in 1973, 29.5 percent; in 1987, 19.2 percent; and in 1991, 27 percent.[1]

Similar longevity has marked the careers of many other Turkish political leaders, such as Bülent Ecevit (the current prime minister and head of the Party of the Democratic Left [DSP]), who assumed his first ministerial portfolio in 1963; Necmettin Erbakan, a thirty-five-year veteran of conservative religious politics (who in 1996 and 1997 served as prime minister of the Islamist-led *Refah-Yol* government and who, though currently prohibited from political participation, remains the éminence grise behind the banned *Refah*'s successor, the *Fazilet* Party); and the late Alpaslan Türkeş, the ultranationalist and one of the leading figures in the 1960 coup, whose career spanned four decades and whose party, the Nationalist Action Party (MHP), made spectacular gains (following his death) in the 1999 parliamentary elections.

The few younger political figures are similarly able to maintain their party leadership positions regardless of performance either in elections or in office. Tansu Çiller, the American-educated economist who heads the True Path Party (DYP), and Mesut Yilmaz, the chairman of the Motherland Party (ANAP), remain firmly in control despite a steady erosion of their electoral support. Çiller's party received 12.5 percent in the April 1999 elections, down from 19.19 percent in 1995, while Yilmaz's 19.65 percent 1995 share dropped to 13.3 percent in the latest voting.

Despite the fact that all these politicians bear their share of responsibility for many of the major problems Turkey faces today, each has managed to remain in control of a party base and to emerge again and again following election defeats and setbacks. Leadership of a party apparatus in Turkey allows one to name the candidates for parliament and to control the purse strings, a fact that prompted one wit to define the current Turkish political landscape as a kleptocracy run by a gerontocracy. One thing is clear: there is little sign of democracy in the way Turkish political parties are run. However they have used their positions (for self-aggrandizement or simply to maintain their political careers), one fact remains consistent: it is a rare Turkish politician who pays heed to the voice of the electorate and voluntarily relinquishes power.

Using the April 1999 Turkish elections as a springboard to move backward and forward in time, this essay analyzes the dynamics of power in Turkey that have evolved over the past seventy-five years.

It begins with an analysis of the Turgut Özal era, the years 1983–93, and the beginnings of far-reaching economic reforms. In doing so, it draws attention to the fact that the country has (since 1983) generally raced far ahead of its political system, which by and large has held it back. This is followed by an analysis of voting trends in the past decade, which show a definite swing away from the traditional center-right–center-left split toward parties of the extreme right. It then focuses on one of the most contentious issues in Turkish public life, the growth of religious political parties. An examination of the way the Turkish state now operates follows, focusing on the military's infringement on civilian functions and powers in the past three-plus years. It moves then to an examination of prospects for Turkish civil society. Finally, it discusses the possibilities for political reform, which has gained an air of expectancy and much media discussion in the wake of the August 1999 earthquake and the improved working this past year of coalition government. What sort of political world may policymakers face in the next decade? New faces? Military control? A new political transformation? The answers will influence much of what happens in U.S.-Turkish relations.

THE ÖZAL LEGACY:
IS IT "BALIK BAŞTAN KOKAR" [THE FISH STINKS FROM THE HEAD] OR THE TURKISH ECONOMIC MIRACLE?

The Turkish society entering the twenty-first century has been shaped less by the state's revered founder, Mustafa Kemal Atatürk (1881–1938), than by Turgut Özal (1927–93), who served as prime minister (1983–91) and then as president (1991–93). This view is largely ignored in Turkey. Photographs and statues of Atatürk adorn every public and private space, and his name is evoked daily in the print and electronic media; references to Özal are limited, and photographs are absent. Indeed, when his name is mentioned it is likely to be in reference to some charge of governmental corruption, typified by the phrase "to turn the corner," his euphemism for making it in the new Turkey.

For most Turks today the memory of Özal is a muddied one: his reforms are inseparable from the enhanced corruption spawned in their wake. His best-known aphorism is the comment he reportedly made in 1986 at a meeting of his ANAP parliamentary group—when queried as to how government bureaucrats could survive on the minimal salary increase he had proposed, he retorted, "my civil servants know how to look out for themselves." Many view that remark as his sanction for practices of corruption long prevalent but never so openly acknowledged, and as his primary political legacy. While the seven years since his death may not be sufficient for a dispassionate analysis of his tenure, it is strange that the immense transformation of life in Turkey that he instituted is accepted with little acknowledgment of his role as its architect.

Turgut Özal was first and foremost a breaker of taboos. Whether it was by his undermining of the powers of the traditional strongholds of the *"Derin devlet"* [hidden or deep state authority], the ministries of Finance and Foreign Affairs, or his varied pronouncements on the need to recognize the Kurdish reality and the fact that Islam is a profound part of the lives of millions of Turks, or his cavalier treatment of the top military brass during the Gulf War, Özal consciously (and sometimes perhaps unconsciously), trampled at one time or another on many of the cherished icons of republican Turkey. All too seldom did he attempt to replace the broken taboos with a new set of basic principles.[2] It is partly a result of Özal's weakening of the traditional bureaucratic pillars of the state and the political system that the military (the one pillar that escaped his efforts) emerged in the late 1990s as the key player on some major issues affecting Turkey.

However Turks remember it, there can be little doubt that the outlook of today's generation has been heavily influenced by the Özal era. From the ever-growing number of private television stations they watch to the cars they drive and the imported South American bananas they eat, today's Turks bear his imprint. Yet no real attention is focused on this obvious fact, and there has yet to appear a single scholarly study devoted to Özal and the reshaped Turkey he left in his wake. Part of the ambivalence with which Turks view his legacy certainly stems from the fact that the changes he introduced were all too often based on finding a practical solution to an existing problem rather than creating a new rule-based infrastructure. He tended to take the easy road and set up parallel systems or bypasses that, although generally far more efficient than the existing systems, supplemented rather than replaced the older forms. Thus, rather than revamping the nation's outmoded tax system, he created a series of "user funds" designed to increase state revenues. Nor were the revenues thus generated always incorporated into the national budget. In many areas this has led to a paralysis of the system: one cannot use two incompatible systems simultaneously without creating friction. Thus, in post-Özal Turkey, where outside every bank stands an ATM and cash is only a credit card away, it can be unnerving to enter the bank and realize that such a simple procedure as changing money still calls for up to five different signatures, a carry-over from the pre-Özal era of tight restrictions on foreign currency.

The other face of the Janus created by Özal largely keeps Turkey moving today: the vigorous market economy (much of it "unregis-tered") fuels the country's rapid transition from a state-controlled econ-omy to one where the Turkish private sector now successfully competes on the world market. In areas as diverse as tourism, textiles, and construction—low-tech industries to be sure—Turkish entrepre-neurs (aided by low-cost labor) have rapidly established themselves as a force to be reckoned with. The income they generate has kept afloat an economy most of whose indicators (such as huge foreign and domestic debt, together with chronic high inflation) are less than reas-suring. Turgut Özal (like Deng Xiaoping) taught a generation that it was good to be successful—to make money and to enjoy the benefits it brings. What he did not give Turks was a new sense of values or, in a practical matter, a revamped tax system that raised sufficient rev-enues, encouraged entrepreneurship, and made some serious bow to equity. While one may lament that the opportunities created by the private sector have largely failed to trickle down to the mass of the population, the fact remains that private investment continues to grow, the private sector share of GNP has expanded considerably, and Turkey is developing a sizable middle class.

Nevertheless, Turkey remains a land of social extremes. The con-spicuous consumption of the nouveaux riches in post-Özal Turkey is a highly noticeable and much-discussed phenomenon. For 90 percent of Turkey's sixty-five million population the flagrant lifestyles of the haves are a disquieting political factor, one that bears watching in the coming years. Those who have failed to find a piece of Özal's pie have not taken to the streets, but their voting patterns have shifted dramat-ically away from those parties they associate with their poor state and the corruption endemic in the new Turkey.

In short, Özal introduced economic liberalization without putting any kind of legal infrastructure or controls in place to regulate and limit its excesses. Indeed, the press widely reported that he went so far as to express publicly his disdain for law when he quipped, "What differ-ence does it make if the Constitution is not abided by on occasion," thereby making it clear that the important thing was "to turn the corner," regardless of the means used to do so. His failure to provide ethical references for his new Turkey weakened the public fabric of the nation. Corruption, though always a factor in Turkey, was generally shunned as evil prior to the Özal era. In the past two decades it has became more or less an accepted way of life.

The interlinked nature of public and private sector corruption was recently illustrated in a most vivid and tragic fashion by the devastation of the 1999 earthquake. Unscrupulous contractors and the politicians and bureaucrats they paid off to overlook the failure of their buildings to meet safety standards were indirectly responsible for the loss of thousands of lives. Although the earthquake was a natural disaster, much of the enormous loss of life caused by crumbling apartments was man-made. It stemmed from those Turks (in both the public and private sectors) who had chosen to "turn the corner" regardless of the means, or the cost their actions might have to others.

Turkey's Swing to the Right, 1989–99:
Islamist and Nationalist Parties to the Fore

The political chaos of the 1990s, which featured no less than ten different coalition governments (most of which were marred by runaway corruption), also must be viewed as part and parcel of Özal's legacy. So too, as we shall see, are the massive voter shifts that have marked Turkish political life in this decade.

Almost without exception the fledgling body of Turkish political pundits and pollsters failed to predict the election results of April 18, 1999. Locked in a mind-set shaped in the 1970s and 1980s, they were predisposed to view Turkey through the prism of its two main traditional blocks of voters: the center-left and the center-right. What they miscalculated was the steady shift throughout the past decade of voters from the center to the extreme (religious and nationalist) right:

- In the 1989 nationwide municipal elections, the far right took some 10.8 percent of the total vote (*Refah,* 9.8 percent, plus 1.0 percent for the MHP, the National Action Party).

- Two years later, in the 1991 parliamentary elections, these two parties (running together for fear that alone neither would meet the 10 percent nationwide barrier) accounted for 16.9 percent of the total vote.

◆   On March 27, 1994, once again in municipal elections, the extreme
    right tallied 28.28 percent of the total (*Refah*, 18.99 percent, plus
    MHP, 8.03 percent, and the newly formed ultranationalist splinter
    party, the BBP or Grand Unity Party, 1.26 percent).[3]

◆   In the December 1995 parliamentary elections *Refah* emerged as
    the single largest vote-getter with 21.38 percent of the popular
    vote, and MHP's share rose to 8.18 percent, for a total radical right
    vote of 29.56 percent.

◆   In the most recent parliamentary voting, on April 18, 1999, the
    vote share of *Fazilet* (*Refah*'s successor) dropped to 15 percent,
    with MHP more than doubling its 1995 total to 18.1 percent (which
    made it the second party, behind Ecevit's DSP with 22.1 percent).
    When one factors in the vote of two other small ultranationalist
    parties, the extreme right vote totaled 34.57 percent.[4]

In only ten years, one-quarter of the Turkish electorate have
shifted their allegiance from the traditional center-left and center-right
parties to those of the extreme religious and nationalist right. Stated differently, whereas in 1989 one out of every ten voters supported these
parties, today three and a half of every ten votes are cast for the
extreme or alternative right.

This startling growth is paralleled by a decline in the vote shares
achieved by the center-right (ANAP and DYP) and the center-left (DSP
and the Republican People's Party, or CHP). The combined votes of
these four parties accounted for 82.54 percent of the total in 1991,
dropping to 64.19 percent in 1995 and further to 56.4 percent in the
April 1999 elections. Most precipitous was the decline in support for
the center-right parties: DYP plummeting from 27.03 percent in 1991 to
12.5 percent in 1999 and ANAP from 24.01 percent to 13.3 percent.

It would appear that the Turkish electorate is far from satisfied
with politics as usual, although there is little indication that the leadership of the centrist parties is heeding their warning. Post-election
polling shows that the voters view the traditional parties as racked by
corruption and most of their leaders as motivated by a desire for personal gain (the one exception being Ecevit). They closely associate
the chronic inflation of the past decade with the mainstream parties.
They are aware of the growing gap in income distribution, which once
again they lay at the door of the parties that ruled Turkey during and

after the Özal years. (International Monetary Fund statistics published in 1997 show that between 1987 and 1994 the real per capita income of the top 20 percent of the population grew by 15 percent, while that of the bottom 20 percent dropped 1 percent.)[5] Finally, the Turkish people are fed up with hearing the same promises from the same tired political figures they see as the cause of their dissatisfaction.[6]

The two winners of the April 1999 election were the center-left DSP headed by Bülent Ecevit, whose vote share doubled from 10.8 percent in 1991 to 22.1 percent in the 1999 elections, and the MHP, currently led by Devlet Bahçeli, whose party's 8.18 percent vote share in 1995 more than doubled to 18.1 percent in the recent voting. Some of the DSP's gain was at the expense of the second center-left party, the CHP headed by Deniz Baykal, whose 10.71 percent vote of four years ago fell to 8.5 percent. However, post-election surveys show that Ecevit also made significant gains as a result of the capture of PKK leader Abdullah Öcalan, which occurred before the April voting while Ecevit was heading a pre-election caretaker government.[7] Though the Turkish media and the traditional elite have devoted little attention to the bloody conflict in southeastern Turkey throughout the past decade, it would appear that the Anatolian peasants and small townsmen whose sons have fought and died are well aware of the meaning of Öcalan's arrest.

While Ecevit benefited from his hard-line Turkish nationalist rhetoric, it was clearly the MHP, whose firm stance against the PKK resonated with Anatolian voters, that emerged as the biggest winner. From a dismal showing of only 1 percent in the municipal elections of 1989, the MHP surged to more than 18 percent in the April 1999 parliamentary vote. When one queries voters who support this party, it is the strong nationalist stance and the fact that it is viewed as the one political party to provide moral and financial assistance to the families of soldiers killed fighting the PKK insurgency that seem to account for much of the surprising gain. It is no coincidence that among first-time voters, in particular males eligible for military service, MHP made exceptional gains. This voting bloc is too young to remember the political violence associated with this party's anti-communist stance of the 1970s but old enough to appreciate both the jobs the party provides its youthful cadres and its strong anti-PKK rhetoric. MHP's support also included numerous swing voters that had gone to *Refah* in 1995. Whether they shifted to MHP in yet another effort to find a party to address their concerns or out of a belief that they would be wasting their votes should *Fazilet,* like *Refah,* be banned is unclear. MHP also picked up votes from DYP supporters tired of the charges of corruption against party head Tansu Çiller.

What remains to be seen is how the MHP reacts to sharing political power. As the second-largest contingent in the present three-party coalition government, its representatives are no longer always the outsiders criticizing the status quo; now they are part of the problem. They have moved cautiously so far in their new role, generally following the mainstream line adopted by Bülent Ecevit and Mesut Yilmaz, their partners in Turkey's fifty-seventh government. They have even joined their coalition partners in passing important legislation to encourage foreign investment, prevent torture, regulate privatization, civilianize the state security courts, and create unemployment insurance. Even on an issue as controversial among their own electorate as whether or not to impose the death penalty on PKK leader Öcalan, they chose to side with their coalition partners and voted to postpone a decision until the European Court of Human Rights has heard the appeal. They have concentrated on using their access to power to find jobs for large numbers of their supporters in the state bureaucracy.

If Ecevit and Bahçeli share anything beyond their Turkish nationalism, it is the perception by the voters that neither is corrupt. Ecevit's life has been an open book; he is one of a handful of late-twentieth-century Turkish politicians (another being Erdal İnönü) who have not used political position for personal gain. Ecevit has even successfully managed to impose his sense of ethics on his party's leaders. The last time he was head of a government was in 1978: many of today's voters are too young to hold him responsible for today's problems. Devlet Bahçeli enjoys the distinction of being totally untested in this regard, that is, he has never before been in a position that allowed access to the public trough. A sizable number of supporters state that it was the honesty of these leaders that attracted them.[8]

The gains of both these parties should sound a warning call to the remainder of the center-left–center-right Turkish political elite. They cannot count on their traditional voters. Ever-growing numbers of the electorate are fed up with corruption and lackluster government and are willing to send their votes in different directions in hopes of finding a new kind of political leader.

Much of *Refah*'s gains in the 1995 elections stemmed also from this element of the electorate, which although tired of the politics of corruption still had enough faith in the system to cast around for options. It may be that the losses suffered by *Fazilet* in the latest voting did not all stem from its short-lived government having shown the electorate that the Islamists were not a serious alternative; some of the loss may be attributed to the numerous media accounts of the enormous personal wealth accumulated by Necmettin Erbakan during a lifetime of public service.

Similarly, the steady erosion of support for Tansu Çiller and Mesut Yilmaz is linked to the numerous scandals tying them both to corruption. They epitomize the so-called new politicians spawned by Özal's philosophy of "turning the corner" and no questions asked. In rejecting them, voters also are signaling their dissatisfaction with this aspect of the Özal legacy.

Despite these facts there is little or no sign that the message of the Turkish electorate has permeated the minds of leaders of the old-guard parties. Of the four clear losers in the 1999 elections (Yilmaz's ANAP, Çiller's DYP, Recai Kutan's *Fazilet,* and Baykal's CHP), only Baykal stepped down from his leadership position (and he may be planning a comeback). Yilmaz, Çiller, and Kutan are still entrenched at the head of their parties. Despite their election setbacks, none of the losers in the 1999 elections (with the exception of CHP, whose failure to meet the nationwide 10 percent barrier means it is not represented in parliament) seems to be engaging in any serious soul-searching.

The 1999 elections would appear to be a clarion call for changes in the electoral system and for an entirely new cadre of political leaders for the new century. The politics of "personalities" and "special interests" have been rejected by a growing percentage of the voters. As emphasized in countless columns and editorials, the eight different coalition governments since 1993 have shown Turks that they can no longer afford the luxury of two center-left and two center-right parties. In short, the voters want reform.

Political reform calls for a complete revamping of the legislation regulating political parties and the electoral process. The present system, wherein incumbents have the authority to place their own supporters in positions where they in turn choose the party leaders, ensures the maintenance of the status quo. Given the vested interests and the power of political leaders, such far-reaching change is unlikely to occur in the near future. Those parties that respond to this challenge will make the transition to twenty-first-century Turkey; those that fail to do so will continue to see their share of the vote shrink.

Just how patient the long-suffering Turkish electorate will continue to be remains to be seen. So far they have shown a capacity to endure much.

Is Turkey in Danger of Becoming an Islamic Republic?

In recent years one of the most frequently asked questions by Western publics and policymakers is whether Turkey could experience a radical Islamic revolution. Before assessing this query we must briefly reexamine the history of religious expression in the Ottoman Empire. From 1299 to 1923 the region encompassing the present Republic of Turkey formed the heartland of the Ottoman Empire, one of the world's longest-lasting multiethnic, multireligious, multilingual states. Throughout this six hundred years personal identity was based on confessional groups. Muslims, whether Turks, Iranians, Arabs, Bedouins, Kurds, or others, were viewed solely as "Muslims." Greek Orthodox Christians, whether ethnic Greeks, Bulgarians, Serbs, or whatever, were simply known as the Orthodox community until the mid-nineteenth century.

Beginning with the Young Turks at the turn of the century, and thereafter with the reform-minded founders of the Turkish republic, Mustafa Kemal Atatürk and his colleagues, there was a conscious decision to replace religion with ethnic-based nationalism as the key to personal identity. With the collapse of the Ottoman polity the overwhelming majority of its non-Turkish peoples became part of a number of newly formed countries, and the Anatolian successor state, the Republic of Turkey, had a majority population that was identified as largely ethnically Turkish. The new state's founders consequently chose Turkish nationalism as the replacement for religious identification.

In the minds of Atatürk and his associates (all products of Western-style education), the collapse of the six-hundred-year-old Ottoman Empire was closely linked to the role of Islam. They viewed religion as having prevented the Western-style reforms and innovations needed to halt Ottoman decline. They saw Islam as a force that had to be controlled and subjugated if they were to succeed in Westernizing and modernizing their new state.

To ensure their success they adopted a draconian—indeed, almost Jacobin—form of secularism. The *laik* or secular state they envisaged, in sharp contrast to the United States (founded in large part on a desire for complete religious freedom), was predicated upon limiting the role of Islam by strictly controlling it. Although from their point of view this was necessary, the fact remains that it was the small band of revolutionaries running the state, not a plebiscite or consensus, that chose this course of action. Likewise, it was the state that used all its power to replace earlier forms of identification (religious, ethnic, or regional) with its own version of state secularism and Turkish nationalism. It was ultimately the inability of Atatürk and his associates to sell their version of the future to a large segment of Turkey's citizens that led to the current difficulties.

Adopting methods more commonly associated with Turkey's revolutionary neighbor to the north (the USSR), Atatürk imposed a state-run bureaucracy to regulate all religious affairs, outlawed the *tarikat*s or dervish religious orders (which for centuries had served as the cornerstone of folk religion), banned formal religious instruction, and even on occasion sanctioned the closing and destruction of religious sanctuaries. In short, the new republic equated religious expression with the past, that is, with opposition to all the things it now sought to achieve. While in retrospect one may debate the wisdom of the republic's founding fathers in this regard, one fact remains: despite their best efforts, a significant portion of the Turkish population has not yet fully embraced the secularist vision set forth in the 1920s. Nor have the ideological descendants of the secular reformers shown a willingness to change their stance in light of the desires of a growing segment of Turks today, who at the very least want to reflect their religiosity in everyday life (be it by wearing headscarves, observing the Islamic holy day of Friday, or teaching their children to read the Koran in Arabic).

With the advent of democratic elections in 1950 (more than a decade after the death of Atatürk), politicians (including devout secularists) began increasingly to play the Islamic or religious card as a means of attracting voters for whom secularism had little appeal. From the early 1950s until the present day every political party in Turkey has at one time or another granted concessions to the religious right in an effort to gain electoral advantage.

Not even the military guardians of secularism have been fully able to escape the trap of appealing to religious values; it was the military junta led by soon-to-be President Kenan Evren that (in the aftermath of the 1980 coup) mandated compulsory religious education to be added to the curriculum of the secular state schools. They did so in the belief that it was the lack of proper moral and ethical training that had led to the anarchy of the late 1970s. They equated the leftist terrorism of the pre-coup period with godless communism and felt that instilling religious values in Turkish youth would counter its appeal. This example highlights the extent to which the Turkish military's efforts at post-coup social engineering often created new problems rather than resolving those they were designed to correct.

This practice of buying the religious vote came to a head during the Özal era, between 1983 and 1993. Özal, a devout, practicing Muslim (unlike any of his predecessors in office), through his personal devotion and the open discussion of the role of religion that he encouraged, repeatedly challenged Turkey's official secularist symbolism: his repeated pilgrimages to Mecca, his open attendance at Friday prayers, his fasting (and even his hosting of *iftars*—dinners ending the fast during the holy month of *Ramazan*—for the foreign diplomatic corps in Ankara), all signaled to the Turkish public that the days of politicians' concealing their religious beliefs and practices had ended—at least in his eyes. Özal's message for Turks was clear: it is possible to be both a devout and openly practicing Muslim and to be head of state in a secular Turkey, but not in the one we have had until now.

Necmettin Erbakan, the leader of the Islamist *Refah* Party, who became prime minister in 1996 after having emerged as the largest single vote-getter with 21.38 percent in the December 1995 elections, picked up Özal's message but went much further in appealing to voters on religious grounds. He had already done this in the 1960s and 1970s, but in post-Özal Turkey a larger portion of the electorate was responsive. Erbakan had a clear grasp of that portion of the Turkish electorate susceptible to religious rhetoric. Even though most voters had little idea of what he had in mind for the future of Turkey, many were attracted by his championing of religious values and condemnation of corruption. Although many voters shared his demand for the liberalization of religious practices, they did not necessarily embrace his more radical supporters' vision of a Turkey guided by Islamic holy law or of a Turkey whose Western orientation would be replaced by an Islamic one. Stated differently, although many voters wished to see an easing of some of the extreme aspects of early twentieth-century Atatürkist secularism, their support of *Refah* did not necessarily translate into agreement with the extremists in the party. Erbakan, who from the outset of his coalition government began pandering to the most radical of his supporters, even acted as if his 21.38 percent of the vote had given him a mandate to institute basic change in Turkish foreign policy by forging closer ties with Islamic regimes such as Iran and international pariahs such as Sudan and Libya.

Erbakan fully realized that while the Turkish population in the 1920s had been given no choice about whether the new nation should be secular or Islamic, the growth of one-man, one-vote democracy meant that the ballot box and a newfound devotion to democracy on the part of the Islamists could serve to challenge the secularist underpinnings of the republic. It is an awareness of this fact and the use that Islamists make of it in the West that worries the military and the traditional elites. Somewhat paradoxically, although Erbakan used the democratic process to gain power, he showed far less devotion to it in the policies he espoused in the course of his short-lived government. There he tended to operate as if the support of two of every ten voters entitled him to reverse the secular path Turkey had been following for seventy-five years.

All these developments were watched with rising concern by the elites—and in particular by the watchdog of "laicism," the Turkish general staff (TGS) and the military element of the national security council (NSC). In the early months of 1997, they determined that Erbakan had crossed the line and was becoming a danger. The timing of their decision to intervene was prompted by a variety of factors including a dinner Erbakan hosted at the prime minister's residence for the leaders of legally banned *tarikat*s, and the public program the *Refah* mayor of the Ankara suburb of Sincan hosted in praise of the radical Palestinian group Hamas, with Iran's ambassador as an honored guest. So incited, they began to engineer the series of events that led to the downfall of Erbakan's government.

It is at this point that we must return to the query with which this examination began: namely, Is Turkey in danger of becoming a religious state? There can be no doubt but that the conditions that could lead to conflict exist. The potential battle lines are clearly drawn.

On one side is the military, supported by the overwhelming majority of the country's Western-oriented educated elite, who are dedicated to holding the existing line on state secularism. They view any attempt to undermine the secularist reforms of the 1920s and 1930s as tantamount to a rejection of Turkey's commitment to becoming a full member of the Western family of nations and as the slippery slope to religious rule and social decline. Their approach is far-reaching in nature and is typified by the list of demands regulating religious practice (discussed in the following section) that were enacted in the February 28, 1997, meeting of the NSC. Their view of the Islamic threat brooks no compromise, and even an issue as seemingly innocuous as women's wearing headscarves in schools and the public sector workplace is equated with a political act, an early effort to reinstitutionalize an Islamic regime in Turkey. In their minds their position is bolstered by the Turkish constitution, whose Article 24 clearly bars the use of religion for political purposes.

Their counterparts on the extreme religious right, who go so far as to support the reintroduction of Islamic law *(Şeriat)* in Turkey, have long recognized the importance of step-by-step gains in the ongoing battle against state secularism. They believe demographics are on their side: an ever-increasing number of generally religiously conservative, poor rural Turks are flocking into the country's major urban centers, where they often find that the only assistance available in the urban hurly-burly is that offered by the well-organized members of the religious party; the birthrate of the rural population far outpaces that of the traditional urban elite. They also are aided by the tendency of the secularist elite (and particularly the military) to equate any overt display of conservative values (such as women's covering their heads in the public workplace or university classroom) with Islamic fundamentalism. This has the effect of lumping many conservative villagers, small townspeople, and newly arrived urban dwellers, who are practicing Muslims, together with the activist religious right as Islamic fundamentalists in the eyes of the authorities. While the growth of the extremists may well lead to serious countermeasures, the problem is that the "line in the sand" that the secularists have drawn may well radicalize those who wish nothing more than to be able to practice their religious beliefs with somewhat more freedom in a secular Turkey.

Indeed, there are many aspects of post-Özal Turkey that disturb a wide segment of practicing Muslims. Nowhere is this more discernible than in the electronic media, where Özal allowed the growth of unregulated private television stations, many of which today feature talk shows hosted by transvestites or soft-core pornography in prime-time viewing hours—leading many conservative viewers to show their own values by wearing headscarves. All this is an attempt to preserve self-identity. When such expressions are undifferentiated by the secularists and considered *İrtica* (fundamentalism and reactionaryism), this threatens to create the very thing they fear.

The goal of the republic from its inception was that a Western-educated elite would take its values to the countryside: as teams of bureaucrats, teachers, and military officers communicated the lessons of the new republic to the rural masses a gradual "Istanbulization of Anatolia" would occur. Now, rather than urban-elite values taking root in the countryside, the rural population is moving to the cities and bringing traditional values with them—the "Anatolization of Istanbul" and the country's other major cities. Chief among the values these new residents bring with them is a commitment to Islam far different from that previously seen in the cities.

A growing number of Turks want to practice the tenets of their Islamic faith both publicly and privately. If Islam requires a woman to cover her hair in public (in school, in the workplace, and in public offices), they argue, then democracy should permit her to follow her religious beliefs without interference from the state. But symbolism has played an important role throughout the history of the republic. It was Atatürk himself who replaced the fez with the fedora and then imposed his choice on the entire nation. In the 1930s he equated failure to accept his example with rejection of his Westernization goals. Today his secularist descendants equate covering one's head with a desire to turn secular Turkey into an Islamic state. Such acts may indeed encourage attachment to an obscurantist, nonmodern mentality, but if democracy in Turkey is ever to mean more than free elections, it will have to learn to encompass those choosing a conservative lifestyle as well as those imitating the latest European and American fashions in dress. What the guardians of Atatürk's legacy seemingly fail to see is that radical secularism has the power to create radical Islamists. If Turkey's leaders stop viewing the gap between secularists and Islamists so starkly, some of the threat they perceive in Islam may well dissipate. Should this not occur (and given the current stance of the military it probably will not), the gap will widen, leading to the cleavage in Turkish society they so fear, particularly should economic conditions worsen.

What has been missing are voices of moderation seeking a live-and-let-live compromise between the radical secularists and the extremist Islamic fundamentalists. Until recently, one voice of moderation appeared to be that of Fetullah Gülen, the head of a large *tarikat*, who sought to establish a dialogue between the opposing forces. His efforts were discredited when the Turkish media were supplied videotapes (doubtless edited but nonetheless authentic) of conversations in which he was shown encouraging his followers to hide their real views and adopt a temporary policy of conciliation that would be discarded when Turkey ultimately returned to its Islamic roots. The discrediting of Gülen decreases the likelihood of a serious effort to narrow the enormous gap between Islamists and secularists.

Underlying all these arguments is the question of whether a secular democracy and political Islam can occupy the same space in Turkey. Stated differently, since Islam traditionally guides all aspects of believers' lives (including legal entanglements), can there be a secular Islamic state? This is of course one reason that so much attention both in the West and in the Islamic world is being focused on Turkey. Turkey has long been hailed as proof that a country with a strong and growing democracy can also be one in which 99.8 percent of the population are Muslims, but will it be able to maintain this balance? Or will the scales tip in favor of the growing power and influence of Islam in the lives of its citizens?

Those who would liken *Refah/Fazilet* to Christian Democratic parties in Europe would be well advised to look at the recent history of Islamic political movements in other parts of the Islamic world, for which the question has become whether or not the state will follow the one true path, that of Islam. Erbakan's ties to radical Islamic leaders in Egypt, the Sudan, and Libya have not passed unnoticed in Turkey, nor can they be overlooked by Western policymakers. As early as 1990 Erbakan had joined Muammar Qadhafi's shadowy "International Command of the Islamic Peoples" organization, a fact Qadhafi publicly announced in October 1996, in the course of then Prime Minister Erbakan's official state visit to Libya. "My brother Necmeddin," Qadhafi said, "is a member of the 'International Command of the Islamic Peoples' which I head," placing Erbakan firmly in the ranks of the most radical international Islamist fringe.[9]

Whether or not it is possible for a secular democracy and Islam to coexist seems to be firmly linked to Turkey's democratic development. Will the unquestioned commitment Turks have to the democratic process mature quickly enough, from its current simple attachment to free elections and orderly transitions of government, to begin to encompass the idea that Turkey is large and strong enough and has no choice but to house both secularists and Islamists? Will the Turkish military be able to overcome their inherent distrust of both the political establishment and the Turkish people who elect them? In short, will Turkey be able to move from a guided democracy to full democracy, wherein the commitment is not only to one man, one vote but to actually abiding by the results of elections?

It was, after all, the failure of the Turkish political system that allowed Erbakan (who represented only two of every ten voters) to emerge as prime minister in 1996. Four years later his successors managed to attract only one and a half of every ten votes. Political Islam—far from growing at a rate that suggests it is going to present a real challenge to Turkey's secularism—may have peaked in 1996. What is strange is that the same elements of society who so fear the growth of Islam are seemingly unmoved by the shift of an even larger percentage of the electorate to the ultranationalist (at times in the not-too-distant past neofascist) National Action Party. While the political Islamists at least pay lip service to democracy, there is as yet no indication that the nationalists have learned to tolerate dissent. Religion is not the only threat looming on the Turkish horizon.

As for the Islamists, will they be able to modify that portion of their dream which calls for reestablishing Turkey as a theocracy guided by Islamic holy law (the *Şeriat*)? Will their commitment to modernization allow them to recognize that they are going to have to find a place within Turkey's secular order, not overthrow it? Most secularists do not believe anything that Erbakan (and now Gülen) say along these lines, but the results of the April 1999 voting raise the possibility that unless they adhere to such a commitment, their appeal to voters will continue to decline.

To the extent answers to these queries are guided by examples drawn from Erbakan's short-lived tenure as prime minister in 1996–97, the jury is still out. As noted earlier, he took steps aimed at changing Turkey's foreign policy orientation (by increasing ties to Iran, Libya, and Sudan) when he had no consensus to do so. His appeal to the extreme fundamentalist wing of his supporters gave the military the ammunition (in the form of videotapes of inflammatory speeches by radical *Refah* MPs such as Şevki Yilmaz and Halil İbrahim Çelik, and of his meeting with fundamentalist *tarikat* leaders) to help convince the elite that he represented a threat to Turkey's secular order.

There is little indication at this time that either side is ready for compromise. Attempts by the military to reimpose 1920s-style bans on wearing religious apparel are not a positive sign. Nor is the tone of much of the rhetoric in the Islamic press. But the republic's seventy-six-year history should teach us that Turkey and its people are long-suffering and slow to action. As the traditional urban elites come to accept the reality that their vision of a Turkey in Atatürk's image is a thing of the past, and as the Islamists come to realize that the Ottoman Empire is finished and begin to find their niche within a rapidly expanding economy, compromise may prevail over conflict, though the issue is far from settled. An Islamic business community is growing that seems to want to be part of the West. As its members move into politics they could well influence change in Islamist thinking and priorities.

For the present the military and secularist elite cannot seem to differentiate between fundamentalism and a growing desire on the part of many for greater religious freedom of expression. The Islamists have yet to learn that they are a minority who cannot impose their values on the secular elite. Until both sides learn to give a little (you cannot enter military facilities—or even universities—sporting a headscarf or a beard, nor can you drink alcohol in most sites controlled by Islamic municipalities), the issue will remain high on Turkey's domestic agenda.

THE ROLE OF DERIN DEVLET OR THE "DEEP-SEEDED STATE"

On February 28, 1997, Turkey experienced its fourth military intervention in forty years. Unlike its predecessors in 1960, 1971, and 1980, this one did not involve troops taking over the streets, the declaration of martial law, and the open assumption of civilian powers by the military. Unique in style, it may best be labeled a "soft coup," or a "coup by demands" issued by the NSC (a mixed military and civilian body chaired by the president), which enjoys broad but vague constitutional powers as a consultative body whose mandate is to "preserve the existence and independence of the State, the integrity and indivisibility of the country, and the peace and security of society." The coup took the form of eighteen measures designed to contain the perceived threat represented by *İrtica* (Islamic fundamentalism and reactionaryism), which were to be implemented by the coalition government headed by the Islamist Necmettin Erbakan and the secularist Tansu Çiller. After an eight-hour marathon meeting both Erbakan and Çiller (together with the other members of the NSC) put their signatures to the demands, thereby seemingly endorsing the power of the NSC to mandate state policy on domestic issues and pledging their government to implement these measures.

From the outset it was clear that Erbakan had no intention of enacting the demands, all of which were directed at regulating the expression of religious practices held dear by most of the voters who had brought him to power, and it was the nonnegotiable nature of the demands pushed through by the military members of the NSC that toppled the *Refah-Yol* government four months later. Erbakan's ultimate resignation resulted from a campaign orchestrated by the Turkish General Staff's (TGS) "Western working group" (WWG, a semisecret branch of the TGS created to monitor *İrtica* and to devise policy recommendations for dealing with it), which won the majority support of all elements of the country's ruling elites. This campaign, playing upon the secularists' fear of an Islamist takeover of the state (a fear that had grown during *Refah*'s tenure, fed by the series of ill-conceived steps taken by Erbakan), led him to resign his post as prime minister under the illusion that President Demirel would have to give the mandate to form a new government to his coalition partner, Tansu Çiller. Instead, Demirel turned to Mesut Yilmaz, who managed (aided by significant military pressure) to patch together a center-right–center-left coalition that nominally ran the country until three months before the April 1999 elections.[10]

One may debate whether or not the demands, which ran the gamut from reform in the nation's educational system to the strict enforcement of laws implemented in the 1920s regulating the wearing of religious apparel in public, actually fall under the purview of the NSC's constitutional mandate of "preserving the peace and security of society" and the "independence of the state." However, the fact that these military-engendered goals were supported by the mainstream media, several leading business associations, labor unions, university presidents and senates, the majority of the intelligentsia, and other members of Turkey's ruling elite created a climate of acceptance, not a negative reaction.

The absence of a public outcry over the interference of the military in the country's political life has led in the past two years to a de facto dual-track government, in which many of the nation's real policy objectives are being generated by the TGS and its various working groups and task forces. In addition to the WWG, the TGS has reportedly created an Aegean working group, a media working group, and an economic working group. Whenever a particular question arises, the relevant working group sets up a task force to produce a study. (The preceding information was provided in a series of interviews in the summer of 1999 with journalists and former government ministers in Ankara.) Recommendations are passed to the military wing of the NSC and fed to the elected officials for implementation. Whenever the elected politicians move outside the boundaries decreed by the military, they are quickly shown the folly of their errors.

Two cases illustrate how the dual tracks work. In March 1998, after the fall of the Erbakan-Çiller *Refah-Yol* government and the coming to power of the coalition led by Mesut Yilmaz, the new prime minister attempted to articulate to journalists a new modus operandi for the military and civilian authorities. He stated that with the fall of the *Refah-Yol* government the need for military concern with *İrtica* had ended (and therefore the need for the WWG as well), and the military could once again focus on the PKK threat. In other words, the control of fundamentalism was the prerogative of the elected government; the fight against terrorism was that of the military. Hardly a revolutionary stance. Within days General Karadayı, chief of the general staff, issued the first of several statements informing the prime minister that the threat posed by *İrtica* would continue to be the primary concern of the nation's military, the NSC, and the still-needed Western working group. Throughout the remainder of his tenure, Yilmaz did not again stray far beyond the confines of the agenda developed by the military.

In early 1999, a multipartisan group of some 160 MPs who were unhappy with their positions (or lack thereof) on the list of candidates put forth by their respective party leaders for the April elections began a movement to postpone the voting. When it became apparent that their efforts were going to be supported by *Fazilet* parliamentarians (the former *Refah* bloc who were attempting to undo the ban on the political activity of Erbakan), the present chief of the general staff, General Hüseyin Kıvrıkoğlu, gave a lengthy interview to Sedat Ergin, *Hürriyet* bureau chief in Ankara. Kıvrıkoğlu made it absolutely clear that the military would countenance no rescheduling of the elections or overturning the article under which Erbakan's political activities were banned.[11] Once the general made his comments, all talk of a parliamentary move to postpone the elections ceased.

In short, for the past three years real but sub-rosa authority on issues seen as crucial to the continued existence of the state has been vested in the TGS (and its working groups and task forces), while the duly elected parliamentary government is limited in these areas to implementing decisions generated by the NSC in its monthly meetings. In light of this, such seeming political incongruities in recent

Turkish policy as the strengthening of the military relationship with Israel on Erbakan's watch and the threatened military action against Syria on Yilmaz's are easier to comprehend. Erbakan, the Islamist populist, could not have been pleased with heightened ties to Israel, nor was Yilmaz (who was in the United States at the time) consulted or even informed in advance when threats of military action against Syria for its support of the PKK were announced.

For the military the advantages of this "soft coup" are clear. They are in a key policy formulation role for some major aspects of both civil and military affairs, without having to bear primary responsibility for running the government or for anything that goes wrong. In the eyes of the world and Turkish public opinion, Turkey is still a functioning parliamentary democracy rather than a semi-military government. Criticism of legislative action or inaction is laid at the doorstep of the country's elected officials, and there is no popular clamor for ending the military's involvement in nondefense matters. The elected civilian officials generally bear the brunt of criticism for anything anyone dislikes. From the economy (which the elected government largely does control) to mandatory eight-year education (the military-imposed formula designed to weaken the role of religious schools and organizations), the responsibility in the eyes of the electorate lies with the several existing political parties that have played direct and indirect roles in the numerous coalition governments since the 1995 parliamentary elections.

From the moment Necmettin Erbakan affixed his signature to the NSC's February 28, 1997, list of eighteen demands, real civilian authority in Turkey, in the areas of policy considered crucial by the military, has been curtailed. The TGS via the NSC, not the Turkish parliament, became the primary architect of major elements of Turkish foreign and domestic policy, and the elected politicians were to a great extent reduced to the role of aparatchiks who assisted in implementing the decisions generated in the monthly NSC meetings. Between the State *(Devlet)* bureaucracy and the elected government *(Hükümet),* the balance has clearly swung in favor of the *Devlet.*

Still, not all the military's agenda has been enacted. To date, only four of the specific February demands have actually been implemented. But the public is fully aware of the configuration of power and that the military-designed agenda is still very much on the table.

Is this the role intended for the NSC by the constitution drafted under military tutelage and approved by more than 90 percent of the

Turkish electorate in 1982? This document's relevant section, Article 118, provides the following in terms of membership and the constitutional role of this body:

> Article 118. The national security council shall be composed of the prime minister, the chief of the general staff, the ministers of national defense, internal affairs, and foreign affairs, the commanders of the army, navy, and the air force, and the general commander of the gendarmerie, under the chairmanship of the president of the republic.
>
> Depending on the particulars of the agenda, ministers and other persons concerned may be invited to meetings of the council and their views be heard.
>
> The national security council shall submit to the council of ministers its views on taking decisions and ensuring necessary coordination with regard to the formulation, establishment, and implementation of the national security policy of the State. The council of ministers shall give priority consideration to the decisions of the national security council concerning the measures that it deems necessary for the preservation of the existence of the independence of the State, the integrity and indivisibility of the country, and the peace and security of society.

Articles 120 and 122 further state that the national security council must be consulted before the Council of Ministers enacts either a "state of emergency" or issues a declaration of "martial law." In short, all the relevant constitutional articles seem to suggest that its framers viewed the primary role of the NSC to be advisory rather than that of the key player in proposing, shaping, and overseeing the implementation of policy. Be that as it may, the vague wording of Article 118, which mandates that the views of the NSC will be given "priority consideration" by the Council of Ministers in all matters relative to the "national security policy *of the State*," has come to be interpreted as putting even religious expression under the mantle of state security.

As noted previously, this is facilitated by Article 24 of the constitution, one section of which reads: "No one shall be allowed to exploit or abuse religion or religious feelings . . . in any matter whatsoever, for the purpose of personal or political influence, or for even partially basing the fundamental, social, economic, political, or legal order of the State on religious tenets." There is no doubt in the minds of secular Turks that *Refah* under Erbakan was clearly violating all of these mandates. Consequently, all steps taken to force this party from power could be justified under the 1982 constitution, even though many of its tenets fall short of Western democratic standards.

That this was the view of the military was made abundantly clear on August 1, 1997, when the Turkish press reported on a "top secret" report prepared by the TGS's western working group. This document stressed that:

> The power of religious organizations, due to years of governmental indifference, had grown to the point that the forces who seek a return of the Şeriat system in Turkey had managed to take over key governmental agencies. Further, that if steps to the contrary were not taken, it is possible that the fundamentalists' political wing *[Refah]* could come to power by itself in the year 2000.[12]

When we link this position to a statement made just three months earlier by the spokesman for the Turkish general staff, General Erol Özkasnak—"Henceforth the number-one enemy of the state is İrtica; that İrtica represents an even greater threat to Turkey than the PKK; and that the same diligence with which the armed forces are striving to eliminate the danger represented by the PKK will now be directed against the danger represented by İrtica"[13]—it is clear that in the minds of Turkey's military leaders political Islam is a national security threat, indeed every bit as serious as the PKK.

That these sentiments are shared by the country's judicial branch seems apparent from the subsequent banning of the Islamist *Refah* party (now replaced by *Fazilet*), the ban on political activity by Necmettin Erbakan and other *Refah* leaders, the jailing and lifetime ban on political activity that was imposed on Tayyip Erdoğan (the *Refah* mayor of Istanbul), and court actions begun against *Fazilet* in 1999.

This situation exists even though the national security council is equally divided between military officers and civilians. Its five military members are balanced by four civilian politicians, with the final member being its chairman the president, also a civilian. Regardless of appearances, the decree of February 28, 1997, which was passed unanimously by the NSC (including at that time Necmettin Erbakan, who disagreed with every one of its eighteen demands), illustrates the extent to which the military not only shape the NSC's agenda but also "persuade" the civilian politicians to accept their views.

Nor is this situation likely to change easily. On September 3, 1999, Chief of the General Staff Kıvrıkoğlu held a press briefing for selected journalists. The briefing was intended primarily to respond to press criticism of what was seen as the military's failure to react more promptly to the August earthquake, but Kıvrıkoğlu (in response to prodding) strayed from his prepared text to address other topics, notably the military's attitude toward the February 28, 1999, decisions of the NSC. Kıvrıkoğlu's comments left little doubt but that the "dual-track government" is still on track:

> On the 28th of February [1997] an 18 article decision was adopted by the national security Council. To date only four of the 18 recommendations contained in this decision (including that concerning basic education) have been enacted by legislation. However, we see no sign that there are efforts to push ahead with implementation of the remaining articles. We are also face to face with an approach which says that "the 28th of February is over." The 28th of February is a process. It began in 1923 and from that date until the present it has continued in keeping with the threat of *irtica*. We accept our role as the defenders [against *irtica*]. If necessary, the 28th of February will continue for ten years. If necessary, one hundred years. If necessary, for the period of a thousand years. We are expecting parliament when it reconvenes on October 1st quickly to take up the matter of enacting legislation to implement the remainder of the February 28th decisions.[14]

Because Turkey has since the general elections in December of 1995 been ruled by coalitions headed variously by center-rightists (Çiller and Yilmaz), an Islamist (Erbakan), and a social democrat (Ecevit), perhaps it should not be surprising that the Turkish military has turned to another institution to provide both a strong posture and continuity in policy formulation. The use of the NSC is logical: it is the one constitutionally empowered body in which high-ranking military and civilian authorities meet regularly. Unfortunately for those wishing to follow developments in Turkey, what happens at the monthly NSC meeting is secret—except when, as with the meeting of February 28, 1997, members decide to release results to the press.

Attempts to clarify the parameters of the "dual-track government" are obscured because whatever government is in power does in fact (acting through parliament) carry on most of the normal day-to-day functions. Much legislation is presented, debated, and passed without military involvement. Taxes are collected and disbursed. Diplomacy is carried out. It is not that the military has assumed the power of governing; rather, they have set much of the contentious political agenda and then put pressure on the government to enact it. The power of the military (exerted through the NSC) has, in the past two years, increasingly encroached on areas traditionally (that is, in periods other than the aftermaths of the coups of 1961, 1971, and 1980) the prerogative of the nation's elected civilian leaders.

An outsider is struck by the tacit or explicit endorsement by large segments of Turkish society (not to mention its political leaders) of the erosion of their rights and power; the general reluctance of the media to discuss what I have defined as the reconfiguration of real power in Turkey; and the inability of civilian political leaders to reassert their own constitutionally mandated roles. All these stem in no small part from Turkey's having over the past decade been focused on, and traumatized by, the twin threats of ethnic separatism (the Kurdish question) and Islamic fundamentalism. The traditional elites (the media, the politicians, the state bureaucracies, and the intelligentsia) are unable or unwilling to criticize the one body seen as possessing policies for addressing these threats.

How may we account for this apparent acceptance of not wishing to take on or weaken the military? The answer may in part be that rather draconian legislation still makes it a crime to do so, but it may likewise reflect the view that the military alone, of all the traditional pillars of the state, is generally untainted by corruption. Finally, the military is seen as the ultimate bulwark against subversive internal forces.

There is an important economic factor involved. Although the state-controlled economy of the early republic began to be replaced by a market economy during the Özal era, the transition is far from complete. Like much of Özal's legacy, it was not accompanied by necessary structural changes such as laws governing competition. As a result, society (including retirees, bureaucrats, and the poor and lower classes) expends much time and effort on keeping up with chronically high inflation. Attention that in earlier years would have been focused on politics is now directed on the daily struggle for survival. Turkey's expanding population, an increasing number of whom are moving to the cities, also has placed huge demands on an already strained infrastructure. Surrounded by newcomers, the urban elite feels threatened. One response is to look to the military as the only stable element in society.

Meanwhile, many westernized Turks see a threat to the state in the large numbers of Turks turning to religion and in the growth of Islamic political movements. With politicians vacillating between outdoing one another for the religious vote and expressing alarm over the growing political strength of Islam, it is the military that is seen as the one arm of the state with the will to hold the line on state secularism, indeed, the ultimate bulwark against subversive forces.

The vast sums expended on what until recently has been a spiraling insurgency by the PKK (supported by many fellow-ethnics in Turkey and Europe) have not only led to an enormous drain on the economy (estimates run as high as $80 billion for 1991–99) but also have caused cracks in Turkey's carefully constructed nationalist identity. Once again it is the military—a dominant fixture in Turkish life—that is looked up to as the ultimate protector of Turkish nationalism.

For those 75 percent to 90 percent of Turks who repeatedly rank the military as the branch of government they most trust, this enlarged role of the military in the country's daily life is not viewed as stemming from a desire by the TGS to seize power.[15] Rather, it is seen to derive in no small part from an increasingly fractured political structure (racked by corruption), which has led to weak coalition governments and a decline in the effectiveness of a bureaucracy badly weakened by Özal's rule.

The military developed its own mechanism (its working groups and task forces) to fill this vacuum. In the NSC meetings it is often only the military that comes prepared with talking points, working papers, and policy briefs. The civilians representing the parties of the coalition government of the moment are unable to speak with a single voice, and—as confirmed by two former ministers in recent governments—it is usually the staff work of the military members that carries the day.

Turkey is in a profound state of transition, and the weak political system has failed even to recognize the magnitude of the changes under way, let alone to come up with solutions for the problems thus created. The vacuum has been filled by the military, which has been least affected by the collapse of the old order. (Paradoxically, it can be argued that, had the military not interrupted civilian rule in 1960, 1971, and 1980, Turkey's democratic institutions and its elected leaders might be better positioned to cope with today's problems.) The successive military interventions have led the electorate and politicians alike to view the military as a kind of *deus ex machina,* ready to descend in times of crisis to solve the ills of society.

Moreover, in today's impasse the military and its organs too see their role primarily as the guardians and protectors of the Atatürk legacy, forgetting that Mustafa Kemal, for all his genius, was addressing the profound problems facing the newly created Turkish Republic in the 1920s and 1930s. However, the Turkey of today bears little but geographical resemblance to that created by Atatürk's impressive leadership. The present population of more than 65 million has little in common with the 15 million illiterate peasants and the tiny educated elite of the 1920s. Turkey is now far too complex to be guided by laws of conduct laid down three-quarters of a century ago. Religious sentiments and divergent ethnic identities can no longer be ignored or suppressed. When will the Turkish military recognize that Atatürk today would use his genius to find answers to today's problems, not attempt to turn back the clock? The immunity of the military from criticism does not necessarily bode well for Turkey in the coming years.

In light of the military's strong public support and the continuing political fragmentation and for the most part weak and ineffective governments, how likely is a reduced political role for the military? A revamping of the existing political parties and the law that governs their activities seems not in the cards in the short term. And in the absence of reform it is even more unlikely that the military's worries about ethnicity and secularism will end soon and its leadership will retreat behind the walls of the TGS. Chief of Staff Kıvrıkoğlu's emphatic statement that if the threat of *İrtica* necessitates it the military will stay involved for "a thousand years" should not be overlooked. We will indeed probably see coalition governments—weak or strong—continuing to dance to the tune of the TGS on many major issues.

WHERE IS TURKEY'S CIVIL SOCIETY?

WHY SO PASSIVE?

Most voters, as has been noted, distrust their elected politicians and trust the military. In a survey published by Yilmaz Esmer in 1999, only 51 percent expressed trust in government, 30 percent in political parties, 52 percent in parliament, and 68 percent in government bureaucrats.[16] Nor do the media rate highly—only 50 percent expressed trust in the fourth estate. All this is in sharp contrast to the esteem expressed for the Turkish armed forces—94 percent of the respondents stated their trust in the military.

It is clear that society in general finds it easy to turn a blind eye to the military's encroachment on the powers of elected officials.[17] Although 92 percent of those surveyed in Esmer's study agreed with the statement "While there may be problems with democracy, it is better than any other kind of system," no less than 32 percent found nothing incongruous in also stating that they looked favorably upon rule by the military. One cannot help but concur with Esmer's conclusion that a significant minority of Turks do not really know what democracy is.[18]

In general, the country's traditional elites—big business and educated urbanites, those most likely to vocally defend their political rights—continue to remain silent because they share the military's concern with ethnic violence (the Kurdish insurgency) and with Islamic fundamentalism. They do not want to take any action that can be equated with weakening the nation's last line of defense. These elites are firmly secular, frightened by the kind of religious-based civil strife that emerged in Iran and Algeria in recent decades, and thus prepared to stifle any concerns they may have over the increasingly intrusive role of the TGS. Only the Islamic press is becoming increasingly virulent in its criticism of the military.

THE FAILURE OF THE FOURTH ESTATE

The 1990s saw the emergence of several large media conglomerates. Three groups in particular, controlling print and electronic empires, are increasingly disinclined to bite the hands that may now or in the future feed them. These conglomerates depend on government-supplied investment incentives and government contracts. And since today's opposition may well be tomorrow's government, the media moguls have little incentive to take unnecessary risk or to serve as a serious watchdog on government.

On occasion the media conglomerates do affect politics. For example, they spoke up in late 1993 when Tansu Çiller emerged as a replacement for Süleyman Demirel, who had assumed the presidency after Özal's death. Çiller was an attractive university professor who met the media's desire to see Turkey represented by a western-educated economist rather than by another Anatolian politician. There is no doubt that the publicity campaign they orchestrated on her behalf played a major role in her subsequent political career.

In 1989 the media generated a campaign on behalf of the Turkish and Muslim minorities in Bulgaria. With clandestine footage depicting the plight of Muslim suffering, the media fanned the flames of Turkish public opinion, forcing Özal to throw open the doors and ultimately accept more than three hundred thousand refugees. When it became apparent to the new arrivals that they were little more than pawns (no real steps were taken to ensure their integration into Turkish society) and when the Bulgarian government backed away from its most virulent efforts at "Bulgarization," better than half chose—even before the fall of the Communist regime—to return to Bulgaria.

While the media and the traditional elites have been slow to speak out against the erosion of civilian authority, Turkish NGOs and human rights groups have emerged in the past decade. Though their voices have not grown to the point that they influence policy, they are documenting a wide variety of human rights violations (particularly of Kurds and their supporters), generating materials widely used in the West. The elites have little trouble in dismissing their complaints, but a number of newspaper columnists (among them Mehmet Altan, Ali Bayramoğlu, Cengiz Çandar, Hasan Cemal, and the late Yavuz Gökmen) and academics (Kemal Kirişçi and Doğu Ergil) have found an audience on the Kurdish question. In general one finds more divergent views expressed on the Kurdish issue than on the question of İrtica.

In the past year, a most unlikely voice has emerged calling for granting full cultural rights to ethnic Kurds. Şükrü Elekdağ, one of Turkey's most distinguished retired diplomats, whose career included stints as secretary general of the Turkish Foreign Ministry and nine years as Turkey's envoy in Washington, now writes a weekly column mostly on strategic issues in the newspaper Milliyet. He is a member of the ruling establishment with close links to the military, and when, in June and July 1999, he began turning his pen to the question of Turkey's "accepting the Kurdish reality" many observers were heartened to see such a figure taking a stand on the issue.

Elekdağ argues that Turkey's failure to address the underlying causes of the support for Öcalan's PKK among the least educated and most economically depressed of Turkey's Kurds must come to an end. Further, that failure to follow up on then Prime Minister Demirel's 1992 call for accepting the "Kurdish reality" and to begin addressing the concerns of Turkey's Kurdish citizens is against the country's long-term interests.[19] Since much of both Ecevit's and Bahçeli's recent electoral gains stem from their hard-line Turkish nationalist stances, it seems unlikely that either is likely to respond (even should there be tacit military agreement) with the kind of far-reaching steps called for by Elekdağ.

Though voices in the press are finally speaking out on behalf of acknowledging the reality of Turkey's Kurds and their desires and problems, no similar voices are raised on behalf of greater realism toward freedom of religious expression.

That the mainstream media can now accomodate opinions advocating limited steps to avoid the further politicization of the Kurdish issue is not unrelated to the upper hand the Turkish military seems to have achieved in the southeast. In September 1999 Chief of Staff Kıvrıkoğlu went so far as to state that Kurdish-language television stations were broadcasting in the southeast without legal status and implied they should continue. Prime Minister Bülent Ecevit praised Kıvrıkoğlu for his farsightedness and said that additional steps were called for in the region.[20] Subsequently, in a very unusual move, the TGS issued a formal statement diassociating themselves from these sentiments.

Even the usually silent Turkish judiciary has begun to grumble aloud about the need for a thorough overhaul of the constitutional restrictions on civil rights. When two of the country's highest jurists recently said as much, shock waves rippled through society. In April 1999 Ahmet Necdet Sezer, then the president of the Constitutional Court and now the newly elected president of Turkey, went public in an address stressing the need for major constitutional reform, and in September Sami Selçuk, first president of the Supreme Court of Appeals, made a similar address. Sezer emphasized the need for a constitutional amendment establishing universal human rights and civil liberties, and Selçuk even argued for the drafting by civilians of a new constitution—1982's having been prepared under military tutelage. Remarkably, he called the existing military-imposed constitution "illegitimate" and "an obstacle to democracy," and said that the current system, in which the centralized state has more rights than the individual, needed a complete revamping.[21] These speeches are another sign that establishment voices are beginning to speak out against aspects of the system they serve.

One indication that Turkish civil society may be learning to speak up occurred in a most unusual manner. In the early morning of November 2, 1996, a car carrying an odd mix of passengers was involved in a fatal traffic accident near the small town of Susurluk in northwestern Anatolia. Among the victims was Abdullah Çatlı, a former right-wing terrorist who had been under indictment since 1979 for his role in the political murders of seven people. In the intervening years he had been convicted as a narcotics smuggler in France. After completing his sentence he had been extradited to Switzerland, where he was sentenced on a separate narcotics charge. He escaped from a Swiss prison in 1992. He was riding with his mistress, with a prominent senior Turkish police official named Hüseyin Kocadağ, and with a Kurdish tribal leader from Urfa, Sedat Bucak, who also was a member of parliament from Çiller's DYP. The only survivor of the crash, Bucak, pleading amnesia, was unable to tell authorities why he had been traveling with such an unlikely group of associates.

Together with a rather large assortment of unregistered weapons purchased by the Ministry of the Interior, the wrecked car was found to contain numerous identity papers with Çatlı's picture and issued in a variety of false names. They did have two things in common: they had been issued by the police and were signed by the then minister of the interior, Mehmet Ağar, who was a close associate of Çiller's as well and a member of her parliamentary bloc.

The failure of the government (the *Refah-Yol* coalition of which Çiller was the junior partner) to conduct a proper investigation led to spontaneous public protests when hundreds of thousands (and then millions) of Turks began turning off their lights for a time at 9:00 every evening. Forced by the stirring of a generally silent public, the authorities belatedly began an investigation. The lights went back on, but the cover-up continues; the connection between a suspected political murderer turned underworld boss, a police chief, and a prominent politician remains unknown. The parliamentary enquiry into the Susurluk event ultimately did conclude that there were state-supported illegal networks operating as paramilitary hit teams (against Kurdish businessmen suspected of providing financial support to the PKK) and that these groups had ties to organized crime. Testimony had established that Çatlı (while under indictment) had been used—first by Turkish intelligence and then by the very Turkish police who were supposed to apprehend him—for operations against "enemies of the state." While this whole mess is unlikely ever to be unraveled, it is significant that it was a public outcry that forced the politicians at least to feign investigating an issue they did not want to touch, even if in the end it was once again swept under the rug.

Another public outcry arose in August 1999, when Ecevit's coalition government (pressed by its Nationalist partner) passed an amnesty bill that would have had the effect of freeing corrupt politicians, murderers, and mafia kingpins (many with links to the MHP) while leaving behind bars those imprisoned for speeches and writings. The protests convinced then president Demirel to veto the act, for him a highly unusual step. In an accompanying statement he made it clear that he took his decision largely because of the public opposition to the parliamentary action.

Several factors have contributed to what can only be termed the slow emergence of a vibrant Turkish civil society. A strong respect for the authority of the state has long combined with Turkish nationalism to calm down the development of a population otherwise predisposed to keep a close watch on government. The media, long dependent on the support of whoever is in power, have traditionally exercised a great deal of self-censorship in their criticism of authority (the coverage of Susurluk being an exception). Above all, a series of military interventions served to interrupt the development of democratic institutions in 1960, 1971, and 1980. Each intervention was followed by the jailing of journalists, academics, and critics, often for stories they had written years earlier, and the 1982 constitution banned groups such as university teachers and trade unionists from forming any type of association (a constitutional ban repealed only in 1995—although it had never been enacted into legislation).

What is changing this situation is the extent to which Turkey's traditional isolation has been crumbling in the face of the vast information and media revolution and ongoing globalization of the past decade. Only ten years ago, Turkish state television enjoyed a total monopoly. Today, not only are there close to twenty independent television networks (and more than three hundred local stations); the major urban centers have cable television that brings CNN and the BBC into homes. The press has recently reported numerous stories of criminal suspects (influenced by their viewing of American and European television series) who, on being arrested, demand their right to have a lawyer present at their interrogations.

Many Turks received their news about the August 1999 earthquake from foreign and Turkish private television stations. These also served to convince the viewing public of the ineffectiveness of government attempts to cope with the chaos, helping not only to mobilize private relief efforts but also to overturn the popular notion that the outside world cares nothing about Turkey. Hour after hour of watching live shots of Israelis, Americans, and Greeks and other Europeans providing relief may have gone a long way toward changing attitudes toward both their own government and others. Clearly the Turkish authorities were not immune to the earthquake coverage provided by the privately owned media outlets; one channel was ordered shut down for a week as a result of its broadcasts. The widespread calls for the resignation of the minister of health (an MHP member of the government) for claiming that everything was under control and there was no need for foreign relief workers, who were only concerned about the cleanliness of their toilet facilities, stemmed in no small part from the Turkish public's awareness that the only effective early rescue efforts were run by foreign volunteers. It would be ironic if it were the tragedy of the earthquake and the state's inability to cope with it that ultimately turned out to be the needed push toward a more robust civil society.

The information genie is out of the bottle in Turkey, and civil society will only be strengthened as a result. The competition among television channels, particularly the private ones, along with the pressure on the print media not to be outdone by their electronic rivals, means that the public is increasingly exposed to variety in the news. Even the military may not be above criticism when millions of viewers have seen with their own eyes that it failed to react in a timely fashion to the earthquake. Talk shows (many of which run for four to six hours) are popular and provide a forum for views across the political spectrum. In a given night one can surf among lively debates on Kurds, on the role of Islam in society, and on the lifestyles of politicians. Television coverage of the earthquake carnage has already led to the formation of civil defense groups, rescue teams, and private earthquake relief groups. Individuals are beginning to take an active interest in areas long held to be the preserve of government.

At the very least the idea of *Devlet Baba* [father state] as the answer to all of society's ills is no longer sacrosanct, and the 1999 earthquake may yet turn out to have been a turning point. There is a view in the country that what remains under the rubble is the very system itself. If public outrage continues—still uncertain—it may well be that the politicians could be left with no option but to enact systemic reform.

CONCLUSION

Despite the vast changes in society and the economy in the past decade, the Turkey of Atatürk, represented by the military and the older bureaucratic elites, continues to exist side by side with the Turkey of Özal, typified by a younger generation of technocrats and businessmen. Stated differently, yesterday and today move alongside one another in parallel, sometimes in sync but more often each oblivious of the other. When their paths cross it is usually the past that prevails, for when the military speaks, society still listens.

Tomorrow's Turkey will ultimately leave yesterday's legacy behind—but not easily. In the end, even the military (which over the past decade have developed into well-equipped, effective modern armed forces) may have no option but to change their thinking as well. When they do come to accept the complexity of the society they are intended to protect, many of the tensions that loom so large today will likely subside. The indirect "soft coup" of February 28, 1997, may be a preliminary sign that the military have acknowledged they cannot take direct power in the complex society that has now evolved in Turkey.

In time, too, Turkey's mainstream political parties will have no option but to reform. Failure to do so will cause their disappearance as their vote shares fall beneath the 10 percent barrier (as happened to the CHP in the 1999 elections). Self-preservation and the global economy clearly dictate the need for far-reaching political reform. Until and unless it occurs, the trend of voters moving to the religious or nationalist extremes will likely continue.

More and more Turks believe that pervasive corruption among politicians, bureaucrats, businessmen, and even ordinary citizens must be reduced. This can only be done by restoring the supremacy of law and providing more equal justice, but this is up to the parliament, and—in a country where being elected to parliament is often viewed as the first step to "turning the corner"—this will not come easily. Ultimately, it is the public that will have to insist on clean government, presumably finding leaders responsive to its dissatisfactions.

Turkey's political future also will depend on its rapidly expanding business elite's deciding to play a role and seriously enter politics. A first step was launched in the mid-1990s by the young industrialist Cem Boyner, whose New Democracy Movement was the right step at the wrong time. Turkey's ruling elites were simply unprepared for an open discussion of ethnic, religious, cultural, and income distribution problems. Boyner, for his part, with his training in the business world, was unable (or unwilling) to make the kind of compromises that would have ensured a wider appeal to voters. The next such movement, when it appears, will at least have the benefit of hindsight.

Until political reform permits parties to garner broader electoral support (in the April 1999 elections no party was able to obtain more than 22 percent of the vote), we will more often than not see weak coalition governments—governments that by their nature are unlikely to find a consensus for drastic political reform. Thus, the military will in all likelihood continue to play a key role in policy formulation.

The 1980s and 1990s represented an immense upheaval for Turkey and its people. Turgut Özal took on a seventy-five-year-old system of vested interests and ideologies. Unlike the USSR, which replaced an outmoded form of government, Turkey has attempted the daunting task of trying to fit a new approach into an old form. Today, the visions of Atatürk (or more correctly, that of his followers, who created "Atatürkism") and Özal are locked in conflict. While historical experience and Turkish dynamism leave little doubt as to the ultimate success of the new at the expense of the old, there is still a long way to go before Turkey reaches a level of democratic development that fully satisfies its critics both at home and abroad. In the short term, direct outside pressure (no matter how well intended) can play at best only a small part in speeding the process and could have the effect of temporarily strengthening conservative and nationalist forces.

Those wishing to see change in Turkey cannot help but be heartened by the outcome of the EU's December 1999 meeting in Helsinki, where Turkey was added to the list of candidate countries for membership. If this is a path Turkey is to follow in the coming years, it will require wide-reaching changes domestically. The role of the military in civilian politics, freedom of religious expression, and cultural rights for minorities are but a few of the areas that must be addressed before Turkey ever achieves full membership in the European Union.

In the coming months and years the phenomena that bear close watching include the increased political role of the military; the trampling on human rights in the name of national security, which, by suppressing religious sentiments, still could produce a permanently alienated and potentially violent Islamic element; the as yet undetermined nature of the new, ultranationalist MHP; the political role of the Islamists; the growing gap between the haves and have-nots; and the collapse of the center-left–center-right political parties that have heretofore guided Turkey's democratic experiment.

Policymakers will have to avoid focusing narrowly on any single problem area. Turkey is not in any immediate danger of being torn apart by either ethnic, religious, or class conflicts; political turbulence, however, is all but certain.

The enormous loss of infrastructure caused by the August 1999 earthquake, together with the anger against the politicians—blamed both for failing to react more effectively and for not having regulated the building contractors whose faulty construction resulted in tens of thousands of unnecessary deaths—does not bode well for political stability in the short term. Public opinion is looking for someone to hold accountable. For the Islamists the answer may be the godlessness of secular Turkish society—where liquor stores have already been destroyed by citizens seeing in the earthquake God's punishment. Even the military was not spared criticism for failing to mobilize relief efforts in the first five days after the tragedy. For most of Turkey's citizens it is likely to be the politicians now in power who serve as an outlet for their frustrations, further encouraging political instability.

Turkey is alive and increasingly vibrant, though still suffering the aftereffects not only of the August 1999 earthquake but also of the changes introduced by Özal in the 1980s and 1990s. Much time will still be needed to digest and react to them. Turkey's rapid pace of social and economic change, the repercussions of its increasing integration into the world economy, and its systemic difficulties will mean that American policymakers can expect considerable political turbulence for the next decade.

CHAPTER THREE

TURKEY AND THE KURDS
MISSING ANOTHER OPPORTUNITY?

PHILIP ROBINS

*The inability of the Turks to apply in Kurdistan the lesson which
they had been taught by bitter experience in the Arab provinces
and Rumelia, is likely to cost them dear.*
— Arnold Toynbee and Kenneth Kirkwood, 1926[1]

Throughout its short life, the Turkish Republic has had a difficult relationship with its Kurdish population.[2] In all its great projects—state-
building, the forging of a political ideology, creating a modern society,
economic development—the Turkish state has met ambivalence and
resistance from many of its Kurds. In part these problems reflect the
marginality of the Kurdish regions in Turkey—the prevalence of tribal
politics, personal piety and social conservatism, low standards of educational achievement, modest levels of per capita income. In part they
reflect a contrasting vision of how to think of state and nationhood.
Whatever the causes, the reality remains that after more than seventy-five
years the Turkish Republic has failed to incorporate a substantial part

Note: Research on which this paper is based was made possible by a generous
grant from the Leverhulme Foundation. I would like to thank Hugh Pope as
well as the other members of the project for their comments and helpful suggestions on the draft.

of its Kurdish population. The fact that in both the 1920s and the 1990s the Turkish state met widespread, organized resistance, both violent and nonviolent, from among significant numbers of Kurds is an illustration of the enduring nature of these problems.

In view of the longevity and deep-seated nature of the problem, no one should underestimate the difficulty of navigating a peaceful course. Nevertheless, in 1999 the political kaleidoscope was given a sharp twist. Not since 1993, with the PKK's first unilateral cease-fire and Turgut Özal's attempts at peacemaking, have circumstances seemed anywhere near so auspicious for peacemaking.[3] On this occasion, new hope has been provided by the Kurdish side as a result of the actions of the Turkish side. The capture, repatriation, trial, and sentencing to death of the PKK leader, Abdullah Öcalan, resulted in his public conversion, whether as an act of bravery or cowardice, from a proponent of armed struggle to a preacher of reconciliation and cooperation. Most important, on August 2, 1999, Öcalan ordered the PKK to end its armed struggle and to withdraw its fighters from Turkish territory.

Such change in the Kurdish problem in 1999 inevitably raises the question of how susceptible the conflict is to the initiation of a peaceful negotiation leading to a comprehensive and durable settlement. This central issue in turn contains three further questions. First, is it possible at all that Abdullah Öcalan and the PKK could become an acceptable partner for Turkey in the resolution of the Kurdish problem? Second, what are the likely scenarios for the future, and what would a settlement look like in the event of a successful peace process? Third, what are the costs of not pursuing such a course of action? It is these three questions that this paper will address. Before that, however, let us review the essence of the problem and the backdrop of historical experience that has conditioned perceptions on all sides.

THE KURDISH PROBLEM

THE KURDS: A REMINDER

The Kurds are a distinct people[4] who overlap the borders of the states of Iran, Iraq, Turkey, and (to a much lesser degree) Syria. Estimating their general population is difficult—making estimates the subject of both scholarly and political dispute—but they probably number in a range of 20 to 26 million. The largest concentration of Kurds is to be found in Turkey, where best estimates tend to put them at between 15 percent and 20 percent of the population, or between roughly 10 and 13 million.[5] The important thing about the demography of Kurds in Turkey, however, is not their precise number but that they represent a substantial element, both in absolute terms and as a proportion of the total population.

Turkey's Kurdish population is strongly identified with the east and southeast of the country. Over the past two decades a combination of economic pull factors from the increasingly prosperous regions of western Turkey and the push factors of warfare, repression, and poverty have seen a migration of significant parts of the population, leaving perhaps less than 50 percent of Kurds resident in their traditional region.

The geographical dispersal of many of Turkey's Kurds is only one of a number of complicating factors. Though it is not uncommon to see statements that the Kurds are one of the most numerous ethnic groups in the world and certainly in the Middle East not to have their own state, in reality the national expression of a Kurdish ethnicity is less than the sum of its parts. Kurds are divided by the fact that they do not all speak Kurmanji, the main Kurdish language in use in Turkey, with Turkish and the dialect of Zaza being its greatest rivals. Kurds also are divided along confessional lines, with perhaps 30 percent believed to be Alevis and the remainder Sunnis,[6] and they are deeply fractured along tribal lines, which in turn is reflected in deep political divisions. For Kurds, in the past at least, Islam rather than ethnic nationalism has been the chief marker of identity; many Kurds have been assimilated, whether out of conviction or expediency, into the national political milieu of the states they inhabit.

Turkey is the best example of this political assimilation. That the majority of both Turks and Kurds are Sunni Muslims aids integration on the mass level, and intermarriage, especially in urban areas, is not uncommon.[7] Indeed, it must be emphasized that Turkish claims of widespread assimilation, especially in the urban areas of western Turkey, are no sham. For example, Kurdish ethno-nationalist parties usually perform poorly in elections outside their traditional areas. Furthermore, a number of leading political figures of Kurdish origin do in fact insist on expressing the primacy of a Turkish over a Kurdish political identity. There are at any one time estimated to be more than

100 deputies of Kurdish origin in the 550-strong Turkish parliament, a figure representing around 20 percent. To the Western eye such a situation often spawns incongruities: Ziya Gökalp, who is often referred to as the father of Turkish nationalism, was born and bred in Diyarbakır and hence is assumed to be of Kurdish origin; one of Turkey's leading Kurdish nationalist politicians bears the name Ahmet Türk.

Of crucial importance to the issue of the Kurdish problem in Turkey is determining what proportion of the 10 to 13 million or so Kurds self-consciously identify themselves as Kurds and wish to express such an identity in a demonstrable way, whether politically or just culturally. Such a judgment is difficult to make in the absence of efficient quantitative indicators and with the illiberal atmosphere that exists in many of the areas where the Kurdish population is concentrated. However, as was the case in estimating the overall Kurdish population, it is the magnitude rather than the exact size that is important.

Rough-and-ready methods indicate that Kurdish ethno-nationalist affiliation is considerable. Take, for example, the vote in the April 1999 local elections in the largest Kurdish regional city of Diyarbakır in support of the People's Democracy Party (*Hadep*), a self-consciously Kurdish party campaigning for greater rights, which was 62.57 percent. Some foreign diplomats go so far as to estimate Kurdish self-consciousness in the southeast of the country in the 70 percent to 80 percent range.

Making a judgment about the Kurdish population outside the east and southeast is even harder. One would expect a greater degree of at least tacit integration based on a more tangible material vulnerability, together with the fear of an ethnic rejection by the majority Turkish population. These parts of Turkey also are subject to considerable unevenness in terms of integration. In some cities, such as Adana,[8] there is a higher level of tension between the state and the resident Kurdish population; in parts of Istanbul there is a high concentration of Kurds in areas such as Gaziosmanpasa. There is also an important chronological divide to be taken into account, relating to when exactly Kurdish population groups moved outside traditional areas of residence. For those who moved to Istanbul, Izmir, Ankara, and other cities before the 1960s, assimilation was rapid;[9] for those who arrived after the 1960s, but before 1989, migration is likely to have been a deliberate act based on a desire to secure a higher standard of living, but with such large-scale migrations hindering assimilation.[10] Those who left the east and southeast after 1989, when the insurgency and the brutal response of the state and its allies intensified, are more likely to have been obliged to leave due to village destruction, intimidation, and the loss of traditional economic roles; they also are more likely to have been politicized as a result of their experience of tension and conflict, and they are still relatively unassimilated.

Overall, it should be noted that in the two successive elections that it has contested in Turkey, *Hadep* achieved a national vote of 4.2 percent and 4.76 percent in 1994 and 1999, respectively. This provides a baseline for estimation. Bearing in mind that Kurdish families tend to be larger than their Turkish counterparts, that the high number of displaced people in the southeast will have hampered voter registration, and that the illiberal atmosphere inside the country also works against Kurdish political expression, these national election figures need to be revised upward to arrive at a more accurate figure. An intuitive estimate of the nationally self-conscious Kurds in Turkey, together with their families, therefore numbers between 5.2 and 6.5 million, or roughly 8 percent to 10 percent of the total population.

IDEOLOGY AND IDENTITY

The essence of the problem between Turks and Kurds is a deep-seated disagreement about the governance of those people inside the territory of Turkey who identify themselves as Kurds. Often the issue is presented in geopolitical terms, with "the southeast problem" being used interchangeably with "the Kurdish problem," although this ignores the geographical dispersal of Turkey's Kurds. At present, the disagreement is first and foremost ideological, with many Kurds increasingly demanding a right to organize politically and culturally as Kurds, while the Turkish state insists on subordinating such aspirations to an all-encompassing Turkish sense of identity. But this is no fleeting problem. Rather, it is one that has spanned the existence of republican Turkey and has its origins in the Young Turk movement of the beginning of the twentieth century. With notions of nationalism and self-determination continuing to be contested concepts of regional and global importance, there is strong circumstantial evidence at the very least that this fundamental disagreement will not fade away of its own accord in the future.

Although this disagreement has been of an enduring nature, its character has not remained static; rather, it has evolved extensively over the past four decades. In the 1920s and 1930s, the challenge from the Kurdish areas to the new state of Turkey was made in the name of Islam, with tribal affiliation also being exploited to mobilize opposition. In the 1960s and 1970s, the challenge was couched in terms of Marxism-Leninism, a convenient ideological mechanism that legitimized both struggle against a national security state and the Kurdish clients of the state. Increasingly, that ideological dinosaur was supplanted by a wave of Kurdish ethno-nationalism, with its ever-present risk of intercommunal violence. This changing nature of Kurdish opposition has resulted in different goals being pursued at different times during these more or less discrete ideological periods. During the 1920s and 1930s the uprisings in the southeast aimed at restoring Islam as the central organizing principle of a state that would embrace both Turks and Kurds mixed with a tendency among the tribes of the periphery to want to circumscribe the power of the state. During the 1960s and 1970s revolutionary politics preached solidarity between the oppressed among both Kurds and Turks for the transformation to a single socialist state for all. It is only in the 1980s and the early 1990s that the maximalist aim of full secession for the southeast of Turkey has come to the fore, an objective that would divide Kurds from Turks irreparably. This separatist aim may too have had its day, being rhetorically abandoned in 1993 to be replaced by talk of federation or even decentralization within a fully democratic Turkish state.[11] If these shifting goals are suggestive of a fluidity on the Kurdish side, whether born of weakness or pragmatism, on the Turkish side the overriding factor is the presence of a coherent, consistent, and uncompromising Turkish ideology, which implicitly—and often explicitly—rejects the validity of Kurdish ethno-nationalism. As the Turkish businessman and former politician Cem Boyner has said, "At the root of the Kurdish problem lies the Turkish state's nationalist policies."[12]

TURKISH NATIONALISM

The creation of a subjective Turkish identity to be the primary focus of loyalty to the new state was an invention both of necessity and of its day. It reflected the need to bind together a number of disparate peoples thrown together in the chaotic aftermath of the disintegration of the Ottoman Empire. In the past, Islam had provided the glue for such ideological solidarity. But Atatürk rejected religion in such a role as backward. Instead, he looked to Europe for the ideas of nationalism that would forge a new identity for a new state. In doing so, however, Atatürk lacked neither imagination nor realism. He appreciated the widely different peoples of Turkey,[13] as well as the need to act quickly to fend off external attempts to decide the political fate of Anatolia and eastern Thrace. He therefore eschewed a solidarity based on blood or race, insisting instead that all that was required to be a Turk was an act of voluntary association. By the standards of nationalism in many parts of Europe in the 1920s and 1930s, Atatürk's ideas were distinctly progressive.

But if Atatürk's notion of Turkish nationalism was an effective response to the necessities of state-building in the context of the turmoil of the 1920s, those ideas have not matured and evolved since then in calmer times. One might have expected that as the divisive Treaty of Sèvres of 1920 receded into the past, and as state consolidation deepened, especially after the Second World War, so Turkish nationalism would have softened. This would after all have been the greatest sign of success, a product of self-confidence and security rather than a reflection of weakness. This, however, has largely not been the case, as the notorious attempt to label Kurds "mountain Turks" illustrates. Indeed, in the case of the 1980–83 military regime some aspects of Turkish nationalism actually became more uncompromising, such as the impractical move, since rescinded, to ban the use of the Kurdish language in public. For the truth of the matter is that Turks have continued to be gripped by an "insecurity complex" throughout most of the state's seventy-seven-year existence. Turks today, especially among parts of the elite, are acutely aware of the international history of the early 1920s—probably more so than they are of much of what has happened since. Many commentators inside the country have drawn attention to the existence of what has come to be known as a "Sèvres mentality," whereby multiple conspiracies are perceived to exist with the central aim of dividing the state. As Turks have begun to rediscover their Ottoman heritage since the late 1980s so they have become increasingly aware of the territorial disintegration of the empire and the part played by ethnically distinct groups at home and great powers abroad. This sense of territorial insecurity has, furthermore, not been helped by the location of the Kurdish areas adjacent to the Middle East, a region where the revision of the state system has been the focus of active debate from decolonization in the 1940s to the Iraqi invasion of Kuwait in 1990. The disintegration of the USSR and the former Yugoslavia, though these states were by no means analogous to Turkey, has given an additional edge to such fears if for no other reason than their proximity and, in the case of the latter, their common Ottoman backdrop.

In turn, the relative harshness of the state's nationalist ideology has been accentuated since the late 1980s by the emergence of an invigorated commitment to pluralism and liberal politics across most of the European continent. For many opinion formers in Europe, Turkish state ideology has appeared in the 1990s to be increasingly anachronistic. For all of Turkey's decades-old support of the Atlantic Alliance, Turkish state ideology has increasingly been perceived as having more in common with the old authoritarian ideologies of Eastern Europe than with the new liberalism of the continent.

While the ideology of the Turkish state has struggled to match the changes in Europe, it also has faced a more potent ideological threat from its Kurdish areas. As long as opposition from among Kurds was based on Islam, it could be faced down by the Turkish state on the grounds of modernity and the eradication of superstition. As long as opposition was based on Marxism-Leninism and notions of class warfare, it could be resisted vigorously in the name of national security and solidarity with the Western alliance. Opposition based on Kurdish ethno-nationalism, however, is harder to combat, as it is more difficult to make a convincing case that it is intrinsically inferior to or less desirable than Turkish nationalism. The proponents of Turkish nationalism are left with little choice other than to argue a sort of implied ideological Darwinism: Turkish nationalism is better than Kurdish nationalism because the former has access to a strength through state power that is unavailable to the latter. Beyond that, another form of Darwinism beckons: the Turks have been the victors of history, the Kurds, its casualty; ergo the Turks are superior to the Kurds. It is little wonder then that from the late 1980s onward the struggle between Turkish and Kurdish nationalism has basically become a function of power politics.

THE CENTRALITY OF VIOLENCE

That, in turn, leads to a second factor that militates against optimism about the future. That is the centrality of violence both in the pursuit of the Kurdish agenda and the state's response to it. It would be reductionist to suggest that violence was somehow the defining feature of Turkish-Kurdish relations, let alone an intrinsic part of political culture. Nevertheless, violence cannot be ignored, either in itself or in its effects. Violence has been an important form of Kurdish resistance,[14] regardless of whether one looks at the fortunes of the Kurds in Iran, Iraq, or Turkey. Moreover, violence has been as integral to Kurdish opposition in the 1990s as it was in the 1920s, while state repression has been equally vigorous during both periods. The fact that in excess of thirty thousand people have been killed during the PKK-led insurgency since 1984 is evidence enough.

Violence is important not only as a political mechanism to which both sides readily resort. It is important in many other ways. First is the psychological impact on the respective communities. Both Turks and Kurds have been traumatized and brutalized by the ferocity of the conflict. Second, it is important because of the cultural practices it has spawned. The apparent alacrity with which Kurdish protesters resort to self-immolation to protest against political persecution is a ready example. Death by fire has assumed the same meaning for dissident Kurds as the hunger strike has for radical Irish nationalists. In turn, the violence also produces its own mythology: each side has its heroes, its Shaikh Saids and its Kubilays. Third, the violence has created bundles of interests based on it, especially economic vested interests.[15] Here, salient examples abound. Everything from the village-guard system to the extortion and racketeering of the PKK in Europe, and from the control of drug smuggling to the protection of military budgets and hardware procurement, is predicated on the imminent prospect of violent confrontation between Kurd and Turk.

To recap, charting a course toward peace and reconciliation will certainly not be easy. Standing in its way is the harshness and inflexibility of Turkish state nationalism, renewed and nourished by a deeply felt sense of insecurity and the perception of plots all around to divide the state. A second significant barrier is the violence that has riven southeastern Turkey for the past fifteen years, and the cultural, psychological, and economic vestiges of the conflict, all of which will have to be overcome if a workable settlement is to be established. To find a peaceful settlement of the conflict and to establish a harmonious setting in which Kurds and Turks can genuinely coexist, the size of the obstacles that need to be scaled should not be underestimated.

THE COSTS OF CONTINUITY

In the cost-benefit analysis of peacemaking, there is a tendency for the Turkish side to underestimate the disadvantages of not proceeding. If the premise is held that the PKK insurgency is to all intents and purposes already over, and therefore that the intensity of the violence of the early to mid-1990s is a thing of the past, the mistake could easily be made that the costs of failing to achieve a historic reconciliation are relatively minor.

In fact, the costs to Turkey of the Kurdish insurgency have been enormous and are likely to continue to be so in the absence of an overall solution to Turkish-Kurdish relations. The costs have both an internal and an external dimension.

THE INTERNAL DOMAIN

When looking at the costs to Turkey of the Kurdish problem there is a tendency to focus on the areas of conflict and to try to quantify such costs. Most obviously, attention is drawn to the cost of the military operations aimed at containing and combating the insurgency in the southeast of the country. Such an issue is plainly important. At the height of the insurgency, the Turkish state had some 220,000 troops deployed in the southeast, together with an additional 50,000 members of the special forces and around 45,000 village guards.[16] In addition, Ankara has spent heavily in the 1990s on military procurement—some $3 billion a year, much of it with the aim of combating the PKK. Everything from Black Hawk and Super Cobra helicopters through night-vision equipment to armored vehicles has been pressed into service in the southeast. Furthermore, one also needs to factor in the cost of the repeated cross-border incursions into northern Iraq, aimed at destroying and disrupting the PKK's base of operations there.

The costs of such aggregated activities are notoriously difficult to estimate. One is therefore instinctively skeptical of the $7–$8.5 billion bill that was routinely cited in the late 1990s (without elaboration) as the annual cost of the conflict. In some respects, the size of the figure is helpful. It signals the fact that the annual bill is substantial, the equivalent of approximately 15 percent of GDP, especially for a country which has some way to go before its economy can be described as developed. Such a figure is also helpful in pointing to the impact of such spending on the country's inflation rate. If inflation has bobbed up and down between the 60 percent and 90 percent mark over the past two decades, a substantial part of this, perhaps on the order of 10 percent, has been caused by the strain on the Turkish economy by the insurgency in the east and southeast of the country.

The absence of a serious attempt to estimate how the total cost breaks down emphasizes the imprecision—if not the almost arbitrary nature—of the estimate. Although one suspects that the military costs have almost certainly been underestimated, say in terms of full cost accounting and the factoring in of the cross-border activities in northern Iraq, it must be admitted that some of the costs would have been incurred in any case: fighting the PKK has helped Turkey to create a better-trained and more mobile force, putting it more in line with the new NATO norm, a goal to which Turkey has been committed since the late 1980s.

There have been even fewer attempts to estimate the cost of the insurgency in terms of its civilian economic and social impact. It is difficult to put a price on the destruction of up to 3,500 villages and hamlets and the displacement of some 3 million people. Suffice it to say that the scale of this displacement over fifteen years has been far in excess of the estimated 100,000 people rendered homeless by the August 1999 earthquake. While relief assistance has flowed into Turkey to help with the humanitarian plight, little by way of help has been made available to the displaced of the southeast. They have largely migrated to the towns and cities of the southeast and beyond, swelling the population and creating whole suburbs of temporary accommodation. A city like Diyarbakır in the southeast has seen its population rise from around 350,000 in 1990 to some 1.2 million at the turn of the century. In addition to the cost of the destruction and the lost productivity of the rural economy, it is difficult to believe that there will not be long-term costs related to the resulting poverty and dislocation—ill health and crime as well as possible political consequences.

However, a preoccupation with the military impact carries the danger of obscuring the impact of the Kurdish issue on the state itself. Virtually since its inception there have been concerns at the lack of accountability of the state in Turkey. In recent times, the 1980 military coup d'état and the 1982 constitution have further increased these concerns. The modus operandi of the Turkish state has, to say the least, often been obscured from view. Revelations since 1996 have shown that the state in Turkey has abused this privileged position, especially in the relationships that have been established with mafia and ultra-rightist gangs. These abuses did not begin with the Kurdish insurgency; the relationship with such notorious ultranationalists and drug smugglers as Abdullah Çatli and Alaatin Çakici was evident in their involvement in armed attempts to end the campaign of assassinations of the Armenian Secret Army for the Liberation of Armenia (ASALA).[17]

Relations forged in the 1970s and 1980s, however, were multiplied and intensified in the early 1990s, as the state struggled to cope with the PKK insurgency. Ultrarightists were recruited, to the elite forces of the gendarmerie in particular, to fight the PKK on the ground;[18] new special forces and intelligence units associated with different branches of the state mushroomed, as did other shadowy organizations like Hezbollah, a fringe Islamist movement, the violent methods of which have only latterly been exposed. At very least the state was guilty of failing to prevent Hezbollah from pursuing an orgy of violence against predominantly moderate Kurdish figures. Hezbollah's activities appear to have formed part of a campaign of extrajudicial executions initiated in 1991, with few if any of its perpetrators brought to justice. At its worst, Turkey's "dirty war" was comparable to the actions of the state in many Latin American countries in the 1970s. In the words of one human rights activist, there was "a lawlessness" about the Turkish state in the 1990s, even compared to the human rights abuses of the previous decade.[19]

Even today, many Turks will defend the excesses of the state during the 1991–94 period on the grounds of national security and the need to face down a concerted attempt at a foreign-backed secession by a movement acting from within. The cry of "Turkey is proud of you," which was given a loud voice by no less a person than former premier Tansu Çiller, can still be heard. While the threat from the PKK has subsided in the second half of the 1990s, the activities of such "state gangs" have not. Such gangs have exploited the free hand the state gave them in the southeast to move in on and take over criminal activities, notably the heroin trade. Up to 90 percent of the heroin on the streets of Britain has a Turkish connection. The state has been disabled in its efforts to rein in these gangs because of its complicity in their earlier activities.

A further irony lies in the nature of the state in Turkey. It has become routine to describe the Turkish state as strong because of its size, the extent of its control, and the power of the coercive forces at its disposal. However, this image of strength has obscured some realities. First, the state has been losing much of its strength, both economically, as the private sector generates an ever-increasing proportion of national wealth, and with respect to information, with the proliferation of independent media. Second, much of the state's reputation for organization is ill founded, as the poor relief response to the earthquake again revealed; rather than being strong and keen, the state is more often bureaucratic and sluggish. Third, and arguably of greatest importance, the strength that the state possesses can better be described in terms of what Nazih Ayubi, writing about Turkey's Arab neighbors, has called harshness or fierceness than in terms of authority.[20] In particular, the state in Turkey lacks the moral strength that can only come from a near consensus that power is wielded legitimately. The absence of this authority springs directly from the state's inability to incorporate significant sections of the population, notably the Kurds. This most serious of deficiencies not only results in an increase in ferocity by way of compensation but also draws attention to the growing size of the normative gap between contemporary European and Turkish conceptions of state and society.

THE EXTERNAL DOMAIN

EU-TURKISH RELATIONS. The growing normative gap between Turkey and the countries of the EU has been one of the most important, yet least remarked upon, elements in EU-Turkish relations in the 1990s. It helps to explain why Europeans, Helsinki notwithstanding, have increasingly come to regard Turkey as "not being like us" far better than does either religion or cultural heritage. Few subjects better evoke this normative gap than the Kurdish issue, with its challenge to preconceived notions of state and ideology in Turkey, its centrality to the pluralism debate, and its strong association with the issue of human rights. While the PKK as an organization has made little headway in arguing its case with European informed opinion in the 1990s,[21] in terms of the Kurdish issue in general there has been, by contrast, much more of a resonance.

When the cold war ended and the Berlin Wall came down, Europeans and Turks were confronted with one another much more as they are. Gone was the glue of the common external threat of the Soviet Union; gone too was the mutual dislike of communism. Shorn of this artificial solidarity, Europeans and Turks have had to confront their own reality; truth to tell, they have not much liked what they have seen. In 1990s Europe, there has been an embrace of the values of liberalism, humanism, and pluralism; state power, now bordering on the distasteful, has been voluntarily constrained; national governments have increasingly shared ideas and tasks with both nongovernmental organizations and suprastate institutions, especially at the EU level; human rights have increasingly emerged as a central plank of foreign policy.

Many in the Turkish elite have watched the assertion of such values with a mixture of suspicion, disbelief, and contempt. Suspicion, in that many Turks regard these ideas as a European convenience for pushing Turkey away from the EU, while such slogans as "a Europe of the regions" take on a sinister connotation when transposed to the Turkish context. Disbelief, in that such institutions as the European Parliament and Amnesty International are easy for Turks to dismiss as irrelevant, even though the former has increasingly acquired considerable power in terms of European external relations, while the latter has emerged as a benchmark of conscience across much of Europe. Contempt, in that many elite Turks regard these normative developments as exuding weakness—in their eyes, only a strong state and a rigid ideological line are sufficient to stave off the chaos that would otherwise ensue.

Against a backdrop of such cognitive divergence, Turks and Europeans have repeatedly clashed over a series of different areas of public policy, with human rights representing the zeitgeist. For Europeans, as laid down in the Copenhagen Criteria for membership, a good record on human rights is the acid test of whether a state and people are fit for inclusion in the European project. Even a cursory look at Turkey in this area immediately raises many questions, to say the least. In Turkey, torture is endemic, especially in police cells; there is a steady trickle of deaths in custody each year; international conventions to which Turkey is a signatory are often disregarded; the death penalty has been retained on the statute books, and there are currently at least forty-seven people on death row whose sentences have been confirmed by the Court of Appeal. Most notably, in December 1992 the Council of Europe produced the "most critical report" ever on torture in a member state, just as Turkey, its subject, was ending its presidency of the organization.[22] It could be claimed that Turkey has been unfortunate to face the Kurdish insurgency during its phase of greatest intensity at the same time as the height of European idealism about building a better world. Nevertheless, it should be noted that Turkey's human rights record has been poor for decades.

The 1990s have seen a growing overlap between human rights and the Kurdish issue, a trend that has not helped mutual understanding. This has partly been because of the waning threat from other and especially radical leftist groups, as well as the growth of the Kurdish insurgency itself. This overlap has intensified Ankara's suspicions of a European hidden agenda while increasing frustrations on the European side at Turkey's apparent unwillingness to change. The perceived failure of Turkey to honor what was regarded as a commitment to improve human rights in the context of the European Parliament's approval of the customs union in December 1995 still rankles in Brussels today. While a little more flexibility crept into the Turkish position in 1997, especially the admission that Turkey did indeed have economic, social, and political problems and they would not be solved overnight, the crushing disappointment of the Luxembourg summit's refusal to formally designate Turkey a candidate member hardly encouraged Ankara in developing a strategy of mea culpa. It remains to be seen whether the reversal of this policy on candidacy at Helsinki in December 1999 brings in its train the mea culpa.

THE MIDDLE EAST

The negative impact of the Kurdish issue on Turkey's external relations has not been confined to Europe, however. Since the emergence of the PKK as a formidable guerrilla force toward the end of the 1980s, Turkey's Kurdish problems have complicated relations with its Middle Eastern neighbors. In the power politics that so often typifies interstate relations in the region, Turkey's immediate Middle Eastern neighbors (Iran, Iraq, and Syria) have, to varying degrees, found the establishment of ties with the PKK to be irresistible. Motives for such steps have varied. For Damascus, sponsorship of the PKK has been viewed as a useful way of exerting leverage over the issue of the use of the water of the Euphrates river basin. For Tehran, relations with the PKK have been used to underline its displeasure at the presence in Turkey of members of the violent Iranian oppositionist grouping, the Mujaheddin-e Khalq. In the case of Iraq, where the PKK's room for operation since 1991 has been much more related to the political vacuum in the northeast of the country,

Baghdad has also dabbled with the PKK as a way of demonstrating its antipathy toward trans-Atlantic policy.

The presence of a Kurdish problem that its Middle Eastern neighbors could exploit has caused extensive difficulties for Turkey, dating back to 1987. It has contributed to mercurial bilateral relations with Syria, as five major initiatives from Ankara raised expectations of stabilization only to see such hopes dashed. In October 1998 the two countries almost came to war over the issue of Syrian sponsorship of the PKK. It has contributed to successive waves of Turkish frustration at the indeterminate situation in northern Iraq during the 1990s. A clutch of major cross-border military operations into northern Iraq in turn exacerbated Turkish relations with a range of countries in Europe and the Arab world. If the Kurdish and PKK issues have been less turbulent in the context of Iranian-Turkish relations, that is tempered by the widely held belief that Iran is currently Turkey's neighbor having the closest relationship with the PKK.

Of course, it must be admitted that the Kurdish issue is currently less problematic as far as Turkey's relations with its Middle Eastern neighbors are concerned than at any time since the late 1980s. Most graphically, Ankara can still point to the swift and ignominious climbdown by Damascus in the face of Turkey's muscular diplomacy in October 1998. It might, however, be advisable not to overemphasize this experience in dismissing the deleterious effects of the Kurdish issue on Turkey's relations with its neighbors. Ankara can hardly expect to be able to use bellicose threats each time it has a Kurd-related problem with its neighbors, nor can it expect such sweeping results as Syria's expulsion of Öcalan. The image of a powerful Turkey was soon replaced by the scenes of destruction and state immobility linked to the earthquake. Power relations can change, while the drift toward nonconventional weapons and missile delivery systems will erode threats from conventional attack. Meanwhile, the uncertain future of northern Iraq shows no immediate sign of being resolved. Whatever happens, it would be naive to think that Turkey's Middle Eastern neighbors will not look again at the Kurdish issue as a potential asset in the cut and thrust of bilateral relations.

A discussion of Turkey's foreign policy toward the Middle East in light of the Kurdish issue also needs to encompass relations with Israel. Since 1991 bilateral relations have been flourishing across the board, with military and strategic matters increasingly dominating since 1996. Only occasionally has this linear advance in bilateral ties been subject to public difficulty; remarkably, two of the most notable examples relate to Turkey's Kurdish problem. The first was the eruption of Turkish-Syrian tensions in September and October 1998 and the consequent fear of war, which prompted Israel to go out of its way to disassociate itself from the rise in tensions.[23] The second came in February 1999 with the capture of Öcalan; the assumption that Israel had helped the Turks in bringing about this end was followed by a series of assaults on Israeli diplomatic missions across Europe, the attack on the Berlin consulate resulting in three Kurdish demonstrators being shot dead by security staff. Israel was surprised and disconcerted by these unexpected by-products of its improving relations with Turkey. They did not result in any discernible revision of Israeli policy toward Turkey, though they did help, together with the issues of Cyprus and Greece, to spark a robust debate within government, political, and specialist circles as to the implications, both positive and negative, of the development of such a relationship. With Israel keen not to assume an enmity with Turkey's nationalist Kurds as part of its package of improved relations with Ankara, further negative experiences such as these may hinder Turkey's pursuit of close ties with Israel.

TOWARD A SOLUTION?

LEADERSHIP AND STRUGGLE

If the Kurdish-Turkish dichotomy represents the central ethnic cleavage in Turkey, its crucial nature has often been obscured by the struggle between the Turkish state and the PKK.[24] This is understandable from both points of view. The PKK has tried to become synonymous with Kurdish nationalism, to become, in Palestinian parlance, "the sole legitimate representative" of the Kurdish people in Turkey.[25] For the PKK to be accepted as the only tenable interlocutor for Turkey's Kurds would already represent a significant political victory in its own right. Yet it is important to recognize that the PKK is first and foremost an organization whose primary loyalty is to itself, its bureaucracy, and its leaders rather than to the mass of people that it purports to represent. In short, there is both a body of people that identify themselves as Kurds and an organization called the PKK.

By the same token, the Turkish state has for much of the time insisted that there is no Kurdish problem, only a PKK problem. That allows the state to argue that the issue is not about politics or culture or identity at all but about terrorism. And terrorism, the state maintains, referencing the Western world's implacable hostility to the phenomenon, must be met by a security response. To paraphrase a slogan from another divided society, there must be "no surrender to the PKK." For the state, then, the PKK *is* Kurdish nationalism. The PKK's use of violence in turn both delegitimizes Kurdish nationalism and legitimizes the use of repression in a single-strategy approach to the troubles in the southeast.

With both the PKK and the Turkish state insisting on this most impolite of fictions, most of the middle ground in Kurdish-Turkish relations has either disappeared or has become extremely uncomfortable— not to mention dangerous—to occupy. The middle ground has been sparsely populated, and those who have sought to occupy it have often been the object of the unwanted attentions of both the state and the PKK. Those from the Turkish side who have ventured to recognize that there might be a Kurdish political reality have found themselves cut adrift and vulnerable. When the social democratic party (SHP) decided out of political expediency to expel seven of its Kurdish deputies for attending an international conference on Kurds in Paris in 1989, it was an instructive illustration of the inability of otherwise liberal politicians to contemplate edging onto the middle ground on the issue.[26]

It has of course been even harder for Kurds to try to occupy such middle ground. Pressures have come from three directions, the first being the Turkish state, with its raft of illiberal measures aimed at restricting discussion and debate in the name of national security. The second is the "deep state," in the form of the extrajudicial violence and harassment that has been meted out to Kurdish activists, especially since 1991. And the third is the entrenched and organized interests on the Kurdish side, whether the PKK and its affiliates or the village guards and the tribes linked to them and maintaining their loyalty to the Turkish state. In 1994, for example, separate attempts to organize a Kurdish party by Şerafettin Elçi and Kemal Burkay were met with accusations by the PKK of being collaborators.[27]

Astride much of this, and indeed painted by the PKK as the personification of Kurdish nationalism, is Abdullah Öcalan. Again, this is a political convenience for both sides. For Öcalan to become "Mr. Kurdistan," as Yasser Arafat has come to be seen over the years as "Mr.

Palestine," is a boon for his leadership. It implies that an alternative
leadership, even a more collegiate leadership, let alone a more democratic and transparent leadership, is both impossible and undesirable.
In keeping with the largely feudal mentality[28] of the organization, "a
strategic importance" has been attached to Öcalan's life by the PKK
since his capture. For the Turkish state, the reduction of Kurdish
nationalism to the PKK and in turn to Öcalan—"the baby killer" as
Turkish state television has routinely referred to him—offers the relatively simple propaganda task of blackening an organization and a
wide group of people through reference to just one man. Yet such
reductionism is not really helpful, especially at more auspicious times
for peace or reconciliation.

That is not to argue that Öcalan is the saint that his followers
would have one believe. Much of Öcalan's decisionmaking was
obscured from view when he was based in Syria. It became easier to
observe between October 1998 and February 1999, during his itiner-
ancy in Europe and Africa. During that time Öcalan acted in a capri-
cious, dictatorial, and foolhardy way. When based in Rome, he refused
to accept the advice of those who argued that a window of political
opportunity now existed and that it was important radically and swiftly
to reinvent the PKK so as to make it more acceptable to a European
audience. In doing so, Öcalan showed how much he lacked strategic
vision, demonstrating as well his ignorance of liberal values and the
European political milieu. In the end he was duped into leaving Rome,
thereby plunging himself into the uncertainty that eventually resulted
in his ill-fated journey to Kenya, where he was apprehended. The way
he insisted on conducting himself there made his capture all the easier.
Öcalan's past conduct may not then make him a palatable interlocutor
from a Turkish point of view, but Kurds too should be concerned
about his suitability to lead them.

THE CENTRALITY OF ÖCALAN: CAN THE TURKS DEAL WITH HIM?

It also can be argued, though such an argument is obviously far more
contentious, that vilifying Öcalan as the killer of thirty thousand people may now not be to Turkey's advantage. Blackening the name of
Öcalan may have made sense from the perspective of state propaganda during the prosecution of a bloody insurgency; during moments

of opportunity for peace or reconciliation such propaganda and the cumulative effects that it has had on the Turkish psyche become distinctly problematic. Öcalan may indeed fit a reasonable definition of what is a terrorist, in the same way that an Adams, Arafat, Mugabe, or Shamir have in the past. But that is not the point. The critical point is whether, with the PKK's violent insurgency in disarray and its leader incarcerated, it serves the interests of Turkey to continue to insist on Öcalan as a terrorist. In the same way that it ceased to serve any purpose for Israel to view Arafat as a terrorist after 1993, so it may be better for Turkey to begin to view Öcalan differently.

Indeed, the analogy between Öcalan and Arafat is instructive. Consider the unpalatable nature of the latter. In the 1960s and early 1970s Yasser Arafat was the leader of an armed insurgency movement; the 1982 Israeli invasion of Lebanon and the subsequent Fatah rebellion showed how his leadership had become reliant on cronyism; the Palestinian camps war in Lebanon showed that he was not above presiding over internecine feuding; much of his diplomacy was characterized by secrecy and the desire to evade political accountability; the Palestinian Authority, over which he has presided since 1994, has been characterized by corruption, political repression, and inefficiency. Though such a record of course differs in certain ways from Öcalan's, there are plainly many similarities.

Yet, in spite of such an inauspicious record, Arafat has emerged as a crucial player in the Israeli-Palestinian peace process. His long road from armed insurgent to peacemaker reflects a process of maturation and the learning of the lesson that violence must be eschewed if there are other means to pursue political objectives. Furthermore, Arafat's unchallenged leadership of the Palestinian movement has given him an authority within his own constituency without which the long haul toward peace would have been much more difficult. Even today, with the peace process still incomplete, it is helpful for Israel to have to deal with only one, authoritative interlocutor. In turn, Arafat is useful in policing his own community to keep in check those who would seek to subvert the peace process in the name of maximalist political objectives.

If Turks are not convinced that Öcalan is an Arafat, they are entitled to that opinion. It took Israel two decades from Golda Meir's denial of the existence of a Palestinian people in the early 1970s through Arafat's renunciation of terrorism in 1988 to arrive at the Oslo process in 1993. After all, Yitzhak Rabin found it difficult to shake Arafat's hand on the White House lawn in September 1993. Even if Öcalan's 1999 statements about ending the armed conflict are genuine, that at best only puts the PKK at 1988 on the equivalent Palestinian time line; in those terms Oslo is still some five years away. Analogies, of course, can be helpful, but one should always be mindful of their limitations. It should be remembered that the Turks have something that the Israelis did not have. While Arafat was free to pursue a global diplomatic strategy, one that made him, his organization, and his cause increasingly better known to and accepted by the world, Öcalan is confined, his big chance to seize the political initiative squandered during his stay in Rome. In great part Öcalan's attractiveness as a political partner for Turkey ought to be the fact that his position is so dire.

Again, an analogy between Öcalan and Arafat can be identified, this time between 1999 and 1991, respectively. In spring 1991 the stock of Arafat, the PLO, and (it must be added) the Palestinians as a whole—after many of their number had danced on rooftops as Iraqi Scuds landed on Tel Aviv—was almost as low as it had ever been. There were many in influential places who argued that Arafat's apparent support of Saddam Hussein during his occupation of Kuwait had morally stripped the Palestinian leader of all of his claims to play a role in Arab-Israeli peacemaking. Arafat should be bypassed in peacemaking, so the argument went, not least as a form of retribution for his effrontery. Fortunately, cool heads prevailed, not least precisely because it was seen how weak Arafat actually was. Because of his predicament, Arafat was willing to accept virtually any conditions as the price of entry into the peace process. Consequently, Arafat and the Palestinians were incorporated into the Madrid process, but only on the basis of the role apportioned to them by the United States of George Bush and James Baker acting as the peace brokers. And so at Madrid the Palestinians were represented, but only in a joint delegation headed by the Jordanians, a subordinate position that Arafat had stoutly resisted in the mid- to late 1980s. In considering whether or not to deal with Öcalan, and Kurdish nationalist sources insist that regardless of the hardness of the line from Ankara the PKK has indeed had dealings with the Turkish state in the past, the future will certainly not take place in a vacuum. Öcalan has already sought to soften the Turkish stance. He first tried to do so during his trial on Imrali Island, when he apologized for the violence of the past and offered to serve the Turkish state in the future.[29] Since his conviction and sentencing he has attempted to do so in a more tangible way, notably through the call for the cessation of hostilities and for the withdrawal of PKK fighters to beyond Turkey's borders by September 1, 1999. Such gestures are clearly to be welcomed and appear to presage an extended reduction in violence.

However, Öcalan can do more to try to persuade the Turkish state that there can be no return either to a strategy based on violence or to a secessionist political agenda. With Öcalan's appeal to the European Court of Human Rights now proceeding, he has perhaps eighteen months in which to set about enacting the confidence-building measures (CBMs) that will be required to win over a critical proportion of the Turkish elite and public. In doing so, he will have to try harder than merely changing the names of the military and political front organizations of the PKK, as was one of the main outcomes of the party's seventh extraordinary congress.[30] More substantive additional moves could include

- seizing every opportunity to indicate his commitment to the cessation of violence and the future integrity of the Turkish state;

- disassociating himself and the PKK from any state that does not fully and unequivocally recognize the sovereignty and integrity of the Turkish state within its present borders, such as Syria and its de facto claim over Hatay and other border territories in Turkey;

- ordering the closure of PKK and front offices in Turkey's neighboring states, to show that the Kurdish national movement will not allow itself to be exploited by Turkey's immediate enemies for their own state interests;

- ordering the dissolution of the ARGK, the PKK's military wing, to demonstrate a commitment to a strategy of nonviolence;

- offering to decommission the PKK arsenal over a period of time, to be overseen by a body to consist of both Turkish and international figures;

- dissolving the PKK as a formal organization in favor of the creation of a broad front representing all shades of Kurdish nationalist opinion; and

- resigning from and forsaking the future executive leadership of the PKK and any broader Kurdish nationalist movement.[31]

In other words, Öcalan would remain an influential figure who would endorse different stages in the healing process between Turks and Kurds but would not have a hand in the day-to-day conduct of relations between Turkey and the Kurds.

Of course, it may well be the case that the Turks, as they exit from the trauma of the PKK insurgency, feel that they just cannot have anything whatsoever to do with Abdullah Öcalan. The presence of the ultranationalist Nationalist Action Party (MHP, the second-largest party in parliament) in the governing coalition clearly does not make the bold, historic change of direction that dealing with Öcalan would imply any easier. More important, standing behind the government of the day are the institutions of the Turkish state, and especially the Turkish general staff. Through the National Security Council, an "advisory" body of civilians and military men, the armed forces will make their will plain to both cabinet and parliament. Hitherto, the army, as the guardians of Atatürk's legacy and the Turkish state, have been unsympathetic to the idea of compromise with the country's Kurds. At the turn of the millennium it would appear to be the case that the Öcalan option is just too ambitious and cannot therefore be considered to be a viable scenario for the future. Prime Minister Bülent Ecevit appeared to contend as much when he ruled out any role for Öcalan in the incipient national dialogue on the Kurdish issue in January 2000.[32] The subsequent decision of the state regulatory agency to suspend the CNN-Turk channel for one day because of a comparison made between Öcalan and Nelson Mandela by an interviewer on a current affairs program has tended to confirm this impression. Consequently, the Turkish state would appear to have a choice among bestowing a unilateral settlement on the Kurds, seeking alternative interlocutors to Öcalan, and pursuing an all-out victory against Kurdish nationalism.

REALISTIC SCENARIOS FOR THE FUTURE

THE UNILATERAL SETTLEMENT. The most straightforward approach for the Turkish state would be to bestow a number of benefits on the country's Kurds and then declare that the "Kurdish problem," insofar as it is admitted that there was one in the first place, is now over. This would have the advantage of requiring no Kurdish counterpart and could be completed without a negotiation. In other words, the process for the provision of benefits to Kurds could be done in such a way as to appear to be a gift from the state. This would arguably be the best method for retaining the dignity of the state, as well as the military's reputation for being the ultimate guarantor of the Turkish political system. The advantages of such an approach would be its speed, its cleanness, and its relative absence of implications for the standing of the state.

Indeed, Ankara might go so far as addressing the Kurdish issue without being explicit. It could, for example, adopt the view of those more liberal Turkish nationalists who believe that there is no Kurdish problem in Turkey, only the problem of a democratic deficit from which Kurds and Turks alike suffer. A package of measures could then be introduced that would strengthen democratic practice across the board: increased press freedom, a more secure foundation for legal political parties, a move toward a more decentralized political system with, for instance, the election of all regional governors. Additional reforms, such as the removal of all "emergency" regulations, also could be implemented in the name of democratization but would clearly be more specifically aimed at the Kurdish areas of the east and southeast. It was just this type of approach that Süleyman Demirel, then Turkey's prime minister, appeared to signal in March 1992, during an earlier and bloodier phase in the Kurdish problem. He stated that his government planned to give more power to provincial and municipal councils but maintained that "decentralization was not specifically aimed at solving the crisis in the mainly Kurdish southeast."[33] His successor as premier, Tansu Çiller, took a similar approach two and a half years later when she said "there will be no political solution to the Kurdish problem"—but "Yes to a solution with democracy. However, there also cannot be any question of a regional democratic solution."[34] On both occasions, however, such trial balloons burst under the pressure of a skeptical state.

Despite the democratic deficit in Turkey and the many voices, both at home and abroad, arguing for democratic reform, the continuation of the Kurdish insurgency represents an untrumpable argument for the retention of the more illiberal measures that still apply. Arguments relating to national security may well be resorted to by the state to fend off the demands for reform that have accompanied the popular backlash over the August 1999 earthquake tragedy. Under pressure for reform from at least two directions, the state may well conclude that its interests are served better by not implementing a program of accelerated democratic reform.

Even assuming the opposite, that the state was willing to go down the democratic reformist road, there would still be areas of reform that Ankara would find more difficult to implement. There are two critical issues in question. The first is an overarching issue of who holds power in Turkey—real reform in this area, for instance, would surely necessitate the adoption of the NATO norm of making the Turkish general staff subject to the political control of the civilian authority. But the military has increased in power in Turkey through the 1990s, so a tame relinquishing of ultimate power—especially in view of other remaining "threats," notably from the tide of political Islam—appears improbable.

The second critical issue relates to the cultural distinctiveness of Kurds and to notions of pluralism, such as the right to broadcast and educate using the Kurdish language. This second issue does not fall easily under the rubric of democratization. Rather, it appears to be related more closely to principles of minority rights, a greatly contested area in Turkey because of the nature and strength of Turkish nationalism. For Kemalists, the only minorities in the country are those that were designated as such at the Treaty of Lausanne in 1923. Under Lausanne, minority status was ascribed exclusively on a religious basis. Hence Kurds, as Muslims, cannot for Turks be considered to be a minority.

Even in this area obstacles are not necessarily insurmountable. In 1995 the Turkish government circumvented the problems surrounding the celebration of Nevruz, the Kurdish new year, by simply appropriating it as a celebration for the nation as a whole. As far as broadcasting in Kurdish is concerned, the state could simply choose to fudge the issue. Since the late 1980s there has been a plethora of radio and even television stations broadcasting in Turkey without license. Ankara could turn a deaf ear and a blind eye to broadcasts in Kurdish.

There are additional problems beyond the issues of cultural pluralism. These relate to the probable contours of a settlement. In other words, just what is the state likely to give, and what will Kurdish nationalists settle for? Such problems involve the likely inadequacy of state initiatives and the absence of two-sided talks. Short of a negotiation, how can the state know that what it has given will be enough to assuage the demands and desires of Kurdish nationalism, and, though this side of the equation is rather more notional at present, how will it know that it has not conceded too much? To date, the Turkish state's record on unilateral gestures toward the Kurds has been, to say the least, somewhat parsimonious. The 1990s have been punctuated by offers of economic packages for the southeast, based on the assumption that the Kurdish insurgency is a function of underdevelopment and poverty alone. Even these packages, however, have tended to be modest and, insofar as they have ever been implemented, one doubts how much of the financial offering has trickled down to provide jobs and economic opportunity for the predominantly unskilled and impoverished population.

Shadowing the economic package approach has been the offer of amnesties for Kurdish nationalists who have fallen foul of the law. As with the economic packages, one doubts the real utility of such offers. The fact that the Turkish state has approved fifteen general amnesties since 1933, one every four and a half years on average, hardly instills confidence in the mechanism.[35] More tangible concerns relate to the experience of the most recent amnesty draft law. The August 1999 repentance bill produced by the Ecevit government was greatly circumscribed in its application to the PKK, excluding both its leadership and its active-service guerrillas, even though facilitating the surrender of its activists had been one of the law's central objectives.[36] Ecevit had been obliged to compromise and limit the scope of the law because of pressure from his MHP coalition partner.[37]

Finally, there is the issue of just what can be considered to be the bottom line for Kurdish nationalists. The key question is surely what reforms will be sufficient to ensure that a critical mass of nationalist Kurds do not at some unspecified date in the future once again resort to arms against the Turkish state. Hamit Bozarslan describes these minimum demands in general as ending the state of emergency, ending the destruction of the Kurdish countryside, respecting human rights, and recognizing cultural rights.[38] Others have emphasized constitutional reform as guaranteeing the irreversibility of the provision of Kurdish rights. But demands can change over time, especially as power balances alter. Demands also can be different depending on the vantage point of the activist: Palestinians living under occupation were routinely more willing to compromise with the Israelis than the mainstream PLO in the diaspora; likewise, Kurdish activists in Europe and the Middle East have often seemed more radical than those on Turkish soil. And what of the specifics of these demands? For example, should the cultural right to teach Kurdish in school be extended to all state schools in the southeast, or could it merely be limited to private schools? And what of compensation for those Kurds who have been driven from their villages and hamlets, especially during 1994 and 1995?[39] In the absence of any serious and sustained exercise in track-two diplomacy hitherto, it is to be doubted whether the detail of any plausible settlement could easily and swiftly be agreed upon.

SEEK NEW KURDISH INTERLOCUTORS. The virtue of seeking new interlocutors springs from the reservations and questions that ended the previous section. The involvement of Kurds from Turkey in a negotiation would have the advantage of establishing a real process, with representation from both sides. A real peace and reconciliation process could better establish a comprehensive agenda of issues. A process could set out a route map of how to go about addressing such concerns, in what order and at what pace. A process would lock in both sides, making recidivism more costly and hence less likely, and facilitating the building of mutual trust. A process would be a tangible and visible effort, to which outsiders, whether friendly powers or international organizations, could contribute if they so desired. Of course, peace processes are often not pretty, as both Britain and Northern Ireland and Israel and the Palestinians clearly attest. But what is striking about the latter in particular is its durability over more than six years, in spite of the often serious difficulties it has faced.

The adoption of this second road is clearly not without its problems. The first and arguably most serious is the nature of the Kurdish interlocutors. After all, the Turkish state and the PKK have very successfully gone about ensuring that no strong and plausible middle ground could emerge in the 1990s. Consequently, the Kurdish "side" has been politically and spatially fragmented. Consider those who could plausibly claim to play a role in Kurdish representational politics:

+   elected mayors in the predominantly Kurdish areas from *Hadep;*

+   the six former MPs from the DEP, *Hadep*'s predecessor party, which was closed down in 1994, some of whom are still serving prison terms in Turkish jails;[40]

+   the six former DEP MPs who reside in Brussels, having opted for de facto political exile;[41]

+   Kurdish members of other (mainly leftist) political groupings, some of whom such as Kemal Burkay are in exile, and some of whom, such as Mehdi Zana, are still in Turkey;

+   members of the recently dissolved Kurdish "parliament in exile," and especially its head, Yasar Kaya;

- members of the ERNK and other organizations affiliated to the PKK, especially those resident in Europe;

- maverick but authoritative figures in Turkey, such as Şerafettin Elçi and Abdülmelik Firat, who have in the past had good links with mainstream parties in Turkey;[42] and

- conservative figures from landlord or shaikhly backgrounds— men like Kamran Inan and Sedat Bucak, even though they have hitherto insisted on a primary loyalty to a Turkish identity; such figures would presumably be wary of a process that was exclusively confined to the state and a range of leftist Kurds.

In the absence of a single, authoritative grouping on the Kurdish side, a sort of Kurdish PLO, it would be tempting for the Turkish state to manufacture a Kurdish counterpart—tempting but misguided. Ankara could clearly find its own Kurdish partners if it so wished, but relying solely on its traditional tribal allies would neither be authoritative nor the basis for a comprehensive end to strife. Given the difficulties involved, the Turkish state could do worse than begin with the *Hadep* mayors, who at least have the advantage of a fresh mandate from the May 1999 local elections and are not encumbered by incarceration. President Demirel's decision to meet the seven *Hadep* mayors at the presidential palace in Çankaya in August was arguably the most constructive response on the Kurdish issue from Ankara since Öcalan's capture.

However, except over all but the shortest of short terms it would seem desirable to widen the Kurdish platform, perhaps through creation of a new umbrella grouping. Men like Elçi and Firat could then be incorporated, to be followed by imprisoned former deputies such as Ahmet Türk. Eventually, if such a process is to work optimally, it must be widened to incorporate those senior Kurdish figures in exile, softened, as the PLO leadership was eventually softened, by the more focused and realistic political agenda of those Kurds on the ground.

Of course, assembling anything approaching a representative body of Kurds would only be the beginning. Not for nothing do the Kurds have a reputation for fractiousness. Moreover, it will take time for many on the Turkish side to accept the wisdom of such a process. Consequently, it would probably be best to think in terms of a long negotiation, and one that initially focuses on generating regular CBMs.

A sine qua non of such a negotiation would be that all sides should desist from violence. In turn, the military presence of the Turkish state in the southeast would be relaxed and reduced, the biggest of all CBMs for the Kurdish side and one that can be undertaken relatively discreetly. Such a course would in any case reflect the ebb of the insurgency and could be justified on the grounds of the need to cut the costs of policing the southeast. In particular, Ankara should be encouraged to reduce its military profile in zones of demographic concentration in the Kurdish areas. Naturally, there will be no diminution of Turkey's external security provision in the southeast; a successful peace process will be one that is seen not to compromise the integrity of the state but to enhance it.

Assuming that the process begins and is successfully consolidated, it will sooner or later have to address the outstanding substantive issues that divide the two sides. The central question here is whether the provision of enhanced cultural freedoms for the Kurds will be sufficient or whether they will insist on concessions more political in nature. There have been many Kurdish activists who would insist on new political arrangements, including such provisions as autonomy for the southeast or even a federative state of Turks and Kurds. The pursuit of such a goal is really not to be encouraged. Ankara, ever suspicious, would interpret such a demand as the first part of a "strategy of stages"; once autonomy had been gained the concession would be pocketed, only to be followed by the pursuit of the ultimate strategic aim of full secession. In view of the poisonous atmosphere that such suspicions would create it would be best that they were never raised.

There is, however, a second reason why political goals should not be pursued. That rests on a pragmatic assessment of power politics. The Kurdish national movement is on the defensive, with the PKK in disarray and its leader imprisoned. The Kurds are in no position to make demands, especially fantastical ones. Furthermore, the plight of the Kurdish national movement in Turkey, or anywhere else for that matter, is unlikely to improve in the foreseeable future. In the absence of the possession of state power, and with Turkey increasing its power relative to regional states that have previously backed the PKK, the Kurdish national movement's position within a negotiation will be more akin to supplicant than equal partner. If the Kurds are to be successful in obtaining a credible list of concessions on the limited agenda of cultural rights, their case must be made calmly, cogently, and in a way that is designed to appeal to the Turkish nationalist sense of overall self-interest.

THE PURSUIT OF TOTAL VICTORY. There will be those in Turkey who will say that there should be no talk of mercy for Öcalan, concessions to the Kurds, or a Turkish-Kurdish negotiating process. They will object to such a strategy for two reasons, one theoretical, one practical. The first objection will be made on the grounds that recognizing a Kurdish reality will loosen the bonds of Turkish solidarity and encourage centrifugal tendencies, which, in turn, will give outside powers even more leverage over the Turkish state; Öcalan, it will be argued, as the source of so much bloodshed and strife, must die—justice demands it. The second argument will be based on the assumption that Turkey has finally won its vicious struggle with the PKK; why, it will be argued, give concessions when the enemy has been defeated?

Both arguments are flawed. The former ignores the centrality of pluralism as a positive value in the modern political thinking of the Western world; Turkey's relations with Europe, but also with the United States and in the long term arguably with Israel, too, will become increasingly problematic if the persecution of the Kurds intensifies. The latter assumes a PKK problem but no Kurdish problem. Neither the military and political defeat of the PKK nor the execution of its leader will do anything to change the conditions that brought about the emergence of the organization in the first place. It therefore remains reasonable to suppose that the demise of the PKK would sooner or later result in the creation of a new organization with broadly similar goals and a similar mix of tactics. Ultimately, both maximalist arguments are flawed because of the difficulty of repacking Pandora's box. When such luminaries as Özal, Demirel, and the son of Atatürk's right-hand man, Erdal İnönü,[43] recognized the "Kurdish reality" in the early 1990s they ensured that there could be no viable return to a purely Turkish nationalist position. The sudden reemergence of ethnic self-awareness in southeastern Europe increased this process of cultural irreversibility while simultaneously acting as a warning sign as to the costs of a failure to accommodate. It is therefore tempting to conclude that the debate is no longer about whether there should be cultural accommodation but at precisely what point cultural coexistence should come to rest.

While in the long term such a view is likely to prevail, to make too many assumptions about Turkish politics over the short to medium term would be misleading and complacent. Plausible contingencies for the emergence of a total victory scenario could be based on anything from Turkish nationalist triumphalism at the defeat of the PKK or the execution of Öcalan to a domestic backlash against the EU once the honeymoon period in the immediate aftermath of the Helsinki summit has worn off. Even in the event of such a development, it would be difficult for the Turkish state to ignore realities both at home and abroad without entering a period of denial.

But if denial does indeed hold sway it would actually be rather easy for the state to push back the achievements hitherto realized by the Kurdish national movement. *Hadep* remains vulnerable to being closed down as a political party and might already have ceased to exist had not the military in 1997 redefined the Islamist threat as at least as grave a challenge to the state as Kurdish separatism;[44] the fate of HEP (the People's Labor Party) and DEP (Democracy Party) shows that the state does not lack the will, the gall, or indeed the precedents for such a move. Elsewhere, the Kurdish cultural reality appears to be equally or more precarious. A Kurdish institute run by Hasan Kaya does exist in Istanbul, but it is unregistered; the Mesopotamia Cultural Centre, also in Istanbul, has recently been raided. There are only a handful of small weekly newspapers and journals that publish in Kurdish in Turkey, and these are often subject to periodic pressures of both a legal and extralegal nature.[45] Thus, a backlash could easily sweep away even the meager cultural rights currently enjoyed by Kurds in Turkey.

CONCLUSION

This chapter has argued that a golden opportunity emerged during the summer of 1999 for reconciling Turks and Kurds. It is the best opportunity that has presented itself since 1993 and arguably since the beginning of the PKK's violent campaign in 1984. The basis for this putative reconciliation is a package of cultural reforms within a broader context of deepening democratization. This is a thoroughly reasonable basis for the establishment of a new deal between Turks and Kurds in contemporary Turkey. It addresses the Kurdish ethno-nationalist desire to explore its own cultural specificity; at the same time it acknowledges the fears of both the Turkish state and the mainstream majority that reform should not breed discord, instability, and division. In drawing attention to the opportunity for reconciliation, emphasis must be placed on the currently auspicious configuration of factors. The military dimension of the PKK campaign has been contained since the mid 1990s; Öcalan's cease-fire and order to his fighters to withdraw holds the offer of a complete cessation of conflict. Support for the PKK among Turkey's neighbors is at a comparatively low point, following Öcalan's expulsion from Damascus and Russia's own problems with its Chechen secessionists. In the immediate run-up to the Helsinki summit, the EU's perception of Turkey was as close to approximating the principally geostrategic view of the United States as circumstances are ever likely to permit. Most important, perhaps, the capture of Öcalan—and his willingness to cooperate—has, for the moment at least, ameliorated the rawness in the adversarial nature of Turkish-Kurdish relations.

With the PKK in disarray and Turkey's Kurds disorganized and fractured, the future is in the hands of the Turkish state and, indirectly and imperfectly, Turkish society. To date, the response of the Turkish side has been inadequate and disappointing. Ankara has been content to pocket the unilateral concessions offered by Öcalan, reflecting the fact that it has the whip hand. As such, it has signally failed to show leadership in substantive matters of strategy. More concessions may indeed follow, in keeping with the PKK's current conciliatory line. However, as other experiences in peacemaking show, the absence of momentum can leave a temporary peace vulnerable to events. For instance, the longer the Turkish side refrains from responding to Öcalan's concessions, the greater the chance of a split within the PKK. With PKK members following the situation in Northern Ireland extremely closely, the emergence of a "Real PKK" or a "Continuity PKK" along the lines of IRA equivalents cannot be ruled out. Contingencies are in any case, by their very nature, unforeseen. In 1993, it should be remembered, the last opportunity for peace broke down because of the sudden death of President Özal.

With the situation delicately balanced, what can Turkey's friends in the West do to help? It may be argued by some that the Europeans and the United States must tread carefully; strident criticism will easily awaken dark thoughts about a foreign agenda to divide Turkey; shrill or half-baked criticism will yield little but contempt. While the presentation of comment and opinion must indeed be considered with very great care, Turkey's friends would be doing their ally a disservice if an undue equivocation in style was allowed to obscure the substance of honest advice. Turkey should be left in no doubt that many of its domestic actions toward the Kurds are incompatible with the Copenhagen Criteria and hence with the standards of entry into the EU to which the country aspires. Moreover, it needs to be pointed out that, in turn, many of these actions have created major problems for other states, not least those in Europe. From the surge in asylum seekers and the intercommunal tensions among migrant communities to the domination of the Turkish connection in heroin trafficking, the negative by-products of Turkey's Kurdish strategy have been legion. It is precisely such issues that exercise the man and woman in the European street and that are likely to form a component of a common foreign policy. For Turkey, the Kurdish issue is now as much of an issue in external relations as it is in domestic politics. Some recommendations to Western governments would include the following:

♦ Use public and private diplomacy to urge the Turks to seize the moment to address the Kurdish issue in its cultural, economic, and democratic forms.

♦ Sustain (in the case of the United States) and increase (in the case of the EU) the number of high-level visitors to Turkey, on the condition that all such figures add calls on senior, authoritative Kurdish figures to their itineraries, while also not forgetting to meet with representatives of mainstream Turkish nationalist associations in order to reassure them about the future.

♦ Commission a serious attempt at track-two diplomacy bringing together authoritative Turks and Kurds (such as the *Hadep* mayors) who eschew the use of violence for political ends, with a view to generating CBMs and a route map for closer, more collaborative relations.

♦ Redouble all efforts to promote democratization and accountable and transparent government in Turkey.

♦ Initiate a serious and sustained dialogue between Europeans and Americans with access to decisionmakers so as to coordinate action on the issue of Turkey and the Kurds, and to ensure that Turkey's closest allies offer counsel of a more compatible nature than has often been the case in the past.

CHAPTER FOUR

THE TURKISH ECONOMY AT THE TURN OF A NEW CENTURY
CRITICAL AND COMPARATIVE PERSPECTIVES

ZIYA ÖNIŞ

INTRODUCTION

The year 1980 ended the biggest economic crisis in Turkey since the early days of the republic and marked a fundamental shift in the Turkish economy. The crisis was in many ways typical of the inward-oriented, import-substituting model of industrialization (ISI), magnified by external oil price shocks. The economy ultimately failed to generate sustainable economic growth and collapsed in a major balance of payments crisis.[1] The reforms introduced in 1980 were designed to transform the structure of the economy and establish a more open, market-oriented economy in line with the global wave of neoliberal reform. The stabilization and structural adjustment programs received major international support from the IMF and the World Bank. Turkey obtained a record five successive structural adjustment loans (SALs) from the World Bank between 1980 and 1984. By the mid-1980s Turkey was described as a success story and a model of structural adjustment.[2] After two decades of neoliberal economic reforms, has the Turkish experiment been successful? How does it compare to the other "emerging markets" in East Asia, Latin America, or Eastern Europe?

The reform process has indeed made profound changes in the Turkish economy. Turkey is now far more integrated into the international economy and has established itself as one of the strongest economies in the Middle East as well as an active and assertive regional power. The results, however, have been very uneven. Turkey maintained moderately high rates of growth in both the 1980s and the 1990s, in sharp contrast to the collapse of the Latin American economies in the 1980s. But these rates of growth never reached the levels set by the first-generation newly industrialized countries (NICs) in Asia such as South Korea and Taiwan or second-generation ones such as Thailand and Malaysia. While progress has been made in trade expansion and capital account liberalization, much less has been achieved in terms of macroeconomic stability, the privatization of state-owned enterprises, and the reform of the public sector in general. The vast public-private connection with its associated problems of favoritism and corruption has remained largely unchanged.

Failure to achieve macroeconomic stability has been costly—such stability would have allowed the Turkish economy to generate a much more impressive performance in both investment and growth. Moreover, one persistent weakness of the Turkish economy—the inability to attract large amounts of long-term foreign capital—is closely related to the failure to produce a stable macroeconomic environment.

TURKISH NEOLIBERALISM IN RETROSPECT: A CRITICAL PERSPECTIVE

In comparative terms the Turkish neoliberal experiment may be categorized as a "radical-gradualist" program. Unlike the situation in Chile, the earliest neoliberal experiment in Latin America and a classic example of shock treatment, the Turkish reform has been a stage-by-stage liberalization process.[3] It is possible to identify four key turning points in the Turkish reform process. The first phase of economic reform, beginning in January 1980, involved a mix of stabilization measures and a major shift toward exports. Movement to liberalize trade and the capital account was limited. The second phase of reforms in 1983 and early 1984 included significant steps in trade and capital account liberalization. The pinnacle of the reform was August 1989, with the transition to full capital account convertibility. Stated somewhat differently, over the course of a decade Turkey was transformed from being one of the most closed to one of the most open capital account regimes in the world. The third phase of economic reform also involved another round of trade liberalization; the process of trade liberalization gained further momentum during a fourth phase in the 1990s, culminating in the Customs Union Agreement with the European Union (EU) in January 1996. Privatization of state enterprises was initiated in 1986 at a relatively advanced stage of the reform program.

Most commentators would agree that privatization in Turkey—both the pace of the program and the scale of revenues generated—has been less than impressive. Privatization to date has been effectively confined to small and medium-sized public companies. Large enterprises, the basic component of the public enterprise sector in Turkey, only emerged as serious contenders for the privatization agenda toward the end of the 1990s.[4] One can argue that rent-seeking behavior and outright corruption are central to an explanation of the limited privatization that has occurred in Turkey. Corruption through insider trading, false information, lack of transparency, and illegitimate business ethics became one of the critical aspects of the Turkish political scene throughout the 1990s.

In evaluating the success of Turkey's twenty-year reform effort, attention needs to be drawn to five separate but highly interrelated criteria: economic growth, export performance, macroeconomic stability (that is, control over fiscal deficits and inflation), investment (private, public, and foreign), and income distribution. In terms of these criteria there are striking differences and significant continuities between the 1980s and 1990s, as shown in Table 4.1 (page 98).

The swift recovery in economic growth and the dramatic increase and diversification of exports were the highlights of Turkey's reform experience (Figures 4.1 and 4.2, pages 99 and 100). Some fiscal success also was achieved with a major reduction in the rate of inflation from the hyperinflationary proportions of 1980 (Figure 4.1). Several factors explain the phenomenal growth in Turkish exports in the early 1980s. A drastic change in government policy played a critical role: major real devaluation of the exchange rate and an increase in direct

TABLE 4.1. A TALE OF TWO DECADES:
TURKISH NEOLIBERALISM IN THE 1980S AND THE 1990S IN COMPARATIVE PERSPECTIVE

	1980s	1990s
Economic Growth	Moderately high	Moderately high; a distinct stop-go pattern
Export Performance	Very strong in the early 1980s, accompanied by a major structural change in the direction of manufactured exports; the same momentum could not be maintained in the final part of the decade	Export growth continues but not at the pace of the 1980s; exports constitute a relatively neglected dimension during the decade
Macroeconomic Stability	Success in reducing inflation and fiscal improvement during the early years of the decade; growing instability toward the end of the decade	Macroeconomic instability is an endemic problem throughout the decade
Investment	Important public investment in transport and communications; private investment in manufacturing is usual; foreign direct investment improves relative to ISI era, but weak by international standards	Public investment is on the decline; a noticeable improvement in private investment; FDI performance remains weak in comparative terms
Income Distribution	Relative inequality is high but not higher than the ISI era; significant wage repression in the early part of the decade followed by a recovery of wages toward the end	Persistence of high relative income inequality; wage growth followed by wage repression in the aftermath of the 1994 crisis

subsidies to exports made exporting highly profitable for the first time since the early 1950s. The stabilization component of the program—significantly compressed internal demand, amplified by drastic wage repression—was one of the striking elements of the Turkish experience in the early 1980s. Low internal demand coupled with wage

FIGURE 4.1. GROWTH, INFLATION, AND FISCAL DISEQUILIBRIUM IN TURKEY

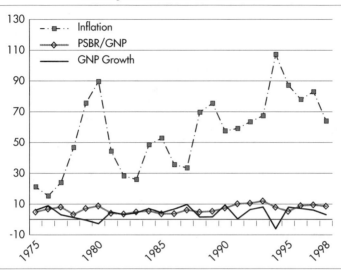

Sources: State Institute of Statistics, *Statistical Year Book of Turkey,* various years; State Planning Organization, *Main Economic Indicators,* various years; State Planning Organization, *Economic Program for the Year 2000.*

repression helped divert significant industrial capacity, built during the years of import substitution, toward exports. The Iran-Iraq war of the early 1980s also added impetus to the export boom.

Toward the end of the 1980s, serious questions began to be raised about the quality of the economy's performance. The momentum of the export drive could not be maintained as the special circumstances of the early phase began to evaporate. While the balance of payments position improved and the internal market started to recover following the restoration of civilian government in late 1983, the policymakers faced a new set of circumstances restricting their ability to pursue the aggressive export-promoting devaluation policy of the early 1980s. Increasingly concerned with rising inflation once again and the burden of external debt, policymakers gradually shifted in the latter half of the 1980s to a policy of keeping the real exchange rate constant.[5] Moreover, it was no longer possible to subsidize exports through tax rebates on a grand scale because of mounting domestic and external pressures. These rebates were subjected to heavy criticism following evidence of misutilization of public funds in the form of "over-invoicing" and "fictitious exports." Export tax rebates were ended in

FIGURE 4.2. STRUCTURAL TRANSFORMATION
IN TURKISH EXPORTS

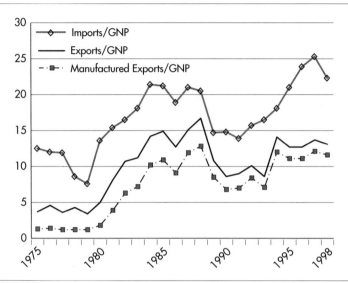

Sources: State Institute of Statistics, *Statistical Yearbook of Turkey,* various years; State Planning Organization, *Main Economic Indicators,* various years.

1988 after heavy pressure from the managers of the General Agreement on Tariffs and Trade (GATT).

By the late 1980s the limitations of the export drive were apparent. Turkey was able to diversify exports toward manufacturing, but closer examination revealed an overdependence on certain labor-intensive manufacturing activities—foodstuffs, textiles and clothing, and iron and steel accounted for a disproportionate share of Turkey's manufactured exports. Indeed, this pattern continued to prevail in the 1990s.[6] Part of the inability to diversify manufactured exports may be traced to the failure to achieve an investment level sufficient to sustain and deepen the initial export boom of the early 1980s. If one examines the experience of countries like South Korea and Taiwan, with their outward-oriented development strategies, one of the striking elements is their capacity to generate rapid growth in exports and investment at the same time. A similar pattern of rapid expansion in private investment has been missing in Turkey, with negative ramifications for exports and growth, although some improvement in private investment performance is evident in the 1990s (Figure 4.3).[7] Macroeconomic instability and high interest rates

FIGURE 4.3. INVESTMENT PERFORMANCE: FIXED INVESTMENT AS A RATIO OF GNP (%)

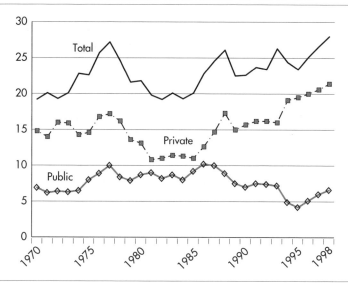

Sources: State Institute of Statistics, *Statistical Yearbook of Turkey*, various years; State Planning Organization, *Main Economic Indicators*, various years.

were among the major reasons for Turkey's inability to generate a major investment boom.

Turning to the 1990s, a striking new element became apparent—the impact of short-term external capital following the full capital account liberalization in August 1989. Large inflows of short-term capital, mostly in response to high domestic interest rates, were instrumental in Turkey's ability to achieve reasonably high rates of expansion and growth in the 1990s. However, the pattern of growth that emerged was one of fragile equilibrium based on a distinct stop-go growth process. This fragile equilibrium became particularly evident after the financial crisis of 1994 and the serious downturn in economic activity following the Russian crisis in 1998 and 1999 (Figure 4.1). Turkey was, in short, confronted with the positive and negative aspects of financial globalization.

In broad terms, one could argue that the main elements of Turkey's economic success were reasonably rapid growth and a profound transformation in the economy's orientation toward exports and open capital markets (Table 4.1). Much less success was evident, however, in other critical realms such as macroeconomic stability,

investment performance, and income inequality.[8] A balanced interpretation would have to acknowledge the fragile nature of economic
growth based on overdependence on short-term capital inflows, failure to sustain the momentum of export growth, weak investment performance, and rising or persistent income inequalities, features not
unique to Turkey.[9]

FISCAL DISEQUILIBRIUM AND
THE CRISIS OF 1994

For analytical purposes it makes sense to consider the years 1980–87 as
having had a considerable degree of continuity. The period of military rule ran from September 1980 to November 1983. A transition to
elected civilian government followed in November 1983. However,
the democracy established during the 1983–87 era was restricted in
terms of both the degree of interparty competition permitted by the
military and the limitations placed on the bargaining rights of labor
unions. The transition to full electoral competition in Turkey followed
the national referendum of September 1987 and the general elections
of November 1987. By the end of 1987, the leading politicians of
the earlier era—Süleyman Demirel, Bülent Ecevit, and Necmettin
Erbakan—banned from participating in politics in 1980—regained their
right to compete for office. The limitations imposed on the bargaining
rights of labor unions were significantly relaxed. The year 1987 also
marks a turning point in the democratic evolution of Turkey's political
economy.[10]

Turkey has not distinguished itself as a successful case of sound
macroeconomic management in the context of a more open, more
democratic polity, a reflection perhaps of the low degree of institutionalization of democracy in Turkey and the limited capacity to manage distributional conflicts. Indeed, there was a marked deterioration of
fiscal balances between 1987 and 1993. Perhaps this was understandable in the sense that the principal losers during the reform process,
namely wage earners and agricultural producers, acquired an opportunity to recover the serious losses they had incurred in the early 1980s
by capitalizing upon their newly acquired political rights. Pressures for
populist redistribution mounted after 1987 and became particularly
acute during the 1990s, after the emergence of a highly fragmented

party system and a series of weak coalition governments. Turkey's encounters with coalition politics have typically been associated with economic and political instability, dating back to the experiences of the 1970s. The more liberal economic environment could not change the image of weak governance and instability associated with coalition politics in the early 1990s, at least until 1999.

Fiscal discipline steadily declined; the rise of the public sector borrowing requirement—the PSBR-to-GNP ratio—reached record levels in 1993. This precipitated the major crisis of the neoliberal era in late 1993 and early 1994 and necessitated a renewed encounter with the IMF (Figure 4.1). The crisis of 1994 was itself a textbook case of a financial crisis originating from unsustainable fiscal disequilibrium. In this respect, there was a clear difference between the cases of Turkey and those of Mexico in December 1994 and Asia in September 1997, where financial crises occurred in an environment of fiscal equilibrium and low inflation.[11] A number of commentators have emphasized that Turkey's transition to full capital account liberalization had been premature, the required fiscal adjustment not having been achieved.[12] In a sense, Turkey's financial crisis highlights the dangers involved when a country is suddenly exposed to the vagaries of financial globalization without having taken the necessary measures to produce domestic macroeconomic stability.[13]

In addition to the great rise in the public sector borrowing requirement (Figure 4.4, page 104), a close examination of Turkey's fiscal disequilibrium—a process progressively acute from 1991—reveals several striking tendencies. First, the trends in public expenditure shifted tremendously in favor of current expenditure and away from public investment. This raises further serious questions about the quality of fiscal management. Public investment performs a crucial complementary role from the point of view of long-term economic growth (Figure 4.5, page 105). Second, in contrast to the steady rise in public expenditures, overall public revenues as a proportion of GNP appear to have registered a decline during the period; although tax revenues as a proportion of GNP rose during the period, Turkey's tax revenue-GNP ratio was low by international standards and remains the lowest among OECD group of countries.[14] The war against the PKK since 1984 as well as the ambitious and expensive South-Eastern Anatolian Project (GAP), financed purely from domestic sources, made significant contributions to growing fiscal imbalances.

FIGURE 4.4. INDICATORS OF FISCAL DISEQUILIBRIUM: BUDGETARY EXPENDITURES AND REVENUES

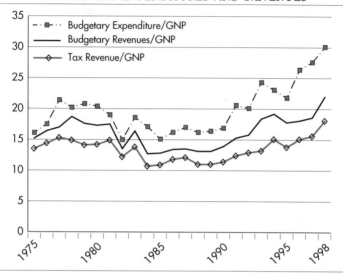

Sources: State Planning Organization, *Main Economic Indicators,* various years; Diş Ticaret Müsteşarliği, *Türkiye Ekonomisindeki Gelişmeler,* 1998.

THE POST-1994 FISCAL RESTRUCTURING: CHANGE VERSUS CONTINUITY?

Fiscal disequilibrium was at the heart of the 1994 financial crisis. The crisis was triggered by the government's decision to respond to strong domestic pressure and reduce interest rates so as to stimulate domestic investment, coupled with the decision of international rating agencies to reduce Turkey's credit rating. These shocks resulted in a speculative attack and a massive outflow of short-term capital. The outflow of short-term capital coming on top of a large deficit in the current account produced a major balance of payment crisis. As part of its IMF standby agreement Turkey had to implement a package involving expenditure-reducing and expenditure-switching policies. The crisis and the subsequent stabilization measures were costly in terms of loss of output and employment losses.

What turned out to be remarkable, however, was the speed with which the economy recovered. The Turkish financial crisis was a minor one by international standards. Its small size was, in part, due to the fact that Turkey was far less integrated into the international economy

FIGURE 4.5. COMPOSITION OF CENTRAL GOVERNMENT EXPENDITURES

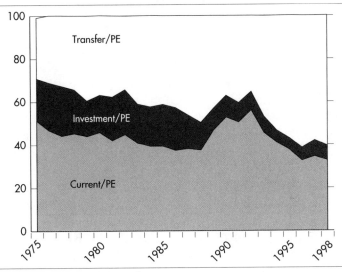

Note: PE = Central Government Expenditures.

Sources: State Planning Organization, *Main Economic Indicators,* various years; Dış Ticaret Müsteşarliği, *Türkiye Ekonomisindeki Gelişmeler,* 1998.

in terms of capital flows than its Mexican or Asian counterparts. Moreover, the Turkish economy also possessed a certain flexibility that facilitated a speedy recovery.[15] It was able to shift the burden of adjustment to wage earners; the share of wages and salaries in national income drastically declined in the aftermath of the stabilization program without serious social and political resistance.[16] Also, large industrial firms managed to shield themselves by continuing to lend to the government at high rates of interest.[17] It is ironic, however, that the comparatively smooth resumption of growth also meant that a key underlying weakness of the Turkish economy, namely fiscal disequilibrium deriving in part from dependence on short-term capital inflows, remained largely intact during the latter half of the 1990s. In other words, the crisis of 1994 did not bite sufficiently hard to provide the shock needed in the government to create a radical change in economic behavior. Turkey's large informal economy—variously estimated at 10–30 percent of the statistical economy—also helped to keep the country going, a situation hardly adequate for a country aspiring to join the EU.[18]

To what extent has fiscal disequilibrium been reversed following the crisis? The critical indicator of the problem, namely the PSBR-to-GNP ratio, continued to remain on a high plateau by international standards during the second half of the 1990s, but it was until 1999 significantly lower than the levels reached just prior to the onset of the crisis in 1992 and 1993 (Figure 4.1). The IMF-assisted program of 1994 involved two radical changes that helped to reduce the size of the PSBR. First, the stabilization package radically reversed the public sector wage booms of 1989 and 1991. Second, the borrowing requirements of state-owned enterprises (SOEs) were substantially diminished through a radical downsizing of investment and employment in existing SOEs (Figure 4.6).

In spite of these profound changes, however, the continuing large public sector deficits still present serious problems for the economy. What is striking in the post-1994–95 era is the changing origins of these deficits. Heavy domestic borrowing at high rates of interest, a practice that started in the early 1990s, has helped to create an enormous interest burden. This is reflected in the progressive increase in the share of transfer payments at a time when the current and investment components of

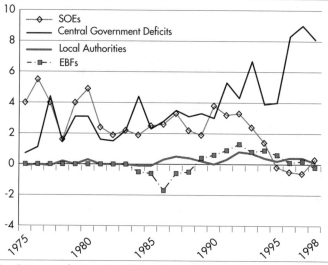

FIGURE 4.6. COMPOSITION OF PUBLIC SECTOR
BORROWING REQUIREMENT

Note: SOEs = State-owned enterprises; EBFs = Extrabudgetary funds.

Sources: State Institute of Statistics, *Statistical Yearbook of Turkey,* various years; State Planning Organization, *Main Economic Indicators of Turkey,* various years.

overall budgetary expenditures display a downward trend (Figure 4.5). Indeed, the interest burden has become the dominant underlying element of fiscal disequilibrium, pointing toward the existence of a vicious circle. The government has increasingly borrowed at high rates. This in turn has caused a lopsided pattern whereby in subsequent years little money has been left for anything but the interest repayment on domestic debt. The domestic debt-to-GNP ratio in Turkey is not particularly high by international standards. What causes a problem is Turkey's weak ability to manage its debt given the limited size of its capital markets.[19] Countries such as Italy and Belgium have larger ratios of domestic debt to GDP but much greater capacity to manage this debt given the size and the depth of their domestic capital markets. Also striking has been the growing deficits of social security institutions in the past few years, a serious structural problem.[20]

THE CRISIS OF 1994 AND THE DOWNTURN OF 1998–99: SIMILARITIES AND CONTRASTS

Although it did not overcome its basic problems of fiscal disequilibrium and high inflation, Turkey nonetheless managed to sustain fairly rapid economic growth, at least until the sharp downturn of 1998 and 1999. There were fundamental differences, however, in the origins of the crisis of 1994 and the severe contraction of the economy in the final years of the decade. The former was primarily a result of domestic mismanagement. The 1999 devaluation was largely an externally generated phenomenon.

Turkey did not feel the effects of the 1997 Asian crisis directly because Asian countries account for only a marginal part of Turkish trade. In contrast, the crisis of July 1998 was a severe blow to Turkey's economy. Turkey's economic relations with Russia had expanded significantly in the 1990s; Turkey exported consumer goods and construction services and imported significant quantities of natural gas. Tourism also provided a significant source of foreign exchange. Hence, the Turkish economy was affected directly by the collapse of the Russian economy in 1998.[21] Indirectly, however, the negative trends in the world economy following the Asian and Russian crises also had serious ramifications for Turkey. The slowdown in industrial growth and world trade seriously hurt Turkish exports. The major withdrawal of foreign funds and stagnation in external borrowing affected economic growth adversely in other emerging markets as well.

Several analysts have pointed out that, compared to many other emerging markets, the Turkish economy had a high degree of resilience to external shocks despite its persistent large public deficits and high inflation. Arguably, the Turkish economy by the end of the decade was in better shape than in 1994. The policy authorities had accumulated experience and appeared to possess greater capacity to manage the economy in the presence of large inflows of short-term capital. Through a flexible exchange-rate system Turkey also has been able to sustain a competitive real exchange rate in the post-1994 period. The basic logic underlying this perspective is that through exchange-rate policy Turkey managed to differentiate itself from other emerging markets and hence has been able to avoid a major crisis of its own.[22] Certainly, Turkey's current account has been better in recent years than in 1994.

Nonetheless, the severe contraction in 1998 and 1999 highlighted once again the vulnerability of the Turkish economy and the fragility of a growth path pursued through excessive dependence on inflows of short-term capital. In this respect, there exists a basic similarity between the crisis of 1994 and the economic downturn of 1998–99. Table 4.2

TABLE 4.2. CAPITAL INFLOWS AND ECONOMIC GROWTH IN TURKEY

Years	Real GNP Growth (Percent)	Net Inflows of External Capital ($Billion)	Net Inflows of External Capital/ GNP (Percent)
1989	1.6	0.8	0.7
1990	9.4	4.0	2.7
1991	0.3	−2.4	−1.6
1992	6.4	3.6	2.3
1993	8.1	8.9	4.9
1994	−6.1	−4.1	−3.2
1995	8.0	4.6	2.7
1996	7.1	8.7	5.3
1997	8.3	8.6	4.7
1998	3.8	0.9	0.5

Source: Central Bank of Turkey, Annual Reports, various years.

illustrates the striking correspondence between size of capital inflows and growth performance of the Turkish economy.

THE TURKISH ECONOMY AT THE TURN OF A NEW CENTURY: GROUNDS FOR RENEWED OPTIMISM?

Where does the Turkish economy stand compared to other emerging markets at the turn of a new century? It is illuminating to compare Turkey's performance with that of NICs in East Asia, Latin America, and Eastern Europe in terms of three basic criteria: per capita income based on purchasing power parity, the human development index (HDI), and the Gini coefficient as an indicator of relative inequality.[23] Turkey's per capita income growth compares favorably with the Eastern European averages but lags behind its East Asian and Latin American counterparts. The difference also is reflected in the respective sets of HDIs. The gap between Turkey and South Korea and Taiwan is particularly striking and reflects the fact that the latter countries have managed to achieve both superior growth and superior income distribution performances. The HDIs of Eastern European countries also are higher than Turkey's, even though their per capita income levels are broadly similar, basically because they have a considerably more even distribution of income on the basis of their Gini coefficients (Table 4.3, page 110).

Indeed, persistently high income inequality between different social classes as well as different regions is a serious and growing problem in the Turkish economy, resembling the situation in Brazil and Mexico. This income inequality is an important contributor to the major internal conflicts in Turkey. The Kurdish problem in southeastern Turkey is one of ethnic identity, but it is also a reflection of the relative economic underdevelopment of the southeast. It is clear as well that, despite the growth and dynamism of Turkey's private sector and the reasonable rates of economic growth achieved during both its import-substitution and neoliberal phases, the rate of expansion has not been sufficient to raise the per capita income to substantially higher levels in the presence of acute population pressures. Given the inability of the state to achieve significant redistribution of income, Turkey has mounting social problems. To absorb its disproportionately large number of young people in the labor market, it will have to achieve much higher rates of economic growth on a sustained basis. Turkey's intentions to

TABLE 4.3. TURKEY AND THE NEWLY INDUSTRIALIZED COUNTRIES IN COMPARATIVE PERSPECTIVE

COUNTRY	REAL GDP PER CAPITA (PPP $) 1995	HDI VALUE	HDI RANK	GINI COEFFICIENT
Turkey	5516	0.782	69	50.4[a]
Argentina	8498	0.888	36	n.a.
Brazil	5928	0.809	62	60.1
Chile	9930	0.893	31	56.5
Mexico	6769	0.855	49	53.7
China	2935	0.650	106	41.5
Hong Kong	22950	0.909	25	41.6[a]
Malaysia	9572	0.834	60	48.4
Indonesia	3971	0.679	96	36.5
Korea, Republic of	11594	0.894	30	34.5
Taiwan	16500	n.a.	n.a.	29.5
Thailand	7742	0.838	59	46.2
Czech Republic	9775	0.884	39	26.6
Poland	5442	0.851	52	27.2
Hungary	6793	0.857	47	27.9
Romania	4431	0.767	74	28.2
Russian Federation	4431	0.769	72	48.0

[a] Observations have been taken from Michael Sarel, "How Macroeconomic Factors Affect Income Distribution: The Country Evidence," *IMF Working Paper,* International Monetary Fund, Washington, D.C., 1997.

Source: The United Nations Human Development Report, 1998.

pursue a more active foreign policy and to play a more assertive regional role also are critically conditioned and constrained by its domestic economic performance.

The foreign direct investment (FDI) received by Turkey has been marginal compared with East Asia and Latin America. Even the Eastern European countries, on the whole, have attracted more FDI than Turkey during the past decade (Figure 4.7). Macroeconomic

FIGURE 4.7. FOREIGN DIRECT INVESTMENT PERFORMANCE OF
TURKEY AND NEWLY INDUSTRIALIZED COUNTRIES IN
COMPARATIVE PERSPECTIVE, 1987–1998

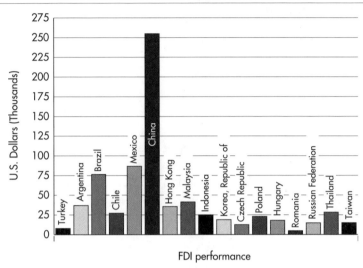

Source: UNCTAD, World Investment Report, 1999.

and political instability have often been singled out as the primary
causes underlying Turkey's inability to attract FDI. Bureaucratic
obstacles, the weakness of the legal system, and inadequate legal
protection for foreign investors also have been serious constraints.
Reforming the public sector and achieving fiscal stability are essential to creating a more conducive environment for both domestic
and foreign investment, resulting in higher rates of economic
growth. Higher rates of economic growth, in turn, are essential if
the state is to provide more for its citizens in key areas such as health
and education.

Although the state will continue to perform an important role in
the Turkish economy, a much more "regulatory state" will be required in
the new global environment. It will have to set high legal standards and
create competitive markets as well as better regulate the operation of
capital markets and the banking system. Transparency and the rule of
law in Turkey are both deficient for a country that seeks to move to a
well-functioning market system and to enter the EU.[24] In addition to its
regulatory role, the state has to increase significantly investment in certain key areas such as physical infrastructure, human capital formation,

and research and development. Finally, in a society characterized by significant inequalities in income distribution, the state has to involve itself in the areas of social policy and poverty alleviation. In the presence of severe fiscal constraints, targeting of the poorest groups in society will emerge as the cornerstone of an active social policy in this sphere.

SOME RECENT DEVELOPMENTS

At present, there are grounds for renewed optimism about Turkey's ability to break the vicious cycle of fiscal disequilibrium, dependence on short-term capital flows, and stop-go patterns of economic growth and to convert it into a virtuous cycle of macroeconomic stability, higher levels of domestic and foreign investment, and higher economic growth. First, Turkey is becoming accustomed to coalition governments and is learning to live with them. There is an increasing feeling that coalition politics may not necessarily imply, as in the 1970s and most of the 1990s, pervasive political instability combined with weak, ineffectual governance. Reconciliation and compromise appear to be entering the vocabulary of Turkish politics.

In fact, the present coalition government in Turkey, the dominant partners the social democratic or left nationalist DSP and the extreme nationalist MHP—parties that tend to draw their political support disproportionately from the poor and underprivileged—surprisingly has managed to implement significant reforms in a wide variety of areas since the general elections of April 1999. These have included rationalizing the social security system, improving regulation of banks and the financial sector, and allowing for international arbitration of foreign investment disputes. In addition, another effort at privatization has begun. The government also has initiated a standby agreement with the IMF, whose support is conditioned on implementation of a far-reaching program of public sector reform, including the politically important agricultural support system. The nature of political leadership is significant in this context. Prime Minister Ecevit's image as a clean politician, one never associated with corruption or scandals, and his conciliatory style of leadership also have been helpful in building confidence concerning Turkey's ability to deal with at least some of its basic economic and political problems.[25] Optimism also is based on a growing sense that the limits of clientelistic politics and populist redistribution have been reached. There is growing awareness that the cost of distributive politics is high and the benefits low, considering that little is left for redistribution because a disproportionate share of government expenditure goes toward the repayment of interest on funds borrowed to finance redistribution in earlier years.

The acceptance of Turkey's candidacy for membership in the EU at the Helsinki summit in December 1999 is expected to have a positive impact on the ability to implement far-reaching political and economic reforms. For countries like Turkey, where clientelistic patterns of politics are predominant, powerful external pressure is often a precondition for the country's ability to engineer radical economic reform. Mexico's experience under NAFTA clearly illustrates how its policymakers employed NAFTA membership to implement far-reaching fiscal reform, trade liberalization, and privatization during the late 1980s and early 1990s.[26]

The Customs Union Agreement with the EU created a powerful impetus for important regulatory reforms in Turkey in such key areas as competition and consumer protection, the establishment of intellectual property rights, and achieving higher technical standards. Yet the customs union has been a weak form of integration, with benefits falling considerably short of those associated with full membership.[27] The logical corollary of this proposition is that the prospect of full membership is likely to provide much more powerful incentives for undertaking serious reforms on both the economic and the democratization fronts.

The growing optimism about Turkey's ability to undertake radical reform and to break chronic inflation should not, however, lead one to underestimate the obstacles or pitfalls on the way. Macro stabilization based on radical reform of the government budget inevitably involves serious short-term losses in output and employment. In the past the losses have been shouldered almost exclusively by wage earners, public sector employees, and other low-income groups, with the inevitable backlash that has subsequently undermined the effectiveness of anti-inflationary strategy. It is imperative that the burden of stabilization and reform be distributed more evenly among the different segments of society and that private corporations share the burden of adjustment. This would, in turn, necessitate a commitment on the part of companies to increase their prices in line with the government's inflation target. Unless the burden of the anti-inflationary program is distributed in a relatively even fashion, it will be difficult for coalition governments to sustain confidence and consensus around the reform program and to prevent adverse reactions from social groups who lose disproportionately in the process.

ECONOMIC RELATIONS WITH THE UNITED STATES: ROOM FOR IMPROVEMENT?

The United States has played a crucial role in Turkey's security during the cold war and its aftermath. In recent years the relationship between the two countries has been particularly positive, reaching a peak following President Clinton's visit in November 1999. The United States has provided active support for Turkey's membership of the EU. Indeed, probably the biggest help that the United States can provide to Turkey, private investment aside, is to encourage the EU to pay high-level attention to Turkey and treat Turkey seriously in the accession process.

The United States also has been strongly supporting Turkey in the building of a pipeline to transport energy from Central Asia and the Caucasus through Turkey to Europe and other markets. The signing of the agreement in November 1999 by the countries involved in the Baku-Ceyhan crude-oil pipeline project has given it some impetus. The United States and Turkey also have agreed to promote a trans-Caspian gas pipeline. Both pipelines are important to Turkey in terms of its energy needs, in generating significant revenues from the transport of energy, and in developing stronger economic and political ties with the countries of the Caucasus and Central Asia.[28] But both prospects seem highly uncertain.

In terms of trade and investment the United States and Turkey have failed to reflect their potential. Turkey's principal trade relationship has been with the EU as a whole. Judged on a country-by-country basis, however, the United States has ranked second among Turkey's trading partners for several years, with a share of about 9 percent in Turkish imports and 8 percent in Turkish exports in 1998. Turkey is one of the few countries with which the United States has a favorable trade balance. Although the trade volume between the two countries has more than tripled in dollar terms since the onset of economic reforms in Turkey in 1980, this increase has been from an extremely low base. Given the size of the American market and Turkey's marginal share of trade with the United States (Turkey accounted for a mere 0.2 percent of U.S. imports and 0.5 percent of exports in 1998), the scope for improvement is considerable.[29] The United States is also crucial in terms of FDI. The growth of U.S. investment in Turkey is currently almost ten times higher than it was early in the 1980s—again, however, from an unusually low base. As of the end of June 1999, 12.6 percent of foreign investment in Turkey comes from American firms. A total of 302

American companies have been operating in Turkey. Foreign investment permits approved by the Turkish treasury for American firms between 1980 and 1998 reached a total of $2.7 billion—not a particularly impressive figure, and much of it in defense industries.

These figures, however, underestimate the true involvement of American investors in Turkey because they fail to include investment by foreign subsidiaries of U.S. firms. The United States has ranked third, behind the Netherlands and Germany, in terms of authorized FDI in Turkey both in 1998 and 1999. Greater Turkish support for foreign investment in build-operate-transfer projects appears to be generating U.S. investor interest. U.S. tourism is also significant for Turkey. The United States ranked fifth, with a share of 4.5 percent in the number of tourists traveling to Turkey in 1998. Nonetheless, the number involved (about 440,000) is exceptionally small compared to the number of American tourists traveling worldwide.

In trade, tourism, and investment there is scope for significant improvement. One long-standing problem is that Turkish exports face protectionist measures in the American market, especially in critical sectors such as steel, textiles, and processed agricultural goods. Import restrictions exist on forty-one different textile products out of fifty basic categories in the market. Still, Turkey's ability to take greater advantage of the American market depends heavily on its own policies and on its ability to diversify its export base in the direction of higher-value-added, more skill-intensive products.

The potential for improvement in FDI is enormous given the marginal position of Turkey in overall investment by American firms overseas. In 1998, authorized investment by American firms amounted to $297.2 million, a meager figure by U.S. standards. The primary impetus for improvement needs to come from Turkey itself. The fundamental problem Turkey has in attracting long-term foreign capital is of course not limited to U.S. firms. Greater security for foreign investors and a reduced perception of risk through a more stable macroeconomic and political environment as well as stronger legal protection are needed. The significance of legal protection is highlighted by the number of U.S. companies waiting for Turkey to implement rules of international arbitration before committing themselves to invest in major energy projects.

CHAPTER FIVE

SOME TURKISH PERSPECTIVES ON THE UNITED STATES AND AMERICAN POLICY TOWARD TURKEY

CENGIZ ÇANDAR

INTRODUCTION

The United States has been Turkey's closest ally since the end of World War II. Along with Greece, Turkey was the early focus of the cold war and occupied a special place in American global policies. Reminiscent of those "golden years" of the 1950s, relations between Turkey and the United States now, at the turn of the millennium, are excellent.

This was not always the case. The bilateral relationship has in fact never been conflict-free. Despite the ostensibly unbreakable security and military ties, there were serious ups and downs in the relationship, and for most of the past two decades its future was in doubt.

The 1950s were followed by a growing popular anti-Americanism that influenced the attitudes of the ruling elite. Attitudes hardened significantly during the second half of the 1970s, following the arms embargo imposed after Turkey's military intervention in Cyprus.

The 1980s, with Turgut Özal at the helm of Turkish decision-making, heralded a new era of Turkish-American relations, crowned by close cooperation in the Gulf War and changing Turkish perceptions of the United States. The change also coincided with the collapse of the cold war's international order and the technology-generated prospects for globalization. The new dynamics, especially the free market reforms set in motion during the 1980s, seem central to the pattern of Turkish-American ties in the first decade of the new century.

The making of foreign policy, as in most countries in the world, is the province of the elite in Turkey. An examination of the evolution of elite perceptions of the United States helps clarify the background and culture of Turkey's political class and produces a better understanding of the complicated and complex bond Turks have with the United States.

THE WATERSHED

It was an unusual appearance for a Turkish president but not un-characteristic of Turgut Özal. It was Saturday, January 16, 1993, three months before his death and on the eve of his last visit to the United States, where Özal was to meet Bill Clinton and be the first foreign dignitary to step into the Oval Office after the inauguration. In a fully packed auditorium at Ankara Gazi University, Özal was making con-cluding remarks on a panel on "Turkey's prospects for the twenty-first century." He was the moderator, not a panelist.

Certainly never before in Turkey (and probably not anywhere else) had a head of state so humbled himself, sitting for seven hours as mod-erator of a panel that gathered a number of mavericks challenging con-ventional dogma and official Turkish positions. He declined to make the introductory speech and said he would come only if he could moder-ate the panel of well-known and controversial pundits—a stunning move even for the iconoclast of Turkish politics. Some of the panelists had a reputation for anti-Kemalist opinions; one was a passionate advo-cate of the "second republic." This was not perceived as "radical reformism" but rather as equivalent to dismantling the Turkish Republic and undoing the legacy of its founder, the sacrosanct Kemal Atatürk.

The calls for transforming the Turkish political system and inaugurating the "second republic" had become anathema within the bureaucratic elite—any criticism of the status quo was immediately dubbed "second republicanism." By moderating the panel Özal was giving a blessing of sorts to the concepts of plurality of ideas and unity in diversity.

These concepts, were, for him, basically American—and therefore had also to be adapted to Turkey so it could meet the challenges of the twenty-first century.

Sitting on his right on that Saturday, I recalled that in one of our meetings at his presidential summer retreat in southwestern Turkey, a book on the table had captured my attention: *Free Speech in an Open Society*. I interrupted the conversation to ask him if he were really reading the book. Smiling, he responded, "Of course I am. Are you one of those who think that I only read Lucky Luke?" In the early 1980s an interview had revealed him to be an enthusiastic reader of the originally Belgian-French comic strip about an American wild west cowboy of that name. Thereafter, thanks mostly to the efforts of leftists who control many of the outposts of the Turkish intelligentsia, an image of Özal was created as someone with a taste for American pop culture. This caricature of Özal, a determined proponent of the free market, conformed to the ridicule in Turkey of President Reagan—by the same leftist intelligentsia—as an American cowboy, an unsophisticated bully leading the most powerful nation of the world.

The *New York Times Book Review*'s synopsis of Rodney A. Smolla's *Free Speech in an Open Society* included the following lines: "This grand tour of First Amendment law underlines the intimate connection between free expression and democratic values as it leads us through the most treacherous and emotionally charged cases in American jurisprudence. Intellectually venturesome."[1] The publisher's description of the book might have contained the clue to Özal's eagerness to read it, possibly the last book he read before his death: "Exploring the question 'What should freedom of speech mean in a democracy?' Rodney Smolla argues that it is a value of overarching significance. Freedom of speech, he says, is not merely an aid to self-governance, but is uniquely connected to all that defines the human spirit—to imagination, creativity, enterprise, rationality, love, worship, and wonder. In a complex modern society, freedom of speech is constantly threatened by other social interests and values, which often seem more important in the short term: national security . . . controlling the corrupting influences of money on the political process, and bringing order to global electronic communications."[2]

Özal's Perception of America

I do not know if Özal ever read that synopsis, but I know those issues preoccupied Özal in that fateful 1991–93 period. One thing was evident to anybody who had any knowledge of Özal's upbringing: he had never been under the influence of Europe's democratic-intellectual tradition; he was not curious about it and did not bother to study it. With his conservative Anatolian background and his training as an engineer in the late 1940s, which corresponded to the beginning of close Turkish-American relations, he had never been receptive to European ideas, nor much attuned to European culture. His references—whether comics or scholarly texts by obscure writers—were American from the days of his early youth. The barely concealed condition was that ideas had to have an American brand. This was true not only for books but also for electronic goods, for which he had an insatiable appetite. He had come to know them in America and kept abreast of developments thanks to his frequent travels to the United States.

In one of his last visits, in March 1991, he was invited to Camp David by President Bush to spend the weekend. A day later, speaking at a dinner in his honor at the University of North Carolina, he discussed his weekend. To the astonishment of his audience, he revealed his obsession with electronic objects. He said that whenever he had been to Washington in the late 1970s and early 1980s, he contrived an occasion to slip away from his meetings to find the latest electronic products in drugstores. Once, a toy called Atari captured his attention. It occurred to him then that if American children grew up playing with it and Turkish children did not, the gap between Turkey and the developed countries would be impossible to narrow. On his return to Turkey in 1979, in the first cabinet meeting as deputy prime minister responsible for economic affairs, he proposed the total liberalization of electronic imports. This met with stiff resistance from the ministers with a military background, who wanted to retain protection for a local electronic production plant facing strong foreign competitors. With a grin of pleasure, he told the 1999 panel, "After three years, military rule ended and my party won the elections; the first decree of my government was to liberalize imports of electronic goods and equipment. On that weekend at Camp David, I noticed President Bush's grandchildren playing with Atari. I want to assure you that my grandchildren are better!"

Özal's moral and material admiration for the American experience had its roots in his first encounter with the United States, on his first day in New York in the early 1950s, as a young electrical engineer on an exchange program. He recalled that encounter to the panel in Ankara: "We were a couple of young engineers with a similar Anatolian background when we had arrived for the first time in the United States. We were both around 5 feet 5 inches and were overwhelmed when we disembarked in Manhattan. Neither of us confessed to the initial and abrupt feeling of inferiority among the skyscrapers. We had all been brought up with the familiar motto that a Turk is equal to the rest of the world. The images of the rural, underdeveloped Turkish countryside passed quickly through my brain. If each one of us is equivalent to the rest of the world, how was it that our land remained as it is? Why were these people, who are supposedly inferior to us, able to construct these wonders?" That panel program was broadcast scores of times and infiltrated the subconscious of millions of Turks.

Özal's remarks were reminiscent of the observations of Ziya Paşa, the well-known Turkish reformist thinker and poet of the late nineteenth century. He summarized his encounters with the West in his poetry, one of whose best-remembered verses, as rhymed in Turkish, is, *"Dolaştim Diyar-ı Garbı hep kaşaneler gördüm; Geldim Mülk-ü İslam'a hep viraneler gördüm"* [I have been to the lands of West and I have seen only mansions; Coming back to the land of Islam, I have seen only ruins].

Özal was awed by America's technological success and might, and this was no aberration: the roots of his response lie deep in the Turkish quest for modernity.

Turgut Özal represented the pro-Western reformist-modernist tendency, which had its roots in the beginning of the nineteenth century. For the modernizing Turkish elite, being "contemporary" was generally synonymous with Western civilization. Western civilization was synonymous with Europe, and in Europe it was France that most influenced the Turkish elite culturally. From the mid-nineteenth century, French standards within the Turkish elite—even among those dissenting from autocratic rule—were supreme. Turkey's administrative structures were modeled after France's. Despite Turkish admiration (mixed with anxiety) for Britain and Germany, particularly the latter's martial credentials, France remained the role model. Notwithstanding the might of imperial Britain and its role in safeguarding the territorial integrity of Turkey [that is, the Ottoman Empire] for nearly a century, the Anglo-Saxon experience did not penetrate the political culture of the ruling elite. The weakness of liberal values in Turkey and the difficulties of creating a civil society have much to do with this history.

The American influence within the elite should be considered a break with a tradition that dates back to the French Revolution. Turgut Özal not only represented a continuation of the painful Turkish drive to modernism and Westernization, he was one of the most striking products of a pro-American Turkey. Former secretary of state James Baker paid him a great tribute in his book *The Politics of Diplomacy:* "Throughout the [Gulf War] crisis, Özal was stalwart in his support for the United States. He was a leader of great heart and courage. . . . America is fortunate to have friends and allies like him."[3]

It was unfortunate that no high-level U.S. official, neither the vice president nor the secretary of state, attended the funeral of Özal, the only Turkish president to pass away in office since the death of Atatürk, the founder of the republic. Even his close relationship to President Bush did not pay off. Baker wrote that he "was proud when as a private citizen and at President Clinton's request, I represented my country."[4] The unexpectedly low-profile American representation did not escape the attention of the Turkish public. For many Turks, whether they were Özal fans or dedicated opponents, the general interpretation of the American representation was that his "dear American friends" had let him down. Years later it was ironic to Turks to see President Clinton and three former presidents of the United States walking after the casket of King Hussein in 1999 and some months later to see Clinton not hesitating to fly across the ocean for the funeral of King Hassan of Morocco.

The result, however inadvertent, was to enhance a perception of the United States opposite to what the deceased Turkish president wanted: the unreliability of the United States and its indifference to Turkey.

BETWEEN DISAPPOINTMENT AND PARANOIA

Despite the half-century-old alliance and even the camaraderie on battlefields from Korea to the skies over Yugoslavia, this basic feeling of the Turks toward America has persisted. Often overlooked or ignored, it constitutes a strong element in Turkish political attitudes toward the United States and serves as a permanent source of mistrust on the part of the Turkish elite.

But the Turks also harbor feelings of betrayal. Most important in producing this are the Johnson letter of 1964 and the imposition of the arms embargo a decade later. The first helped prevent Turkey's Cyprus intervention, the second came as a result of it. For the overwhelming majority of the Turks Cyprus was a national cause. Both episodes were devastating in their effects on both elite and general public perceptions of America—which, on these two rare occasions, coincided.

The two events became so entrenched in the institutional memory of the Turkish establishment that any close cooperation between the two countries in the decades that followed came to be seen as a "marriage of convenience" dictated by realpolitik and Turkey's troubled relations with Europe rather than arising from a genuine feeling of alliance. This lack of trust showed up in the opposition to Özal's pro-American stand during the Gulf War and its aftermath, when the Turkish government worried obsessively about a Kurdish entity emerging in northern Iraq because of U.S. policy.

The republic that replaced the Ottoman Empire after World War I was "security oriented." Founders of the republic were, after all, the top military brass and civil servants of the Ottoman state, which had experienced steady territorial losses for more than a century. The distrust for outsiders stemmed from that Ottoman experience and was deeply embedded in the ruling elite of the new state. Their urge to modernize—that is, Westernize—was more a pragmatic effort to secure the survival of the state than an ideological posture. Their interest in Western institutions and techniques was aimed mainly at strengthening the state to thwart those perceived Western (including Russian) designs on the territorial integrity of Turkey.

After the establishment of the new secular, Western-oriented state, Turkey had to survive in an unfriendly neighborhood with a constellation of new states that, once part of the Ottoman Empire, scorned Turkey's long domination over them. These new neighbors were considered the wards of the victorious Western powers. Negative attitudes also developed against the European powers, who had tried to dismember Ottoman Turkey for more than half a century. This defensive mentality of the Turkish elite resurfaced with a vengeance against Wilson's Fourteen Points, which envisaged carving out from Anatolia an independent Armenian state and an independent Kurdish state. The Wilsonian principles culminated in the 1920 Treaty of Sèvres, still a hated word in Turkey. All these factors became part of the intellectual makeup of the new Turkish bureaucracy. The outside world, including the United States, was unfriendly to Turkey.

Sèvres has never been buried in the Turkish psyche. The frequent evoking of its memory in the aftermath of the Gulf War, in relation to American policies of protecting the Iraqi Kurds from Saddam, reflects this congenital paranoia of the Turkish elite. Despite incessant American assurances, most in the Turkish political establishment have doubted the intentions of Washington.

The Turkish accusations against the United States on the accidental firing of an American missile into a Turkish destroyer during naval exercises were in great part an expression of the general staff's displeasure and irritation over American Iraq policies in the post–Gulf War period. So were the charges that American helicopters belonging to Operation Provide Comfort were dropping aid to PKK insurgents in northern Iraq. These charges were expressed through a manipulated Turkish press, without committing the generals to a hostile stand against the United States. They also were intended to warn tacitly the United States to be much more cautious in its Iraq policy.

FRENCH JACOBINISM VERSUS ANGLO-SAXON LIBERALISM

If there had been some traditional cultural affinity of the Turkish elite for the United States, and better knowledge and understanding of the American experience, the nature of the Turkish reading of America would have been different. However, the educational roots of the Westernizing Turkish elite had essentially been French. French administrative centralism corresponded to Turkish traditions and the preference for an autocratic and centralized mechanism. American federalism did not present an attractive model for the Turkish elite, always wary of dismemberment given the diverse peoples inhabiting its territories. While Anglo-Saxon liberalism never much penetrated into Turkish political culture, French Jacobinism had an appeal to that Turkish elite looking for ways to overthrow Islam, which in their eyes was anathema to progress and whose demise was a prerequisite for survival of the state. "There were many similarities between the Ottoman-Turkish reformers and, especially, the Jacobins who dominated the French state between 1793 and 1794, in terms of the puritanical zeal with which each approached the task of remaking their respective state and society."[5]

It was not strange that the first educational institution established on the Western model had its curriculum in French. Galatasaray Lisesi— Lycée de Galatasaray—was established with the intention of Westernizing education and producing a modernizing ruling elite. It had a reputation of being "the window opened onto the West." Since the mid-nineteenth century, Galatasaray, with its French-language curriculum, was the primary source of Turkish intellectual life. Mekteb-i Mülkiye-i Şahane, today's Faculty of Political Sciences of Ankara University, literally means "The School of Royal Administration" and was founded in 1859, right after "Islahat Fermanı"—Royal Decree of Reform—a landmark commitment in Turkish history to Westernization that followed the Crimean War of 1856. This school of higher education was modeled on France's Ecole Nationale d'Administration. Until the 1990s it was the principal institution for training nearly all Turkey's diplomatic personnel, the civil servants of finance, treasury, and foreign trade, and the high bureaucrats of the Ministry of Interior, whether they were governors of provinces or heads of security.

Knowledge of Anglo-Saxon men of letters and thought was almost nonexistent. The Turkish intellectual elite, from the last decades of the nineteenth century to the second half of the twentieth, had only a vague familiarity with the works of John Locke or David Hume, or of Thomas Jefferson, Thomas Paine, Alexander Hamilton, or Benjamin Franklin. In my elementary school during the 1950s and as a high school and university student of the 1960s, I was taught the name of Benjamin Franklin as the scientist who discovered the lightning rod. My generation of Turks was given no deeper educational exposure to American thought and practice.

On the other hand, French thinkers, above all Auguste Comte and Emile Durkheim, but also names like René Descartes, Jean-Jacques Rousseau (a Francophone Swiss), Voltaire, and Montesquieu had an enormous impact on the Turkish intellectuals who laid the foundations of the constitutional monarchy at the turn of the century and the new Republic of Turkey in the 1920s. They were called *Jön Türkler*—Young Turks—the founding fathers of the secular nation-state of Turkey. This political and intellectual elite was influenced by the French Enlightenment and by the French schools of rationalism and positivism. Ziya Gökalp, the most famous propagandist of Turkish nationalism and the creator of the theoretical framework of the Turkish nation-state that came into being in the early 1920s, was a disciple of Durkheim.

The French cultural influence even extended during the 1960s to the Marxist thought that flourished in Turkey's universities, engulfed in the radical wave of that decade. *The Principles of Philosophy,* a kind of *Dialectical and Historical Materialism for Dummies* by an unimportant French Communist academic named Georges Politzer, was translated from French and became the main reference book for scores of young Turkish activists. Turkey's new left had acquired a simplistic comprehension of Marxist thinking through an obscure French author.

At the beginning of the twentieth century, the dissenters against Ottoman rule had found refuge in Paris. The pattern repeated itself during the 1950s and 1960s. Because of the harsh cold war circumstances, which did not allow overt close contacts between Turkish leftists and the neighboring Soviet Union, the void was filled by the French Communist Party, the most pro-Soviet of the West European Communist parties, exerting an influence on the Turkish émigré leftist community in Europe.

THE IMPACT OF THE 1960S

The 1960s witnessed the eruption of anti-Americanism in countless lands, and Turkey was no exception. The attitudes of Turkey's present opinion makers—media pundits, columnists, or television anchors— and key financial and business executives, even some military officers, were largely shaped during that period.

The 1960s were of course marked by America's unhappy experience in Vietnam and the rise of radicalism on the international scene. In Turkey this was secondary in importance to the bitter episode of President Johnson's letter that prevented Turkey from taking action in Cyprus in 1964. Turks felt let down when they wanted to rush to rescue their kinsmen, and Cyprus fueled Turkish nationalist passions for two decades.

The Johnson letter had ramifications far beyond the period in which it was written. Not only did it leave a deep imprint on Turkish views of the reliability and friendship of the United States; it also triggered a lively debate on Turkey's place and role in global affairs.

The crucial paragraph of the letter read: "I hope you will understand that your NATO allies have not had a chance to consider whether they have an obligation to protect Turkey against the Soviet Union if Turkey takes a step which results in Soviet intervention without the full consent and understanding of its NATO allies."[6]

Dankwart A. Rostow, in *Turkey: America's Forgotten Ally,* wrote, "In Washington, Johnson's letter had remained a secret among five or six top officials; in Ankara, Prime Minister Ismet İnönü was obliged to share it with his cabinet; and the text was leaked to the Turkish press. The damage to US-Turkish relations was severe. Only a decade earlier, Turkey had eagerly dispatched its troops to help the United States fight communist aggression in Korea; now Johnson's letter amounted to threatening America's Turkish ally with the common Soviet enemy. The feeling of betrayal in Turkey was widespread."[7]

It is important to note that this feeling of "betrayal" preceded the heavy anti-American sentiment in the spectacular student demonstrations against Sixth Fleet visits to Turkish ports, the most striking example of the heightened leftist radicalism during the second half of the 1960s. The publication of the deliberately leaked text was expected to spark a heated public debate. It did, causing Prime Minister İnönü to make his unforgettable statement: "A new world can be constructed and Turkey find its rightful place in it." What he meant amounted to blackmailing the United States, during those peak days of the cold war, with the threat that Turkey might move toward the nonaligned group—one of those rare moments when the views of the anti-American left and the establishment overlapped.

İnönü was a historic personality of the Turkish republican era. He was among the founders of the republic, ranking second only to the "eternal leader" Kemal Atatürk. His response to Johnson's threatening message unleashed the nostalgia of the Kemalist elite for the early republican period, the "golden days" of Kemal Atatürk. That period is always interpreted by its proponents as the time when Turkish national pride was high and when Turkey was not a junior partner of any alliance but an independent power center in its own right.

Turkey's NATO membership had resulted from Turkey's strategic choice that its territorial integrity was threatened by Stalin's Soviet Union in the aftermath of the Second World War. Turkey became the recipient of American military aid thanks to the Truman Doctrine, and it was Adnan Menderes's Democrat Party that ended the one-party rule of İnönü in 1950 and saw Turkey into NATO. To impress the

United States and to secure membership in the alliance, Turkey had participated enthusiastically in the Korean War. The souring of relations with the United States over different approaches to the Cyprus problem, the strongest manifestation of Turkish national pride, mobilized doubts over the wisdom of the alliance with America.

And the cleavages within the Turkish establishment were revealed again. In 1964–65 İnönü, representing the Kemalist faithful, stood for "national pride" and "independence," while the former Democrats and their political offspring, according to the traditional Kemalists, were on the other side. Although the military, for whom İnönü was unassailable because of his nationalist-Kemalist credentials, had declared its allegiance to Turkey's NATO ties and did not try to alter its America-oriented foreign policy, it had a tendency to view the Democrat Party and its successor as being too ready to compromise Turkey's national pride. After the İnönü-Johnson showdown, there was a tendency to see the Democrats' former prime minister, Menderes—who had been executed in 1961 following the military coup of 1960—as the culprit in aligning Turkey too closely and too servilely to the United States. İnönü's mention of a "new world to be constructed" in which "Turkey will have its rightful place" struck a responsive chord among many Turks, from the military to the left-leaning intelligentsia.

PERCEIVING "PLOTS"

But after a few months of bravado, İnönü was removed from office when his budget for 1965 was rejected. He was replaced a year later by a young engineer, Süleyman Demirel. Demirel's rise was quickly interpreted by the Kemalist pundits as an "American plot" to punish İnönü for wanting to steer Turkey away from the United States and toward nonalignment.

From the moment Demirel stepped onto the Turkish political stage, he had a meteoric rise. He first climbed to the chairmanship of the Justice Party, which opened the road to political power. Justice was the successor to the banned Democrat Party. Initially, Demirel was given little chance of success since he was running in his first campaign against a politically experienced rival with strong grassroots support. He nonetheless won media backing, and his campaign team distributed a photograph showing him in the presence of President Johnson in the White House, a memento of a group visit to the Oval Office when Demirel was in Washington as an Eisenhower Fellow. His supporters were trying to impress delegates to the Justice Party congress with Demirel's international experience and American support. Once Demirel was elected, the Kemalist circles tended to regard him as an American stooge. Though he was a brilliant young bureaucrat in the late 1950s, supervising the ambitious project of constructing dams, he was more often portrayed as the representative of Morrison-Knudsen, an American construction company, where he was employed after the 1960 military takeover; the streets of Turkey's big cities were rocked by the slogan "Morrison Süleyman" during the anti-American demonstrations of the late 1960s. Demirel's replacement of such a historic figure as İnönü had the effect of underlining existing Turkish suspicions, which saw American moves as a part of a grand scheme or a plot.

Metin Toker, a veteran Turkish journalist and the son-in-law of İnönü, who was considered his unofficial spokesman, reflected the mood of that crucial period of Turkish-American relations:

> As far as I know, we seriously intended to land on Cyprus for the first time during the summer of 1964. That initiative was blocked by that famous letter of Johnson. . . . This is the emotional basis of the anti-American sentiment that would be felt in Turkey for years to come. . . . A short time later, Johnson also had a diagnosis of Ismet İnönü. As a result of this diagnosis, he tried to find a prime minister to replace Ismet İnönü. . . . An American general whose name is Porter arrived in Ankara. He was sent to Ankara by President Johnson himself. His mission was to find a prime minister who would accept the various propositions that İnönü had rejected. General Porter's visit coincided with reports of CIA agents conducting surveys in Ankara. Turkey saw the real face of America on that occasion and the debate on America in Turkish public opinion started. . . . This is exactly what the United States would not permit to continue. Eventually, General Porter and the CIA's agents found what they were looking for. This was Demirel . . . to whom the destiny of Turkey has been entrusted since 1965.[8]

Deep suspicions concerning American "plotting"—allegedly through visiting American military officials—and the association of the

United States with the frequent military interventions in Turkey have not been limited to political observers; they have often been shared by the political actors who helped to shape recent Turkish political history and frame Turkish public opinion. Bülent Ecevit, the present prime minister, is one of them. Ecevit, who served also as prime minister during 1973–74 and 1978–79 and was a victim of the military interventions of 1971 and 1980, emphasized the linkage between the United States and military coups in Turkey:

> This is a fact: what I mean is when you bring together a number of newly collected data, the fact revealed is that all the military interventions in Turkey, even if not provoked—although they may have been so—were carried out with American support and American consent. For instance, the first announcement following the coup on May 27, 1960 started with the assurance that Turkey would remain loyal to the USA, NATO and CENTO. I believe the resistance of the civilian political forces to [American] pressures to ban opium growing played an important background role in the military intervention of March 12 [1971]. . . . I have a strong feeling that the September 12 [1980] military intervention was encouraged by the United States.[9]

He went even further in alluding to an American involvement in the transition from military to civilian rule by referring to the visit of General Alexander Haig to Turkey in 1983, when the military turned power over to a newly elected government.[10]

The belief in the American conspiracy—usually synonymous with the CIA—against the elected authority in Turkey is entrenched in the Turkish political class. In great part this is owing to the longest-serving foreign minister of Turkey, Ihsan Sabri Çağlayangil, and his remarks on the role of the CIA in ousting the Demirel government in 1971. Çağlayangil, in a 1974 interview with the prominent Turkish journalist İsmail Cem (who himself became foreign minister in 1997), explicitly described a supposed CIA involvement in the "military coup by memorandum" of 1971. The interview, published in a book by Cem, has served for more than two decades as the touchstone for the political class in Turkey in understanding Turkish-American relations.

"The CIA was behind the 12 March [1971] coup. It was involved to a great extent," said Çağlayangil. He went further than his allegation of

CIA involvement in the military intervention and characterized American foreign policy imperatives: "The United States does not care if there is a democratic or a chauvinistic or a fascist rule in a country. This is not what it cares about."[11]

His bitter remarks left a strong imprint on the Turkish establishment. Çağlayangil, conveying his long experience as a leading figure of Turkish diplomacy, sounded convincing to many in Turkey. In the same interview, he mentioned other specific cases: "The pressure [from the United States] was exerted on different issues. I was obliged to confront them personally. . . . In fact, they were very polite. The American ambassador in each visit would either bring President Johnson's or President Nixon's special greetings. We received the greetings of Johnson on the issue of the airplanes [U-2s] and of Nixon on the issue of opium growing."[12]

Çağlayangil was not only a titan of the foreign policy elite. During the 1930s and 1940s, he had been an official of the security apparatus. During the 1950s he was a prominent governor. After serving as foreign minister between 1965 and 1971 and 1975 and 1978, he became the chairman of the Senate and finally the acting president of the republic until the military coup of September 12, 1980. With such a rich and diverse record of public service, he was the quintessential figure of the Turkish political class, personifying the Turkish establishment. His cynicism about U.S. policy toward Turkey is illustrative of how the most eminent representatives of Turkish decisionmakers felt about America.

It is ironic that Süleyman Demirel, widely believed to be "Washington's choice" to replace the revered İnönü, was also resentful of the United States, as reflected in Çağlayangil's assessments.

RESENTMENT FROM RIGHT TO LEFT

Notwithstanding the facade of a solid alliance, there were deep contradictions between Turkey and the United States on bilateral issues. These ranged from using Turkish base facilities for espionage flights over the Soviet Union to the ban on opium growing that would affect thousands of Turkish farmers.

The latter half of the 1960s had already witnessed an upsurge of anti-American feeling in Turkey that paralleled the same phenomenon worldwide, in large part owing to the war in Vietnam. The appointment of Robert Komer as U.S. ambassador to Turkey in 1968 was perceived by the Turkish public as adding insult to injury. Turkish-American relations had already been scarred by the Johnson letter. When Turkish student unrest—with its anti-American overtones—erupted, the appointment of a former CIA official as the U.S. ambassador had strong repercussions. The profile of an American ambassador whose main function, as widely reported in the Turkish press, was to "subdue by any means the opposition to U.S. policies" and who earned his reputation being the "chief pacification expert" in Vietnam helped to fuel the militancy of the student movement and increased the general skepticism of the Turkish public about U.S. intentions toward Turkey.

Komer's term as ambassador coincided with sometimes mammoth street demonstrations against American Sixth Fleet visits to Turkey's ports. The Demirel government took heavy police action to quell the growing anti-Americanism, which it sensed also was directed against itself. Ultimately, Komer became the target of student violence in 1969, and his car was overturned and burned while he was visiting a university campus in Ankara, one of the bastions of student radicalism.

The trial of the student culprits turned into a celebration of "national heroes," and the court acquitted them.

The identification of the Demirel government as pro-American created an uneasiness in the decisionmaking apparatus. Embarrassed with the label, the government diminished its cooperation with the United States on many issues, including the implementation of bilateral (mostly military) agreements signed in the 1950s and the restriction of opium growing. Referring later to those years of turbulence in Turkish-American relations, Demirel and his close associates sought to resurrect their "nationalist" credentials by claiming that they were also "victims" of American-orchestrated military coups because they stood up to American pressures.

One of the decisive effects of the 1960s on Turkish perceptions of the United States was to foster an equation of Turkish national interest with distance from Turkey's transatlantic ally or with resisting American requests, whatever their content.

The pressures of the cold war and Turkey's global security concerns kept relations with the United States within certain limits but no longer fostered deep sentiments of friendship and affection on the part of the Turks. Turgut Özal's tenure represents an aberration in Turkish perceptions of U.S. policies.

THE UNITED STATES IN THE EYES OF THE TURKISH MILITARY

The military as the self-appointed guardian of republican values and its belief in being "the backbone of the state" and a main channel for the conduct of Turkish-American relations deserves special attention. The military occupies a special place in understanding Turkish perspectives on the United States.

The military was the first and foremost Turkish institution to establish tangible and often intricate relations with the United States. Since the bond between Turkey and the United States did not originate in cultural affinity, emigration, or commercial ties but rather from a pragmatic response to common security needs and goals, the military became for a long period the preeminent Turkish institution in dealings with the United States. It also was the biggest recipient of American aid.

Given its pivotal role in U.S.-Turkish relations during the cold war, one might expect the military to take a benign view of the United States, hostile to the adverse sentiments of the left, which the military allegedly saw as a fifth column. The reality was somewhat different.

The military's role as guardian of the Kemalist-nationalist legacy, the principles of the republic and "national unity," intrinsically frees it from identifying with any foreign power. Hence, the close military arrangements and links with the United States after Turkey's accession to NATO in 1952 were always presented or justified as dictated by collective security needs against the Soviet Union, a contribution to protecting the territorial integrity of Turkey. Other than the requirements of collective security, the military was always keen to demonstrate and assert its nationalist credentials. It was sensitive to being pictured as "pro-American."

The 1960s accentuated this self-image. It was a decade of upheaval within the armed forces and ended the (overt) noninvolvement of the military with politics. Atatürk, himself a soldier, kept the military out of politics and, thanks to his immense prestige and talent, exercised influence by remote control. Ismet Inönü, also originally a soldier and enjoying high prestige among the military, used his influence similarly.

The subsequent Menderes rule witnessed Turkey's new and exclusive relationship with the United States and membership in NATO, and marked a departure from the established pattern. The free market–oriented Menderes government, with its American-inspired motto "a millionaire in every neighborhood," conflicted with the spartan traditions of the military. Bad blood developed between the two from the outset of Democrat Party power (1950). Further alienation of the military from the decisionmaking process ended with the first military coup in the republic's history, on May 27, 1960. Thereafter the military not only refrained from identifying itself with the Menderes government stance of close friendship with the United States but also permanently involved itself in the power-seeking or power-sharing dramas of Turkish politics.

The 1960s, inaugurated by a military coup in Turkey, was marked by a growth in the numbers of the nonaligned and newly independent countries. The Turkish military, through its active involvement with politics in the post-coup period, became susceptible to radical third-worldist tendencies—Middle East Baathism included. In its Turkish version Baathism was cloaked in the coat of Kemalism and of social progress. Upholding anti-Americanism and a nostalgia for a Turkey with "full national independence," it penetrated down to the rank and file and became a drive to topple the allegedly pro-American government of Süleyman Demirel (1965–71) in order to enact "progressive" reforms.

Shrouded factional disputes and personal rivalries in a politicized military framed the pattern of politics during the latter half of the 1960s and led to the March 12, 1971, military intervention, often referred to as the "coup by memorandum." Although the pseudo-progressivist faction with its putschist tendencies was presumably purged by the high command, which was controlled by more conservative and rightist generals, the residue of the former remained intact among officers who were ultimately to climb to positions of responsibility and leadership during the 1990s. They were instrumental in staging the "soft coup" or "postmodern coup."[13] In looking at the present composition of the Turkish officer corps, it is not irrational to conclude that feelings of ambiguity toward U.S. policy and intentions concerning Turkey have been passed on.

The military establishment as a whole became outraged by the 1975 arms embargo against Turkey after the Turkish landing in northern Cyprus. The embargo was in no way justifiable in the eyes of the Turkish military, which saw it as an unjust punishment by an ally for an action that was a national cause and in Turkey's strategic interest. The arms embargo of 1975 was even more devastating to Turkish perceptions of the United States than the Johnson letter of the preceding decade.

The military as an institution was affected directly, seeing the embargo's crippling effects as reducing Turkey's military advantages compared to Greece. Since even cold war tensions had not prevented the United States from imposing the embargo, the "betrayal" was even more acutely felt.

It took nearly four years and painful negotiations to lift the arms embargo. But the damage was done. Nothing could alleviate the distaste and lack of confidence in U.S. policymaking in the Turkish military psyche.

The 1980s did not have the continuing drama of the 1960s and the 1970s. Nevertheless, during this decade U.S. military aid to Turkey was tied to military aid to Greece, and the 7:10 ratio proved to be unchangeable despite the conviction of the Turkish military that its strategic requirements demanded otherwise. The military saw American arms supply as hostage to Greece's leverage over the United States. With an active Greek lobby and no Turkish counterpart, any change in the ratio seemed hopeless.

A lack of understanding of American political complexities and projection of its own political style also played a part in Turkish misperceptions of the United States. The Turkish side could never be persuaded that deep differences often separate the U.S. executive and legislative branches. The Turkish military, convinced of its indispensable strategic value, would not accept any argument on the inability of the administration to lead Congress on issues of strategic importance to the United States.

Turkey gave an enormously warm welcome to President Bill Clinton during his five-day visit to Turkey in November 1999, the longest of any American president. But this warmth in Turkish-American relations was unable to dispel totally the mistrust of the Turkish military for Turkey's Western partners, including the United States. A twenty-one-page booklet titled "Main Issues," distributed by the general staff to the armed forces in November 1999, did not spare the United States from vitriolic criticism. It said:

> While refraining from selling Cobra helicopters to Turkey under the pretext of they might lead to human rights violations, the US has not seen any problem in selling them to Morocco for the same purpose (to be used against terrorists) under the special order of Carter, in October, 1977.
>
> The same US government, while blaming Turkey for its human rights violations, has not refrained from according most-favored-nation status to China, which has a very bad

record on this issue. President Clinton, despite intense pressure of public opinion, did not bring up the matter of human rights during his negotiations with Chinese President Jiang during the latter's visit to Washington in early 1997. In his own visit to China, he has confined himself to addressing this issue in an implicit manner. Meanwhile, when Boris Yelstin killed many people including some parliamentarians, in shelling the parliament, Western countries accepted this as a necessary measure to restore democracy. . . .

The US, again, had found Turkey's intervention in Cyprus, which is based on the right of guarantee given to it by international agreements, unjustified and has applied an [arms] embargo for many years. By alleging, however, that the lives of a few hundred students are endangered, it had not refrained from invading Grenada or, under the pretext of 'introducing democracy,' from landing troops on the territory of Haiti. Moreover, it has brought to justice in the US and condemned the chief of staff of a foreign country whom it blamed for conducting narcotic trafficking to America. The United States, holding Bin Laden responsible for the bomb attacks against its embassies in Africa, bombed Afghanistan and Sudan for allegedly harboring his terrorist camps; it also bombed Libya for producing chemical weapons. It is not difficult to predict the American response should Turkey, for example, using similar pretexts, undertake such actions against the Greek Cypriot administration or against Syria. It is contradictory for the United States to put forward the precondition of human rights when it comes to arms sales when it is the main arms provider for Saudi Arabia and provides $2 billion in military aid to Egypt annually. Another issue to be registered on the American criminal record is the distribution of the money it earned from selling weapons to its main foe, Iran, to terrorist organizations in South America.[14]

These lines are ironical for those who have championed close cooperation between the Pentagon and the Turkish military and believe they have achieved it, such as former assistant secretary of defense Richard Perle. He said in a recent speech: "Ambassador [Robert] Strausz-Hupé understood the importance that Turks attached to the security relationship with the United States and Turkey's need for assistance from the United States to modernize its military forces. Turkey had the largest army in Europe and the most disciplined and courageous officers. . . . Robert knew that the Department of Defense was far better positioned to gain the confidence of the Turkish government than was his own department."[15]

GULF WAR WORRIES

The Turkish military's deep-seated suspicions of an "unreliable" United States were again manifest in the military's reluctance to cooperate during the Gulf War of 1990–91 and in its implicit resistance to the policies formulated by Turgut Özal. The military was convinced that Özal was blindly following the American line, which could lead to serious dangers to Turkey's territorial integrity after the war.

The defeat of Saddam Hussein and the de facto fragmentation of Iraq, with the emergence of a virtually autonomous Kurdish zone under the protective umbrella of the United States, came true. The new regional status quo was seen as affecting Turkey's Kurdish population and ultimately its territorial integrity. The military presented it this way to the Turkish public, and it generated frictions between the two allies during implementation of Operation Provide Comfort, launched in 1991.

The comments of General Sabri Yirmibeşoğlu, in his memoirs, are indicative of the outlook of many of Turkey's top brass. General Yirmibeşoğlu, now retired, held the powerful post of secretary-general of the national security council when Saddam's armies invaded Kuwait. He wrote, "It needs an impartial analysis to determine to what extent Özal's Gulf policy was compatible with the interests of Turkey. It is worth examining the large costs inflicted upon us from Özal's desire to increase his personal prestige. There is no doubt of the countless benefits from being in NATO and a friend of the United States, but only under one condition: The United States and NATO, besides their own national interests, should also respect and support Turkey's national interests."[16]

Another retired general, who had commanded the Second Army facing Iraq during the Gulf War, expressed his opposition to Özal's wartime alliance with the United States. General Kemal Yavuz, former director of the War Academy and informal spokesman of the Turkish general staff after his retirement, said in a TV program on February 6, 1998, "I told him [Özal], if you follow somebody else's furrow, you are led to somebody else's target. If you want to proceed to your own target, then you must trace your own furrow."[17]

General Yirmibeşoğlu referred in his memoirs to the difficulty of getting Turkey's president and prime minister appointments with the American president and complained about the lack of reciprocity. He wrote that the doors of Turkey's president "are wide open for assistant secretaries and undersecretaries. The extraordinary reception enjoyed by some [American] ambassadors and their pronouncements on our domestic developments do not bring any benefits; on the contrary they cause a loss of [national] prestige. On every domestic issue of concern to us, the White House spokesman is condescending. Turkey is not a colony and these are issues that require us to show independence."[18]

General Yirmibeşoğlu could have climbed to the highest positions of authority and responsibility. His observation that "no one should try to deny the games the United States plays, even extending to the dimension of military coups, in our domestic political life"[19] is thus worth noting as embodying the outlook of the Turkish officer corps on the United States. An even more interesting observation is contained in his memoirs: "In October 1995, at the annual security and cooperation conference in Antalya, I delivered a speech, whose main theme was 'For how long are we going to serve American national interests while ignoring ours?' My speech received a standing ovation. While ladies hugged me, bureaucrats and diplomats whispered 'We cannot say all these things. It is good that you say them.'"[20]

By 1999 they could reflect these feelings more openly. Lt. General Batmaz Dandin of the Turkish general staff expressed his resentment in a public speech in Washington. During a panel at the eighteenth annual American-Turkish Council meeting, Dandin, putting forward the considered opinion of the TGS, complained that the United States "is day by day becoming a more unreliable supplier"[21] and called for revision of the bilateral Defense and Economic Cooperation Agreement (DECA) signed in 1980.

The uncertainty about the United States accumulated over three decades was not limited to the military leadership. The civilian elite, almost without exception, opposed Turgut Özal's allegedly "pro-American" moves and also harbored anxieties about "obscure" American intentions.

The Gulf War and its aftermath, especially Operation Provide Comfort to protect the Iraqi Kurds, brought Turkey's concern for its territorial integrity to a high level. It was reflected mainly in the deep mistrust in the functioning of the multinational force. Neither the Turkish authorities nor the public in general ever called it an operation to provide comfort; it was always named, with pejorative intent, Poised Hammer.

Provide "Discomfort"?

After becoming foreign minister, Mümtaz Soysal responded sarcastically to the British ambassador's question on Provide Comfort, "We will see how comfortable it is."[22] Former president Kenan Evren, the leader of the military coup of 1980 and at the opposite end of the political spectrum from Soysal, was equally adamant. In a television interview on June 23, 1995, he stated, "We witness several initiatives of the United States. They put forward some demands. If you give them a finger, then you cannot free your arm. Whoever is in power cannot cancel Poised Hammer; because we have been too dependent on the United States, both economically and politically."[23]

Evren was also against deployment of the multinational force. "According to my opinion, the poised force should be disbanded," he said, because "a force claiming to protect the Kurds in northern Iraq can also make a pledge to defend those in Turkey's southeast. Or, those in the southeast may request it for their own protection in an attempt to create an international problem. The periodic extension of Poised Hammer was a mistake."[24]

The underlying worry of Turkey's political class has been the same since the foundation of the republic: the territorial integrity of Turkey. It has been what has united many diverse political personalities, even irreconcilable rivals. For Bülent Ecevit (before he again became prime minister), Operation Provide Comfort was "suicidal." According to his reasoning, "If Poised Hammer is extended and Turkey does not take the initiative in resolving the question of Iraq, in a few months the de facto state in northern Iraq [meaning the Kurdish entity] will have an official status and the influence on Turkey of the winds blowing from Northern Iraq will be inevitable."[25]

His archrival Erdal İnönü, the son of the former president, was no less unequivocal: "Poised Hammer has a commander and we are placing our own force under that [foreign] commander. These are the things that may pull Turkey into a [undesired] war. Turkey should liberate itself from this deployment."[26] Süleyman Demirel, who formed a coalition government with Erdal İnönü in 1991, extended the polemic beyond the boundaries of political criticism: "Is Özal trying to make a bid on Turkey's defense? Defense cannot be an issue of bidding. It is a national property." Contrary to his reputation as standing for unprincipled pragmatism and well known for his famous motto ("Yesterday was yesterday; today is today"), President Demirel in 1995 had the same contempt for Operation Provide Comfort as the Demirel in opposition of early 1991: "The snakes came out from under the umbrella. These snakes are the consequence of the Gulf War and of our consent to Provide Comfort."[27]

The allusion to snakes was to the armed activity of the PKK in the southeast, making use of the power vacuum in northern Iraq. For many in Turkey's ruling elite, the "protective umbrella" of the United States for the Iraqi Kurds against Saddam's onslaught was creating fertile ground for secessionist violence and threatening Turkey's territorial integrity.

Resentment over American policy also coincided with unprecedented Turkish cooperation with the United States. As a Turkish political scientist points out, "It is true that there were people who opposed the American-inspired participation in Turkey to the Korean War in 1950. It is also true that especially after the Johnson letter of 1964, which disappointed Turkey as a whole, the 'Uncle Sam' of the 1950s was replaced by 'imperialist America.' Yet this was not the tendency of all Turkey; but rather, mostly of the left and of those influenced by it. Those opposed to Poised Hammer were not only leftists, however: among the public, also within parliament, a great majority even of the most rightist members hated it like poison."[28]

REVISITING SÈVRES

More than a decade ago, Dankwart A. Rostow was quite reassured about the Turkish ruling elite's benevolence toward the United States when he noted, "Of recent Turkish prime ministers, Süleyman Demirel was an Eisenhower fellow in the United States; Bülent Ecevit, a Robert

College graduate, worked in the Turkish press attaché's office in London and received a postgraduate fellowship at Harvard; Admiral Bülend Ulusu held an assignment with the NATO Mediterranean forces; and Turgut Özal spent a year working at the World Bank in Washington. The Social Democratic Party, which in 1984 emerged as the major opposition, was founded by Professor Erdal İnönü, a theoretical physicist of international renown who received his training in Istanbul and California and became a faculty member and administrator at two of Turkey's English-language universities."[29]

Despite these affiliations of high Turkish leaders with American educational institutions, they have had only a limited effect on the Turkish political class's focus on territorial integrity. Three developments on the immediate periphery of Turkey transformed the already very high sensitivities in this respect into an obsessiveness: the dissolution of the Soviet Union, the dismemberment of Yugoslavia, and the effective fragmentation of Iraq.

The so-called Sèvres syndrome haunted the Turkish ruling elite frequently during the post–Gulf War period. Previously rarely raised, Sèvres became a common word in the Turkish political lexicon in the 1990s. The Treaty of Sèvres partitioned Turkey's territory, creating an independent Armenia and a Kurdistan to be autonomous in the first phase and ultimately to achieve independence under the aegis of the League of Nations. It remained the only defunct treaty in the series of treaties linked to Versailles that legally ended the First World War. Long a dormant issue for the Turkish political class, "Sèvres" was revisited after the Gulf War, when the Kurdish question again came to the fore.

President Demirel made frequent reference to Sèvres in 1997 to enhance his credibility with the Turkish general staff. The "Sèvres syndrome," reflecting the deep worries of the Turkish military, helped deflect domestic opinion from the necessary task of finding a political solution to the Kurdish question and blocked any American attempt to stimulate such an effort. On many occasions when Sèvres was brought up, there was reference to American nonrecognition of the Lausanne Treaty, whose Wilsonian principles were seen as also behind Sèvres. This may presage a major confrontation if irreconcilable divergences emerge between Turkey and the United States over the future of Iraq, the Iraqi Kurds, and Turkey's Kurds.

The erosion over time of the basic tenets of Kemalism and the social and political transformation of Turkish society contributed to the ruling elite's extreme sensitivity to the fundamental tenet of "territorial integrity." Caught unprepared for the dazzling changes of the post–cold war period, the elite sought refuge in two concepts: "territorial integrity" and "unitary state." The changes in the lands surrounding Turkey aggravated their worries, which were reflected in an allergy toward any American or American-led international move that the military feared would have domestic repercussions for Turkey and might undermine the "unitary" quality of the state and endanger its "territorial integrity." Any public remark on Kurds by a minor U.S. official could generate attention and resentment; references by President Bush, Secretary of State Baker, and National Security Adviser Brent Scowcroft in their memoirs to American intentions to keep Iraq a unitary state and preserve its territorial integrity, and their awareness of Turkey's sensitivities, passed unnoticed in Turkey. Even the comments of Centcom general Anthony Zinni at a congressional hearing, expressing doubt about the Iraqi opposition's ability to oust Saddam and implicitly counseling the United States to refrain from jeopardizing Iraq's territorial integrity,[30] did not get much attention in the Turkish media. Turkey's worries on this score have not been easy to alleviate.

ON TURKEY AND THE TURKS

In his monumental work *The Labyrinth of Solitude,* Octavio Paz explored the contradictions of the Mexican character and people, a result of roots in both the Spanish and pre-Hispanic cultures. Turkey resembles Mexico not only in being "one of the big emerging international markets" but for our purposes here in also having identity problems.

Turkey has a multiple identity. It is heir to an empire that survived more than six hundred years as the sovereign of the most contested territories of today's world. It was regarded as the standard-bearer of Islam for hundreds of years and the leader of the whole Muslim world in its confrontation with Christendom. It has Turkic Central Asian roots predating Islam.

But the country also has had an undeniable European vocation for nearly a millennium. Always present is a sense of inhabiting historic territory and of the continuity of centralized statehood going back more than fifteen hundred years to the Byzantine Empire.

Turkey has a young, vibrant population of whom 65 percent are below thirty years of age. They face gross problems of poverty, unemployment, and low education. Turkey has an uneasy and contentious political environment. It still suffers from the traumas of a shrinking empire. Turkey is a nation-state formed out of human calamities and cannot overcome the ambivalence of contradictory feelings. It is listed among the developing countries but resents being treated as undeveloped. It has retained the uneasiness of being alienated from both the Muslim and Western worlds but yet of being part of everywhere: the West, the Muslim world, the Turkic world of Central Asia and the Caucasus, and the Mediterranean.

A "siege mentality" has remained. Octavio Paz played down inferiority and put forward loneliness as a defining Mexican characteristic; Turkey's situation is quite similar. After a triumphant past, today's relative retardation does not lead to feelings of inferiority. It could not. Turkey was never colonized. For only a brief episode, between 1919 and 1922, Turkish territory was invaded by Greece, supported by some Western powers. The national resistance led by Atatürk that produced an independent Turkey is presented in the Turkish education system as the first national independence war waged against global imperialist forces, a war that constitutes a role model for all the oppressed peoples of the world. While the Turkish elite aspires to see Turkey counted among the family of modern nations, it also sees the origins of the modern Turkish state as enhancing its leadership role in the world.

In the post–cold war period, Turks never neglected to boast of their country as at least a "regional power." Foreign Minister İsmail Cem spoke of Turkey as—literally—"a world state," meaning a "global power." Any violation of this inflated self-image leads to an extreme touchiness, which may quickly transform itself into outrage. Any unpredictable act of an ally not corresponding to Turkish expectations culminates in traumatic disappointment.

As Morton Abramowitz notes gently in Chapter Six, "It is also true that Turks have had difficulty coming to grips with some of their history." The difficulty is not only in coming to grips with some of their history but also with digesting even friendly advice and criticism of political practices. The uproar in the Turkish media against U.S. deputy secretary of state Strobe Talbott's 1998 Turgut Özal Memorial Lecture is testimony to this mood.[31] While underlining the importance the administration attached to Turkey, Talbott also drew attention to its violations of human rights and democratic principles. The reaction in the Turkish press was immediate and violent. After remarks in Turkey's southeast in August 1999 by U.S. assistant secretary of state for human rights, democracy and labor Harold Koh on the necessity of resolving the Kurdish question through nonmilitary methods in the best interests of Turkey, the Turkish Foreign Ministry complained to the American embassy about Koh's "violation of Turkey's sensitivities."

DIFFERENT OUTLOOKS: THE DIPLOMATIC COMMUNITY AND THE BUSINESS COMMUNITY

The Foreign Ministry generally holds that friendly advice or benign criticism from an ally is an irritating interference. Such absolutism is a reflection of the nature of the reverence in Turkey for the apparatus called the "state," of which the Ministry of Foreign Affairs is considered one of the pillars. There has always been a distinction in the Turkish political lexicon between "state" and "government." The Turkish diplomatic community is regarded as virtually autonomous with respect to the government constituted by political parties, although less so than the military.

This is a heritage of the Ottoman administrative edifice. The diplomatic community represents the continuity of the state and stays aloof from the tribulations of "dirty" daily politics, which is the domain of the interactions between the government and parliament. Thus, the political personality of the minister is secondary in importance to the apparatus of the ministry. The relationship is somewhat similar for the military. The chief of staff, as the acting commander-in-chief, is higher hierarchically and in protocol than the minister of national defense.

The military is both ideologically and physically the guardian of the security of the state. The Foreign Ministry is the diplomatic instrument for safeguarding security, and it is institutionally excessively cautious even with an ally. The ministry and its diplomats have been skeptical about the United States.

In the words of Richard Perle, who carried much of the responsibility for the American-Turkish security relationship during the administration of Ronald Reagan, "There was a sense among many Turks, widely promoted in the press that the DECA was a favor conferred on the Americans by the Turks, for which an appropriate price should be paid. The idea of an agreement providing extensive cooperation on security and other matters for our mutual interest was beyond the comprehension of many of those with whom we had to deal. This was certainly the attitude of certain Turkish diplomats, some of whom were transparently anti-American."[32]

Nonetheless, slowly but surely, the recent positive evolution of Turkish-American relations has been changing the outlook of Turkey's diplomatic establishment. Bilateral relations have flourished on many issues of crucial importance to Turkey; the United States stood as the most reliable friend and ally of Turkey in the rapidly changing 1990s. On several occasions the Americans stood as Turkey's only ally.

The Turkish business community has had a considerable role in contributing to this positive evolution of Turkish-American relations. Globalization has made its impact on Turkey's business community. And the private sector, more self-confident after the free market reforms of the 1980s, has sought to free itself, however gradually, from the "official dogma," to become more influential in foreign policy. Two magnates of the Turkish economy, Vehbi Koç and Sakıp Sabanci, were harbingers of a new Turkish view of the United States. Koç, in his 1973 autobiography, described America vividly and was stunningly perceptive on its guiding characteristics. Sakıp Sabanci went beyond Koç in his positive impressions of the United States of the Reagan era. The impetus of that period, aided by the vision of leading Turkish industrialists, gradually led to the institutionalization of Turkish-American business ties. The Turkish-United States Business Council, which was formed in April 1985 following Turgut Özal's visit to Washington, was a landmark. A few years later, its counterpart in the United States, now the American-Turkish Council, began to play a pivotal role, with its annual conference soon becoming the biggest bilateral event in Washington, bringing together nearly two thousand people, including legislators, ministers, diplomats, and businessmen.

The business community has been steadily moving to the forefront of Turkish-American relations, dominated for half a century by security cooperation. The quarterly international review published by the Turkish Industrialists' and Businessmen's Association (known in Turkey as TÜSİAD), *Private View,* devoted its Spring 1999 issue to redefining Turkish-American relations. TÜSİAD's secretary-general, Haluk Tükel, wrote, "Whereas during the cold war most Turks looked to Europe for economic and political relations and relied on the United States for security arrangements, in the last decade a new approach has increasingly gained ground. Turkish firms decided to explore the American market and Turkish businessmen began efforts to lure American capital into Turkey for cooperation on a variety of grand, ambitious, and lucrative investments. Turkey has begun to pay more attention to the political developments in the United States." TÜSİAD's present chairman, Erkut Yucaoglu, writing about the role of businessmen in the next century, says that Turkey,

> in her attempt to integrate with the world under the impact of the tide of globalization, . . . had to make use of the synergy of cooperation between business and state at home and abroad. For Turkey to succeed in the globalized economic and political order of the 21st century, the businessman's relationship with the government must take on new dimensions. We at TÜSİAD have called for a series of economic, social, and political reforms on numerous occasions. These range from establishing macroeconomic balances to reforming the social security system to ending oligarchic rule in political parties. We aim to get closer to the American public, American policy makers, and to the leaders of the American business world to learn from the [American] experiment.

CHANGING TIMES, CHANGING PERCEPTIONS

It would be misleading, therefore, to think that Turkish elites today see the United States only or primarily in negative terms. Worries, suspicions, differences of opinion, or different interpretations of national interest certainly continue to exist in the most elite groups, but Turkey has been undergoing a transformation since the Özal reforms of the 1980s and mentalities have changed. Free market reforms and the emphasis on exports imbued Turks with a new sense of entrepreneurship, and the political culture—though lagging behind the pace of economic change—benefited. Along with these changes has come a changing comprehension of the United States.

The end of the cold war and the emergence of the United States as the sole superpower also have contributed to changed Turkish perceptions of America. Despite the recurrent concerns about an uncertain future, Turks drew closer to the United States than ever. Despite the fears over Iraq, the partnership professed during the Gulf War opened new avenues for Turkish-American relations, while Turkey's anxieties about its diminishing strategic importance with the end of the cold war were soon alleviated by an America that promoted Turkey as an important strategic ally.

Positive feelings reached their zenith during President Clinton's visit to Turkey in November 1999, when Clinton's flattering speech to parliament was interrupted eleven times by the applause of the not-so-pro-American, 550-member chamber and greeted at the end by a standing ovation. Islamist deputies were among the most enthusiastic of the cheering audience.

"For better and for worse," Clinton said, "the events of that time when the Ottoman Empire disintegrated and a new Turkey arose have shaped the history of this entire century. From Bulgaria to Albania to Israel to Arabia, new nations were born, and a century of conflict erupted from the turmoil of shifting borders, unrealized ambitions, and old hatreds—beginning with the first Balkan war and World War I, all the way to today's struggles in the Middle East and in the former Yugoslavia. Turkey's past is key to understanding the twentieth century. But, more importantly, I believe Turkey's future will be critical to shaping the twenty-first century."[33] His words struck a chord among the Turks, so much so that the legislature could digest his thin and polite criticism of Turkey's embarrassing human rights record and his mention of "Kurdish citizens of Turkey."

Only a week before this speech Clinton had pointed to Turkey's importance for America in remarks at Georgetown University on the tenth anniversary of the fall of the Berlin Wall. He said,

> I believe the coming century will be shaped in good measure by the way in which Turkey, itself, defines its future and its role today and tomorrow. For Turkey is a country at the crossroads of Europe, the Middle East and Central Asia; the future can be shaped for the better if Turkey can become fully a part of Europe, as a stable, democratic, secular Islamic nation . . . and if there is a real vision on the part of our European allies, who must be willing to reach out and to believe that it is at Turkey where Europe and the Muslim world can meet in peace and harmony, to give us a chance to have the future of our dreams in that part of the world in the new millennium.[34]

A few days later National Security Adviser Samuel Berger elaborated on the American assessment of Turkey:

Turkey's relationship to the United States is more important now than it was in the cold war. Turkey, by reason of geography, by reason of religious diversity, will either be in the 21st century a bridge, a democratic bridge of stability between East and West, between the Islamic world and the non-Islamic world, or it will be a source of instability, of conflict, both with respect to its neighbors and the region. The President, from the very beginning, from the first term, felt that this relationship was extremely important. This is why, for example, he has supported so strongly the EU's providing candidacy to Turkey for membership.[35]

Both Clinton's and Berger's remarks went unnoticed by the American public, but they aroused great interest in Turkey and inspired many commentaries and discussions. Most important, they served to punctuate the changed climate of Turkish-American relations; they also helped convince broad segments of Turkish society of the genuineness of American friendship for Turkey.

The Turkish public, after being essentially snubbed by Europeans during the course of the post–cold war period, felt flattered to receive the support and warm feelings of the most powerful player in the international system. It made a considerable impact on the elite's increasing emotional preference for America over Europe. The relentless modernizing of Turkey's secular population and its historically rooted Western vocation shifted more toward the United States.

The variance in American and European attitudes toward Turkey is understandable: it is the European Union and not the United States that Turkey is seeking to join. Nevertheless, when the whole European architecture was being rebuilt, it was America that prevented Turkey's isolation from the Western world when it was confronted with rejection from Europe. It was the United States that helped Turkey to pursue one of its most cherished goals: to be a part of the modern (that is, Western) world.

The United States during the second half of the 1990s constantly drew attention to Turkey's increasingly important geopolitical role at the end of the cold war. As the energy-rich Eurasian landmass takes on much greater prominence, the convergence of interests between Turkey and the United States has added new dimensions to Turkish-American relations, which had been basically security oriented and military in nature. The new relationship involves the profound interests of the business community as well as the Turkish political establishment.

Moreover, the loneliness that Turkey felt during the 1990s and the uncertainties of the Middle East brought Turkey even closer to the United States. The Turkish-Israeli rapprochement further enhanced Turkey's warm feelings toward the United States.

With elite perception of the United States undergoing a major transformation in the late 1990s, bilateral relations looked remarkably promising.

LOOKING TO THE TWENTY-FIRST CENTURY

What is to be expected in the next decade? Turkey's outlook will be shaped by developments in the liberalized economy and by globalization, education, democratization, and administrative reform. The vast expansion of civil society will ultimately produce a demilitarization of political life, leading to a change in political culture and eventually in the ruling elite itself. But that will be a long haul.

The national calamity of August 17, 1999—the devastating earthquake that hit the industrial heartland of Turkey, including Istanbul—may be considered a milestone. The rapid and effective international humanitarian assistance effort, in which scores of countries took part, shook the foundations of Turkish xenophobia, undermining the frequently heard motto, *Türkün Türkten Başka Dostu Yoktur* [There is no friend to the Turk but the Turk]. Strong and effective international solidarity had led to a significant reconsideration of the conventional Turkish perception of the international system.

In the aftermath of the earthquake also came a decline in Turkish-Greek tensions and, more broadly, positive developments in Turkish-EU relations, culminating in the historic decision of the December 1999 EU summit that formally declared Turkey a candidate member. The Helsinki decision was also the acknowledgment of Turkey's place in the Western family and rewarded its pro-Western elite's traditional European vocation.

A Turkish public jubilant over the European decision believed that the radical change in Turkey's fortunes in Europe would not have come without firm American support for Turkey and intense lobbying on its behalf. The Helsinki decision consolidated the growing sympathy for the United States—even though in the long run integration might make Turkey "more European" and less "pro-American."

Nevertheless, relations with the United States will obviously not be free of differences. The main one will be over Iraq, since it is central to the threat perception of the Turkish military. As long as uncertainty over the future of Iraq prevails and Turkey's Kurdish question remains unresolved, difficulties will beset bilateral relations. Removal of the issue of Iraq from the international agenda in manner guaranteeing Turkey its territorial integrity will eliminate an important bone of contention between Turkey and the United States.

Equally important is the resolution of Turkey's internal Kurdish question, the main source of its human rights problems, a major obstacle to democracy, and a constant threat to the rule of law. The United States as a global leader committed to democratic principles will find it increasingly difficult not to address these issues publicly. Resolution of the Kurdish problem will heavily impact the future of the U.S.-Turkish relationship.

Hopes for Turkish democratization and political reforms have steadily risen in recent years. One notable expression was the speech inaugurating the new judicial year by Chairman Sami Selçuk of the Courts of Appeal on September 6, 1999. His speech, delivered before the president of the republic, the prime minister, political party leaders, the military top brass, and the high judges, and televised a number of times nationwide, has been hailed as a "manifesto of democracy." As the highest judicial authority, he defined Turkey "as a state with a constitution but not a constitutional state" and advocated the supremacy of the universal values of democracy over Jacobinist republican practices. Interesting to note was his attribution of Turkey's administrative wrongdoings to adoption of the continental European system. He emphasized the France of 1789 as the source of Turkey's chronic illnesses of regime while praising the historical experience of Anglo-Saxon democracies, which he pointed to as the role model that Turkey needs to follow.

Dr. Selçuk characterized the military constitution of 1982 as a disaster. His views reflect the increasing adjustment within the Turkish elite to the demands of the age of globalization. The speech heralded greater Turkish-American rapprochement in the political cultural sphere.

NEW PHENOMENA

The first quarter of the twenty-first century also could witness the emergence of a new political elite in Turkey that the United States may find itself unprepared to deal with: modern Muslim politicians, businessmen, and intellectuals quite different from stereotypical fundamentalists. The political Islamists, after many blunders and excesses, paid a heavy price in Turkey in the 1990s. But the setbacks they suffered and the undemocratic measures against them set in motion a slow grassroots transformation.

A Turkish Muslim generation open to the world, quick to benefit from the incentives of the globalist era, different in its outlook toward the United States, and differing from the traditional view of political Islam *may* be in the process of taking over. Many of these Muslims are aware that the United States is a country upholding individual liberties and guaranteeing freedom of religious faith. Their attention will likely be increasingly focused on the United States rather than on the Muslim world, and they will come to demand more from the United States in showing real concern for their grievances. The United States also is replacing Egypt and other Muslim countries as a venue for long, temporary residence for popular Islamic political figures. The first quarter of the twenty-first century should be decisive in overturning the traditional cultural-ideological outlook of the Turkish elite.

The cultural gap between the United States and Turkey also should diminish with the increasing numbers of Turkish students at American universities. From an annual average of two thousand Turkish students in American higher education institutions before the 1990s, the numbers by 1997 reached as high as fifteen thousand to twenty thousand annually. After the "soft coup" of February 28, 1997, the Turkish Higher Education Council cut funding to alleged Islamist students in the United States; by the end of the century, the number had dropped to around seven thousand to eight thousand. Compared to forty thousand students from South Korea, these numbers may sound thin. Nonetheless, more than a hundred thousand Turks armed with globalist insights and different views of the United States will penetrate Turkey's ideological, political, and business market within a decade, to be followed by even greater waves of students.

It is likely that within two decades some prominent members of the new Turkish elite will be the classmates or schoolmates of American presidents, senators, congressmen, or other high officials and influential personalities. An overall transformation in the structure of the Turkish elite will undoubtedly mark the future.

Meanwhile, within Turkey itself, America set the trends followed especially by young urban generations. The American movie industry's latest presentations are on screen in Turkey the day they appear in New York, Los Angeles, or Boston. NBA stars have become household figures.

Intellectual influences do not trail behind the global commercial onslaught. The Turkish intelligentsia is no longer Francophile or Europe-oriented. The names of Paul Kennedy, Samuel Huntington, Francis Fukuyama, Alvin Toffler, Noam Chomsky, Bernard Lewis, Paul Krugman, Zbigniew Brzezinski, Peter Drucker, and John Naisbitt are as familiar to an average Turkish intellectual as the names of the thinkers of the Enlightenment were to the Turkish intellectuals of 1960s and 1970s. American experts studying Turkey are followed even more closely and sensitively. An Amazon.com survey indicated that the book most ordered by Turkish readers was *Turkey's Kurdish Question* by Henri Barkey and Graham Fuller. Paul Krugman's *Return of Depression Economics* ranked high in the same survey, suggesting the Turkish intelligentsia's sensitivity to global issues.

The breathtaking advances in information technology and globalization are already molding future generations of Turks. Thousands are connected to each other and to the whole globe through the Internet and are inevitably developing radically different outlooks on the world from the older generations now mostly occupying the stage. The rapid organization of NGOs helping the victims of the 1999 earthquake and networking through the Internet stimulated the growth of civil society in Turkey.

Thus, the ground is increasingly fertile for a new political class with a global outlook. This generational change in Turkey will be the business of the first decade of the twenty-first century, and, with it, the prospects for better understanding between Turkey and the United States have never looked brighter.

CHAPTER SIX

THE COMPLEXITIES OF AMERICAN POLICYMAKING ON TURKEY

MORTON ABRAMOWITZ

PROLOGUE

My wife and I went to bed in Ankara late the night of January 16, 1990. It was difficult to sleep. I knew the war with Iraq would begin soon, but I did not know when.

Around 2:00 A.M. our time Washington called. It was Dick Clarke, a close colleague, then assistant secretary of state for political-military affairs and now a senior National Security Council official. He said the B-52s had just left Spain for Iraq. We need overflight rights over Turkey immediately.[1]

"When will they reach Turkey?" I asked.

"Six hours or so."

"Can they fly over Syria?"

"No."

I told him I would call back after I got to President Turgut Özal.

I was never thrilled, as an ambassador, to call the country's leader in the middle of the night. The president of Turkey actually lived across

---

the street, but I picked up the phone and called. It took about a minute to get through, after I told someone on his staff that the call was urgent. Özal was a night owl and was in fact up, as he said when I apologized for waking him.

I told the president the United States needed overflight rights over his country within the next five hours. His only question was, "Can they fly over Syria?"

I simply said no, we didn't want to ask and they wouldn't agree. Özal said he would call back.

He did, a short while later, and asked if the planes could fly close to the Syrian border so the overflight could be plausibly denied in Turkey. I said yes and would tell Washington immediately. He gave his approval.

I then went on to remind the president that we had discussed many times the American need to use Turkey's air bases to bomb targets in northern Iraq. The matter was now critical. We urgently needed his government's permission. "When can we get an answer?"

Özal always had a kernel of doubt about U.S. determination to deal decisively with Saddam Hussein. He feared that in the end the United States would not go to war and force Iraq out of Kuwait. The moment of truth had finally arrived. He said he would, "of course," have to get parliament's approval and would propose legislation as soon as possible. I asked when. He sort of chuckled, I think, and said, "Today."

That same day Özal asked the parliament for approval. Many Turks opposed it, in and out of parliament, including those running Turkey during 2000, such as President Süleyman Demirel and Prime Minister Bülent Ecevit. But Özal's party had a majority—the only one Turkey has had since the military gave up power in 1983—and parliament gave its approval that afternoon. In the early evening Özal called, and his first words were, "Well, Mr. Ambassador, are you satisfied?" I confessed to it and thanked him.

Özal's responses were very much in character. He disliked Saddam intensely and the way he ruled his country; more important, he felt Saddam's control of Kuwait's oil directly threatened Turkey's economic security. High oil prices almost destroyed Turkey in the 1970s. In January 1990, seven months before the invasion of Kuwait, Özal told President Bush in the Oval Office that Saddam was the "most dangerous man in the world." He urged Bush to lead an international effort to rid the world of him. The president listened carefully. U.S. policy toward Iraq at that point was "constructive engagement," and that did not change much until Iraqi tanks rolled into Kuwait.

Özal could make bold decisions quickly. He threw Turkey's lot in with the United States after the Kuwait invasion despite public skepticism and a long Turkish tradition of staying out of Middle East disputes. Over strong domestic political objections, he quickly shut down the pipeline transporting Iraq's oil through Turkey. Not only did he believe that was necessary to counter Saddam, but he also feared that failure to close the pipeline would create a crisis with the United States. He was convinced that close ties with the United States were profoundly in Turkey's interest; the United States was Turkey's major defense partner and its principal source of science, technology, and training. From his days as a World Bank official in Washington in the 1970s, U.S. drive, openness, and technical innovation always dazzled him. Özal wanted to show that at a critical time Turkey was not on the fence and was prepared to accept political and economic costs in the short term to support the United States in a vital joint strategic effort. He also thought this policy would serve Turkey well in its relations with the United States and other allied countries after the war.

The United States wanted three things from Turkey during the Gulf War: the use of bases for a sustained air campaign in northern Iraq, the movement of more Turkish troops to the Turkey-Iraq border to help deter Saddam from moving his troops in that area south to the Kuwait front, and the dispatch of a Turkish battalion to Saudi Arabia to join the allied forces assembling there.[2]

The essential requirement was the ability to use the bases. It was probably the most controversial issue in Turkey at the time. Many in Turkey did not want to go to war with Iraq in any way or feared blatantly antagonizing a difficult and powerful Arab neighbor, who, many Turks would frequently remind Americans, would "always be next door." When the base issue was raised in August 1990, Özal was sympathetic but in fact did not commit himself to allowing the United States to use the bases to wage war against Iraq. He did not want to draw political fire in Turkey until he had to. More important, if he had sought parliamentary approval beforehand for American use of Turkish bases and the United States did not go to war with Iraq, he would have expended enormous political capital for nothing, while Turkey would be left facing a hostile Iraq with a real ability to help stoke up a Kurdish insurgency in Turkey's southeast.

Özal ultimately did turn the United States down on sending a Turkish unit to Saudi Arabia. Here too he was prepared to agree to the U.S. request, but he faced strong opposition from the Turkish general staff. Since Özal considered the deployment request of much lesser importance given the level of forces the allied coalition was assembling in Saudi Arabia, he apparently thought it would be political folly to confront the Turkish military on this issue.

A Complex Strategic Relationship with Domestic Complications

I cannot help thinking about that episode often. For the United States, Özal's was a bravura performance. It also marked the beginning of the renaissance in a somewhat battered Turkish-American relationship. Under the Clinton administration U.S.-Turkey relations blossomed; despite occasional flare-ups they are probably as close as they have been since the 1950s. President Clinton's relatively lengthy visit in November 1999, the first presidential one since 1991, symbolized that vast improvement, occasioning an outpouring of affection for him and goodwill toward the United States.

   This chapter deals with the American policymaking environment—the elements, starting with the strategic, that have helped shape Washington's thinking on policy toward Turkey over the past decade. It inevitably strays a little into the substance of policy, which is discussed in detail in the chapter on American policy but also partly in other chapters, particularly the one on Greek-Turkish differences. It concludes with an evaluation of aspects of the U.S. policy approach toward Turkey and a brief examination of prospects for change in the policymaking environment.

Iraq and Other Strategic Considerations

Unintended consequences always follow from major events. For Turkey the outcome of the Gulf War produced new uncertainties and economic grief. Indeed, it made Iraq a major issue in U.S.-Turkey relations because of the creation by the allies of a protected zone for Iraqi Kurds returning from the mountains along the Turkish border, where a half million fled after their uprising against Saddam failed. (Another million fled to Iran.) This allied effort came about because of the plight of the Kurds (perhaps also some guilt) and the need to protect Turgut

Özal from a political catastrophe if he allowed a half million Iraqi Kurds into Turkey. The United States and its allies sought to deter Saddam from moving against the Kurds by a continuous air cover of the protected area, and that required the use of Turkish bases. This allied air operation from Turkish bases (originally called Provide Comfort, now designated Northern Watch) became perhaps the most important specific factor in U.S. policymaking toward Turkey for much of the past decade.

Turkey did not much relish the allied air operation because it did not want to see an independently operated Kurdish entity emerge next door. But it also did not want to face another Kurdish refugee influx. Until recently the United States had to make a strenuous diplomatic effort twice a year when the Turkish parliament would review and authorize the politically contentious air operation. Turkey's leverage on U.S. Iraq policy from this operation has been important because after Özal's death in 1993 the two countries held divergent views on the Kurdish protected area and on getting rid of Saddam. Turkish authorities mostly have viewed Saddam as the best barrier against Iraq's disintegration, a development that could lead to the establishment of a Kurdish entity in northern Iraq—with a baleful impact on Turkey's own Kurds. Even a social democrat like Bülent Ecevit has had kind words for Saddam. Despite the considerable Turkish evasion of UN sanctions on Iraq, the economic costs to Turkey from sanctions also turned out to be sizable in terms of lost trade, construction, and transportation revenues over the past nine years. Few in 1991—neither Turks, Americans, nor Iraqi Kurds—believed Saddam would still be around a decade later.

More fundamentally, the Gulf War and the still continuing American military action against Saddam brought home to Washington once again the major strand in official thinking about Turkey since World War II: its political and strategic significance, including the value of Turkish bases for operations in the Middle East—even while the military necessity of the NATO alliance and Turkey's role on its southern flank was being diminished by the implosion of the Soviet Union.

Turkey is one of the few states in the world that is not a major player but has sufficient size, power, and economic potential—and a sufficiently critical location—to give the question of its strategic importance real relevance to American policymakers. But trying to balance a variety of often conflicting policy considerations raises occasional differing emphases among policymakers on managing specific issues, including security ones. Nevertheless, by and large that sense of Turkey's strategic importance has remained the dominant factor in American policy thinking on Turkey among conservatives and liberals, Republican and Democratic administrations alike. Congress, on a number of issues no supporter of Turkey, has generally accepted that conclusion.

After the Gulf War and the Soviet collapse, emerging American strategic perceptions were no longer fixated on NATO and the possible longer-term resurgence of a dynamic, hostile Russia. The new perspectives influencing American post–cold war policy toward Turkey stemmed from changed geopolitical realities and over time from worries about internal developments in Turkey. Most important in the short term were the consequences of leaving Saddam Hussein in power in 1991 and the need for Turkish bases both to protect the Iraqi Kurds and confront Saddam should the need arise. Turkey's deepening involvement in the Turkic states of the former Soviet Union with their oil and gas resources added new political and economic considerations to U.S.-Turkish relations. It also highlighted Turkey as a competitor with Russia and Iran for influence in these new states. The continued fighting in the Balkans generated some fears in the U.S. policy community—frequently voiced publicly to defend intervention in the Balkans—that the Balkan wars could spread to Macedonia and ultimately engulf Turkey and Greece in a new phase of an old hostility. The United States also had a growing interest in Turkish participation in peacekeeping in the NATO protectorates created in Bosnia and Kosovo. Finally, the emergence of an Israel-Turkey axis added grist to a continually revised official view of Turkey's place in the world and helped generate political support for Turkey in the United States.

By the mid to late 1990s, American officials also noticed that Turkey had developed sizable ground and air forces with some capability of projecting power outside the country. Massive military expenditures, new weaponry, better training, and combat experience from many years of war against the PKK, including large-scale incursions into northern Iraq, have made Turkey the most powerful state in the area. With the end of the Soviet Union, Turkey's security situation is the best it has been, in stark contrast to the beginning years of the twentieth century. The Turkish military like to say they are now "producers" of security, not "consumers."[3] Turkey's military strength and its new close link to Israel were probably the decisive factors in "persuading" Syria to expel PKK leader Abdullah Öcalan in 1998 from his long-established residence in Damascus. In short, Turkey could not easily be discounted—although it might be taken for granted—and the United States did not want it drift-ing away from its side. But as Turkey's strategic significance was being renewed in the outside world—much to the relief of Turks, whose lead-ers kept publicly repeating Turkey's indispensability—another factor had arisen that made American policymakers fear a disruption in Turkey's basic strategic contribution: its internal instability began to be a matter for concern.

The rapid rise of political Islam in the 1990s and the continuing and intensifying Kurdish war in southeast Turkey with its impact on inflation, human rights, and national cohesion made policymakers focus on Turkey's internal health and even its basic Western orien-tation. These concerns served to highlight—particularly for those used to taking it for granted—the fundamental value to the United States of a secular, stable, friendly, Western-oriented Turkey in a very turbulent area. Once more Turkey was anointed a major U.S. security interest, perhaps best encapsulated in Assistant Secretary of State Richard Holbrooke's public characterization of Turkey before a congressional committee in March 1995 as the preeminent "front line state," surrounded by nasty or chaotic neighbors, a central element in our strategic thinking. Greater American interest and effort to promote Turkey's integration into Europe followed from this perception.

Thus, strategic considerations in some form continue to be a ver-ity in Washington's collective thinking about Turkey. But, just as Turkey's internal scene had its impact on Washington's perception of Turkish stability and how the United States should deal with Turkey, so also have American domestic politics affected the making of U.S. pol-icy toward Turkey. Indeed, domestic political considerations have been a prominent feature of U.S.-Turkish relations for many years, but over the past decade they have become somewhat more complex, with more domestic players. Moreover, as American power and pre-eminence have grown ever greater, so has the influence of domestic political considerations on foreign policy formulation. Perceptions of a strategically important Turkey—much greater in the United States than in Europe—may fill the thinking of policymakers and the would-be policymakers in America's numerous think tanks, but strategic cal-culations are not always sufficient to counteract a host of domestic political difficulties raised either by specific issues involving Turkey or by Turkey's internal troubles. The political complexities affecting American decisionmaking on Turkey deserve elaboration.

PRIVATE COOKS STIR THE POLICYMAKING STEW

Like many other foreign policy concerns, Turkey has not been much an issue in the United States, except among a number of small but influential interest groups. Indeed, Turkey is hardly noticed unless a war is going on or a huge earthquake occurs. Until the earthquake of August 1999, the general public knew or saw little about the country. There was a surge of popular interest and positive feelings toward Turkey in 1990, when President Özal shut down the Iraqi pipeline and Turkey became an ally in the Gulf War. But that did not last long. More gripping were the images of the 1999 earthquake, which stirred American television viewers for about two weeks and generated plenty of sympathy and private contributions; that attention, as with most natural disasters, vanished quickly. President Clinton's visit in 1999 stimulated enormous interest in Turkey but little in the United States. Turkey's admission to EU candidacy aroused the cognoscenti in the United States but few others. Rapidly growing tourism may ultimately have the biggest impact on the public's awareness of Turkey; it has become a better-known travel spot, and tourism seems to generate positive feelings among Americans toward Turkey. Some 440,000 Americans visited Turkey in 1998, numbers that should rise significantly if continuing tremors in western Turkey do not scare tourists away. Fifteen to twenty thousand Turkish students in the United States annually also contribute to a wider public awareness of Turkey.[4]

Because of the perceived lack of public interest, Turkey has traditionally received little media attention. U.S. official statements or comments on Turkey are rarely covered. Few people know when a Turkish president or prime minister is visiting Washington. For a long time one had to read British journals like the *Financial Times* or the *Economist* to get some sense of what was happening in Turkey on a regular basis. Media interest invariably has focused on the darker side of developments in Turkey. The image of Turkish justice conveyed in Alan Parker and Oliver Stone's popular movie of the seventies, *Midnight Express,* is still extant, if declining. The rise of the Islamist *Refah* Party to power in 1996 probably received the most recent sustained—if still modest—media attention, embodied in the inevitable question, "Is Turkey going fundamentalist?" More recently the Kurdish issue has received considerable attention, particularly with the drama of PKK leader Öcalan's flight and eventual arrest.

Interest in Turkey in the United States seems to have risen slightly in the last few years, largely because of the *Wall Street Journal* bureau in Istanbul and, more important, the opening of a *New York Times* bureau, also in Istanbul, in 1997. An enterprising *Times* reporter—bureau chief Stephen Kinzer—probably has had more stories on Turkey published in one year than appeared in the *Times* for the whole period from the end of the Gulf War and the return of Kurdish refugees to Iraq in 1991 to 1997. The growing number of articles on Turkey on a regular basis has helped bring Turkish developments to a little wider American public, not always to the Turkish government's unalloyed pleasure. There is, for example, now more public awareness in the United States of the relationship of the Kurdish issue to Turkey's human rights problems. All this greater awareness may better serve the purposes of the various private American groups antagonistic to Turkey than those of Turkey's supporters.

In short, as with the bulk of foreign policy matters, Turkey is largely an elite issue, centered in the American government. But a number of private groups, mostly ethnically based, have achieved significant influence on American decisionmaking on Turkey because of their domestic political clout, particularly in Congress. Ethnic politics continue to play an important role in the making of American policy toward Turkey.

Concerned private groups are divided in their attitude toward Turkey. The most focused on bringing political pressure to bear on policy toward Turkey—and the most nettlesome to the Turkish government—are two ethnic lobbies with sizable populations in the United States, the Greek-American and the smaller and less powerful Armenian-American. Both groups work hard to convey their views to Congress, the executive branch, and the media. They are well organized, well funded, and knowledgeable, and they have sought to make common cause with other groups having differences with Turkey, such as human rights organizations. The concentration of Greek and Armenian Americans in a number of politically important states gives them added political weight. So too do they make use of the help and cooperation of legislators of Greek and Armenian origin. Important American Jewish organizations, meanwhile, have joined the fray in support of Turkey.[5]

THE GREEK-AMERICAN LOBBY. This interest group, composed of a number of different organizations, focuses on Greek-Turkish issues and generally sees the interests of Greece and Cyprus as congruent with American interests. (On other issues like terrorism or Kosovo it may part company with Greece's policy perspective.) For the past four decades it has heavily influenced the way the U.S. government deals with Cyprus, the biggest issue in Greek-Turkish relations.

Given the disparity of power between Greece and Turkey, the approach of the governments of Greece and Cyprus and Greek supporters abroad has been to try to internationalize the Cyprus issue as much as possible—to get the nations of the West, many with Greek-origin populations, to back the Greek Cyprus position for settling the issue and to isolate and pressure Turkey in world forums.

The Greek-American lobby has been effective in persuading legislators in Congress (and similar groups in other Western parliaments) that the Cyprus issue began with the Turkish military takeover of northern Cyprus in 1974 and the ensuing occupation of 40 percent of the island by Turkish Cypriots. Ethnic history is always disputed everywhere, but the creation and destruction of the Cypriot state in the years prior to the Turkish occupation of northern Cyprus and the damage inflicted at that time on the Turkish population of Cyprus get little notice anywhere these days. The Cyprus issue for the Greek-American lobby is mostly about getting the Turkish military off the island and less about ways to reconcile two antagonistic populations with a bad history. Athens has been successful in keeping pressure on Turkey and the Turkish Cypriots by blocking any international recognition of the Turkish Cypriot government other than by Turkey and, until it changed course at the end of 1999, in hindering Turkey's efforts to benefit from the EU.

The international approach to resolving the Cyprus problem for the past twenty years has been to work through UN-sponsored negotiations supported by Western countries and based on numerous UN resolutions to broker a deal involving the establishment of a federation of the ethnically separate parts of the island ("bizonal, bicommunal"). The substance of this effort is discussed in detail in Chapter Seven. The domestic politics of decisionmaking on Turkey are the concern here.

Many interested Americans, both in and out of Congress, have long believed that the Cyprus problem persists because the United States government does not use its "great leverage" on Turkey to force a settlement. The two times the U.S. government forcefully intervened—the Johnson letter in 1964 and the arms embargo of 1974—were disasters and produced nothing but Turkish rage and renewed determination. Nevertheless, to ensure that the executive branch seriously pursues a negotiated federal solution, Congress in the 1980s variously created one or more ambassadors to serve as negotiators and facilitators. At any one time this small land could have three American ambassadors roaming around it—not a bad ambassador per population ratio! It is the U.S. negotiators as well—who have to be concerned with domestic American political repercussions—who do most of the heavy lifting in Cyprus negotiations. Congress also requires the president—not the State Department—to send it a report every two months to the Congress setting forth the administration's efforts on the Cyprus issue and generally testifying to its determination to pursue a Cyprus settlement.

The executive branch tries to weave its way between the demands of the Greek-American lobby and Turkey's determination (and military capability) to protect the interests of the Turkish Cypriots—without seriously damaging other aspects of American relations with Turkey. Every year or so the international community, led in effect if not literally by the United States, marches up the hill with a similar if slightly varied proposal for a negotiated agreement on a bizonal, bicommunal federation among the parties. Later in the year or the following year it marches down the hill after the proposed deal has been rejected by one or the other or both of the parties. Indeed, getting the parties to talk to each other in some fashion is frequently difficult: the current effort to promote proximity talks took almost a year to arrange and was the beneficiary of an earthquake and an EU summit. To be fair, the proposed settlement makes a good deal of sense and has been honed after many years of negotiations. But for a variety of reasons negotiations have always failed.

One would think after so many years of failed negotiations that a different approach to the Cyprus problem might be in order, but administrations find it politically difficult to depart from the tried and true. A serious departure could be politically disastrous domestically, and, given that the United States has nationwide elections every two years, no administration has been willing to test that possibility. Certainly all administrations would love to solve the Cyprus problem and put Greek-Turkish relations on a better footing. Incoming-administration senior officials frequently believe they can succeed where their predecessors have failed. At least once in every administration a "year of Cyprus" is proclaimed, and 1999–2000 seems to be the Clinton administration's. President Clinton has made repeated public statements on the importance of dealing with the Cyprus issue now and on his dedication to trying to resolve the issue before leaving office. In a speech in January 2000, National Security Adviser Samuel Berger listed the beginning of proximity talks between the two sides as one of the administration's foreign policy successes—not a particularly high standard for success.[6] But administrations also have to survive this issue politically, and the minimum goal each year is to continue to export the Cyprus problem to the future in the hope that new developments—acceptance of Turkey as a candidate for EU admission, for example, or the departure from power of Rauf Denktash, the only leader the Turkish Cypriots have ever had—could open better opportunities for a settlement. The sad fact is that, after more than three decades of often intensive involvement in Greek-Turkish problems, the U.S. government has made little progress on Cyprus or any other major issue, although it has helped to prevent skirmishing between the two sides.

And indeed new elements did emerge in the last four months of 1999—a significant improvement in Greek-Turkish relations and EU acceptance of Turkey's candidacy for admission. The United States had tried—quite creatively—in 1997 to use Turkey's great interest in joining the EU to promote changes in Turkey's position on Cyprus, including encouraging the Turkish Cypriots to be more accommodating in the negotiations. That tactical strategy failed when the EU at its 1997 Luxembourg meeting refused to go along by admitting Turkey to candidacy. The EU reversal in 1999, generating a greater perceived need in Turkey to solve the Cyprus problem, the willingness of Greece to drop progress on major differences as a precondition to improvement in relations between Turkey and Greece, and Turkey's seemingly more flexible posture on Cyprus have changed the negotiating environment. Whether environmental change ultimately produces the necessary substantive changes in the positions of the parties remains to be seen. Cynicism is understandable, but the externals are now significantly different and quite promising.

THE ARMENIAN- AMERICAN LOBBY. The Armenian-American lobby, with its supporters concentrated in politically important California, until recently had one great foreign focus: its quarrel with Turkey. That antagonism is a carryover from a long, tortured history during the Ottoman Empire; a new dimension was added in 1991 by the creation of two states from the former Soviet Union—Azerbaijan and Armenia. The Armenian anger focuses on terrible events of almost ninety years ago, the destruction and deportation of well in excess of a million Armenians in Anatolia during World War I, the final years of the moribund Ottoman Empire. Although the numbers and circumstances are deeply disputed by the two sides, it is also true that Turks have had difficulty coming to grips with some of their history, even that before the existence of the Turkish Republic. The Armenians have labeled these wartime events a genocide; like the Greeks they have tried to internationalize their issue and use their political influence in the United States and other Western countries to push the passage of legislative resolutions (including in some American states) commemorating the Armenian genocide. One Armenian terrorist organization (ASALA) between 1979 and 1986 carried on this historical antagonism by killing 34 Turkish diplomats and their family members and wounding 424 others in the United States and elsewhere.[7] The Turks have denounced the Armenian charges as a slur on Turkey; they look upon the genocide resolutions as one step in an effort ultimately to win some form of reparations. They have worked zealously to defeat the Armenian efforts in the United States and elsewhere.

Every year Armenian-American groups in the United States have sought a commemorative "genocide resolution" in Congress blaming the Turks, in some years making a major effort, in others proceeding much less intensely. The biggest push took place in 1990 in the U.S. Senate, when the resolution produced a great and unusual personal battle between two titans of that institution, Robert Dole for the Armenians and Robert Byrd for the Turks (a contest that was barely mentioned in the national media but played heavily in Turkey and Armenia). Byrd went all out to call in the support of his colleagues and won the vote narrowly after two days of intense debate. The whole episode led to vitriolic outpourings from Ankara and a brief but severe downturn in U.S.-Turkish relations because the Turks viewed the Bush administration at its highest levels as staying on the sidelines rather than supporting a NATO ally on a matter it characterized as of the utmost importance. Senator Byrd, however, became something of a national hero in Turkey; enormous crowds greeted him everywhere he went when he visited Turkey in 1990, shortly after Iraq's invasion of Kuwait.

The genocide issue continues with somewhat diminished intensity in recent years. Nevertheless, the Turkish government watches the issue closely and does everything it can to keep the issue quiet in the United States and Western Europe. The genocide resolution has been joined as a political issue in the United States by the struggle between Azerbaijan and Armenia over the status of Azerbaijan's ethnic Armenian enclave of Nagorno-Karabakh. Turks and Armenians worldwide act as surrogates for the two countries. Because of Armenian-American efforts

Congress has effectively prohibited any U.S. aid to Azerbaijan, while Turkey prevents any goods crossing its territory from reaching Armenia. Amazingly, the U.S. government is proscribed by law from sending humanitarian assistance to Azerbaijan, the only such instance in the world. The major negative impacts of this legislation are the denial to Azerbaijan of much-needed help to reinforce post-communist political and economic reform, the further souring of the atmosphere for a negotiated settlement of the Nagorno-Karabakh dispute, and perhaps the rendering of dealings with Turkey on other issues a bit more difficult. Azerbaijan's oil and gas holdings have commanded the attention of energy companies, and some of the companies' influential lobbyists and some Jewish groups keep trying to get the ban on aid to Azerbaijan lifted, so far unsuccessfully. The Nagorno-Karabakh issue, however, does not appear to generate the passion of the genocide resolution in the Armenian-American community.

The "alien influences"[8] in the U.S.-Turkish relationship, as the Turkish government likes to call the Greek- and Armenian-American lobbies, still make Ankara livid despite their long-standing exposure. And year after year the Turkish government solicits the executive branch for support in Congress and expends enormous effort and some monies to counter the congressional efforts of the two ethnic lobbies. In great part this is because Greek-Turkish differences have recently been displayed in Congress over military sales to Turkey, a matter of fundamental importance to the influential Turkish military. Indeed, the holdup of arms exports in Congress, with its associated lobbying by American ethnic and human rights groups who decry the use of some arms purchases in the fighting in southeast Turkey, have generated much of Turkey's sharpest acrimony against the United States. The Turks profess to find it difficult to accept these lobbying efforts as an integral part of American democracy. They want the U.S. government to disregard these opposing voices, whatever the merits of their case or the potential political costs to any administration. The phasing out of grant military assistance because of Turkey's own economic growth has probably lowered the overall temperature on this issue, although military sales of important items like helicopters have become big political playthings. And in fact the U.S. government patiently pursues the sales of most, not all, items. Over time, deals are made, both with Congress or Turkey, Congress usually relents, and Turkey gets to buy or receive the vast bulk of equipment it seeks, albeit sometimes far later than it wanted. But much greater scrutiny of

Turkish arms sales and performance by both the executive and legislative branches has raised considerable angst in Turkey on purchasing U.S. arms.

The 1999 Turkish earthquakes produced a radical change in attitudes among Turks and Greeks. There was much sympathy for Turks from all quarters in the United States—including the Greek- and Armenian-American communities—as well as from Greece and Armenia. Greece's rapid assistance to earthquake victims was heavily praised in Turkey. The vast improvement in the atmosphere of Greek-Turkish relations has occasioned some reassessment of domestic lobbying efforts and their focus. Turkish- and Greek-American associations even collaborated in statements praising the effort of both countries to improve relations. Whether there will be any substantial longer-term change largely depends on what happens on major and continuing Greece-Turkey issues like Cyprus.

THE PRO-TURKEY LOBBIES

Not surprisingly, Turkey—like many other countries—has learned to play in U.S. domestic politics. The Turkish government would like to alter its lobbying disadvantage but cannot count on a comparable number of Turkish-American citizens. Turkish Americans also are widely dispersed in the United States and affect no state in any serious political way, as the Armenians do in California, although they have a good number of important legislators deeply sympathetic to them such as Senator Byrd and Representative Dick Armey. Turkey has tried to level the congressional playing field the past decade by spending between $2 million and $4 million a year for assistance from American lobbying firms.[9] This effort has helped mobilize Turkey's supporters in Congress and present its case better in the United States, but the monies have never yielded the benefits the Turkish government had hoped for. Far more important, Turkey has found a potent ethnic ally in helping its efforts in the United States.

THE JEWISH LOBBY. Over the years many organized American Jewish groups have quietly supported Turkey. Turkey was the first Muslim state to recognize Israel in 1948 and established diplomatic relations in 1949. For Israel, having a nearby friendly Muslim state in a sea of hostile Arab ones has been a matter of political and psychological importance. In the second half of the 1990s, Israel-Turkey relations took a great leap forward, including many forms of military and intelligence cooperation, far in excess of what had ever been imagined by either state or by other states in the region or by the United States. This impressed many American Jews.

The Turkish government, particularly the military, saw the expansion of relations with Israel as leading to significant intelligence, defense, economic, and political benefits. It also recognized the possible squeeze that a close Israel-Turkey relationship could put on Syria and its longtime support of the PKK, invariably denied by Damascus but virtually open. Ankara downplayed the negative impact of its growing Israel connection on its relations with Arab states, in part because it felt the Arab states never gave Turkey much support anyway. The Turkish government also sought another benefit from its Israel connection, support from another powerful American lobby.

The Turkish government believes that American Jews have great influence in the executive and legislative branches and in the media. For the past decade it has tried hard to expand ties with the American Jewish community. It rolls out the red carpet for visiting American-Jewish delegations. It also sees Israel's influence with American Jews and concludes that a close Israeli connection also could help cement ties with the organized American Jewish community, which, although not providing the constant, complete support Turkish officials would like, is nevertheless a generally friendly influence on such important Turkish interests as military sales and the Baku-Ceyhan pipeline project and helps generate a more sympathetic political hearing and a better public image for Turkey. There was a strong outpouring of support for Turkey by Jewish groups after the earthquake, with organizations like the American Jewish Committee taking strongly emotional, full-page advertisements in major papers to emphasize the close ties between Turkey and Jews since the expulsion of the Jews from Spain in 1492 and their acceptance by the Ottoman Empire.

The Jewish lobby has multiple interests, Israel of course being the biggest. For some American Jews Turkey is an important, not a vital, concern. Some pay little attention or are hostile on human rights grounds. There also are many prominent American Jews—mostly conservatives and many ex-government officials—who have become deeply interested in Turkey and are dedicated to preserving a strong U.S.-Turkish relationship. They go to bat for Turkey on military assistance, emphasizing Turkey's strategic importance to the United States and to Israel. Such support is frequently quiet and behind the scenes. On some issues, like the Armenia genocide resolution, Jews both in Israel and the United States are divided. The close Turkish-Jewish connection has produced tensions among the ethnic lobbies, which they all recognize and try to limit. But the clashing ethnic interests involved in Turkish issues are far from resolution.

THE DEFENSE LOBBY. Ever since 1947 Turkey has been a major recipient of American defense equipment. Another American supporter of Turkey, small but influential, has been the defense industry. Moreover, at a time of less robust overseas military sales, Turkey's annual billion dollars or so in arms purchases are important to the dwindling number of U.S. defense firms and to the Defense Department's efforts to keep equipment costs down. Sales of big-ticket items like helicopters have been impressive. The Turkish military plan many billions of dollars of arms purchases abroad the next decade, including airborne early warning craft, helicopters, and tanks. Not surprisingly, defense contractors see a congruence between their sales of military equipment to Turkey and the security interests of the United States. The Turkish military in turn has become heavily dependent on U.S. procurement for technology, training, and the development of Turkey's own defense industries.

For a long time, particularly in the 1980s, the defense industry was virtually the only private American group actively supporting Turkey's interests. Defense firms helped establish and finance Turkey's major private supporters in the United States—the American Friends of Turkey (AFOT), now the American Turkish Council (ATC). By and large their lobbying has been directed to getting congressional and executive branch authorizations for military sales and preventing or removing congressional restrictions on sales of defense equipment. Nondefense American trade and investment in Turkey is growing, but until Turkey seriously encourages foreign investment, a broad business lobby for Turkey in the United States is not on the horizon.

ENERGY INTERESTS. There is one important business group that has recently become very interested in Turkey—the energy companies, which see considerable commercial promise in Turkey's growing energy requirements, including construction of generating facilities, and have generally been supportive of Turkey and strong backers of Azerbaijan, where they produce much of that country's oil. Still, oil companies have been reluctant to support a major enterprise of the

U.S. and Turkish governments: to construct a pipeline for transporting a million barrels of Caspian and Azerbaijan oil a day through Turkey (Baku-Ceyhan) to international markets. Both U.S. and Turkish governments have zealously pursued this effort in part supposedly for strategic reasons—to reduce the dependence of the states of the area on Russia—and the United States has created a special presidential envoy with the rank of ambassador to see that it happens. For the most part companies have considered the pipeline as not competitive and have doubted the availability of sufficient oil in the area to make it cost-effective. They are also loath to offend the Russians, and some may reckon that a far more economical route will be available through Iran once U.S.-Iran relations improve. After much effort, in November 1999 Turkey and the United States obtained an agreement in principle among the relevant countries to have the pipeline built, but so far they have not been able to persuade the oil companies to start construction. They are not likely to do so without drastic changes in oil prices, or the assurance of adequate amounts of oil, or major subsidies, which the United States—despite its insistence on the pipeline's strategic importance—is not prepared to provide. Relentless U.S. efforts have quieted vocal company opposition but so far no more than that.

THE HUMAN RIGHTS LOBBY. The various human rights groups also have become an important part of America's Turkish political turbulence. Their focus, of course, is on Turkey's numerous human rights failings, including police torture, extrajudicial killings, and infringements on freedom of expression. They also have concentrated on the war in the southeast and the way it has been carried on. The restrictions on free speech and the highly publicized jailings of poets, novelists, and a blind lawyer have resonated in important quarters of the U.S. media, which have publicly honored long-imprisoned Turkish journalists. Such groups as Human Rights Watch and Amnesty provide support to Turkey's own human rights groups, who do much of the actual investigation of abuses, often under difficult conditions. Human rights groups are very active in Congress and the media, propagating their reports, which are full of detail and carefully done—and help shape Turkey's image abroad. They play an important role in helping produce the State Department's annual human rights report, a document that arouses significant media interest and has become increasingly attentive to the Turkish situation. These groups often seek to impose conditionality—for example, trying to tie human rights considerations to military sales programs—making common cause with Greek- and Armenian-American groups.

THE TURKEY SPECIALISTS. Lastly, a small, heterogeneous group—lobby would hardly be the right word—deeply interested in Turkey but the least influential of all, are Turkey specialists outside the U.S. government (some of them contributors to this book) and clustered around universities and think tanks. Some are Turkish-Americans. Many are former officials who have worked on Turkey either in Washington or in Turkey. Some have ties, formal or informal, with the U.S. government and are occasionally consulted by government officials. They play a small role in shaping public images of Turkey in the United States, doing much of the limited media explanation of developments in Turkey and some of the small amount of congressional testimony, although, not surprisingly, they often disagree on how to interpret Turkish events. They get plenty of attention, however, in the Turkish media, where their views are followed closely and are often read as official. Indeed a number of them have become public figures in Turkey. The significance of their work is probably mostly in giving the Turks useful feedback on their own policies and actions. These specialists have tended to stress Turkey's strategic significance and to focus attention on political Islam, the Kurdish issue, and other internal difficulties.

∗   ∗   ∗

What is the significance of these often contending private "players"— from ethnic groups to defense firms, human rights groups, and think tanks—in the formulation of American policy toward Turkey? It is hard to measure, but it is clear that the U.S. government pays serious attention to most of them, particularly the ethnic lobbies, and factors their views into the development and implementation of policy. Their influence is largely issue specific, but some issues, such as Cyprus and military sales to Turkey, are of great importance and can cause turmoil in American-Turkish relations. These groups generally make senior policymakers and bureaucrats more cautious and more hesitant. It is noteworthy that under the pressures of politically important domestic groups with negative views of Turkey, successive administrations have done what they believed needed to be done to preserve and expand U.S.-Turkish relations, even though having had to circumscribe important parts of relations heavily affected by domestic ethnic politics.

THE TURKISH DOMESTIC SCENE AND U.S. POLICYMAKING

The Islamist *Refah* Party's emergence as the leading political party in Turkey in 1996 shook Washington. If U.S. domestic politics complicate American policymaking on Turkey, so also have domestic developments in Turkey. Unlike most U.S. allies, Turkey has internal difficulties that can significantly affect American policy deliberations. They have created some doubt about Turkey's basic stability and orientation—less over the past year—and have caused domestic political problems for the administration.

In the past, military coups in Turkey were the principal domestic political problem for U.S. policymakers. Turkey, after all, had duly elected governments, and military coups were an embarrassment, momentary to be sure, for the NATO alliance. The three Turkish coups (1960, 1971, and 1980) were not protracted events; they usually succeeded in one quick swoop and were essentially bloodless, although many in and out of governments were often imprisoned, and in 1960 the prime minister and foreign minister were hanged. These coups also took place in the depths of the cold war—the 1980 one following years of increasingly intense daily public violence. All this made it easier for the U.S. government to get over any political difficulties, usually with Congress or the media, or with other allies, over supporting authoritarian states and being unwilling to limit aid to Turkey as pressure for a return to civilian rule. In contrast, Turkey's internal political difficulties of recent years have at times caused hand-wringing at policy levels in the U.S. government. Unlike the earlier coups these difficulties appear protracted and hard for Turkey to deal with; they seem to threaten the sustainability of close ties with Turkey or, worse, possibly to lead to a shift in Turkey's orientation in a volatile region where many American interests are at stake. Worried senior policymakers have frequently exhorted subordinates to reexamine U.S. efforts and find ways to improve support to Turkey.

Turkey's ability to solve its major internal problems—uneven economic growth coupled with chronic high inflation and a bloated state sector, the growth of political Islam, and the Kurdish issue and the war against the PKK in the southeast—has been hindered in turn by its political fragmentation and weak political leadership. Military domination of major aspects of the internal political scene continues and inhibits free expression, institutional development, and the growth of democracy. These and other internal issues were discussed in detail in Chapters Two and Three of this book.

Turkey's domestic political problems raise practical difficulties for policymakers because it is not clear, for example in the case of the rise of political Islam, what the magnitude of the problem is or what the United States can do or should do to help. And even if the United States government decided it knew what to do or propose, it is questionable whether the Turkish government would listen. (Indeed, if Turks themselves had better answers to their internal difficulties, getting them adopted in the existing weak political system would still be a far from simple matter.)

The United States can help Turkey economically, for example through promoting private investment, increasing textile quotas, or facilitating IMF support, but the prescriptions are far less clear in dealing with Turkey's religious or Kurdish problems, the issues that trouble the U.S. government and its Western partners the most. They generate value conflicts among Americans and thus enter American domestic politics. The Kurdish problem is the major source of human rights violations in Turkey, while the rise of political Islam raises familiar dilemmas about our dedication to democracy, our willingness to accept the results of free elections, and the proper role of the military in a democratic society. Discussions within the U.S. government on such issues as dealing with the now proscribed Islamist *Refah* Party can often end up in arguments over the wording of official public statements designed more to deter criticism in the United States than to cause ripples in Turkey.

Both on religion and on the Kurds U.S. policymakers have generally sought to help preserve or at least not undermine internal stability in Turkey. In considering the Kurdish issue the U.S. government first focused not on Kurds in Turkey but on the need to be able to continue Operation Northern Watch to protect the Iraqi Kurds. While recognizing the costly drain to Turkey of the war against the PKK and its major contribution to Turkey's inflation and internal strife, policymakers emphasized the same point that Ankara did, the need "to combat terrorism" and defeat the PKK. The U.S. government, of course, has not been oblivious to the human rights consequences of Kurdish problems and from time to time has spoken of them, usually quietly or indirectly. That willingness to speak out has increased in the past few years with the major decline in the military capabilities of the PKK, the broad political acceptance in Turkey of Operation Northern Watch,

and domestic political pressures in the United States. The U.S. government usually fended off domestic political efforts to tie its hands on
military sales to Turkey because of human rights concerns, though at
times it also insisted that Turkey make some very modest internal
changes before certain arms could be sold. EU countries often have
been more vocal than the United States on human rights abuses and
more willing to use conditionality in their dealings with Turkey, particularly with sales of military equipment. Had there existed in the United
States an organized Kurdish lobby like the Greek-American one or just
a sizable number of Kurdish immigrants, the American policy dilemma
could have become more painful, as it sometimes is in Europe because
of periodic outbursts of public violence by Kurdish émigrés.

More complex, and for the years 1996 and 1997 a daily reality for
policymakers to contend with, were the practical difficulties raised by
the coalition government established in 1996, led for the first time by
the Islamist *Refah* Party and its leader, Necmettin Erbakan. Washington
wanted to avoid doing anything that could lend support to the notion
that the United States welcomed an Islamist-led government, but it did
not want to say it could not work with such a government. It was, after
all, the duly elected government of Turkey, and the U.S. government
had plenty of real business to conduct with Ankara. It worked with
Prime Minister Erbakan on a variety of important issues such as
Operation Northern Watch over Iraq, issues where there was some
common ground, but it also sought to minimize whatever political
benefit the *Refah* Party might get from its dealings with the U.S. government. It also did as much business as possible through then Deputy
Prime Minster and Foreign Minster Tansu Çiller, the leader of the other
party in the coalition.

This approach encouraged, or certainly did not discourage, the
Turkish military from eventually squeezing and successfully forcing
the *Refah* Party from power in 1997, in what has been called a "soft
coup." The *Refah* Party was soon legally banned. The U.S. government said little about all this; indeed, it was obviously relieved by the
outcome—as were most other Western countries, whatever their
protestations. U.S. government spokespersons developed wonderfully
tortured public statements that defended democratic principles but
were meant to have no practical application in Turkey—at least in the
short term.

None of this may be particularly virtuous, but dynamic Islamic
political movements pose a real dilemma for policymakers. The United

States wants Turkey to remain stable, secular, democratic, and allied with the West. Turkish governments meet these criteria more or less. The U.S. government does not like to intrude in sensitive political matters in a friendly country; knowledge is limited, particularly on Turkey's politically active Islamists, and its involvement could well be counterproductive, affecting the Turkish scene in ways no one is wise enough to foresee. The Kurdish issue can set off a truly paranoid reaction by Turkish leaders toward any U.S. government statement or action; some still believe, contrary to all American statements and policy, that the United States wants to dismember Turkey and help carve out a Kurdish state from Turkey's southeast—the so-called Sèvres syndrome.

Presidents this decade usually have not liked to talk candidly about such problematic issues with Turkey's leaders or to preach. They generally have other issues they consider more pressing. Turkey is also a good friend; they prefer a more positive atmosphere, and they tend to make uplifting general statements when they meet Turkish leaders. It is easier to avoid confrontation and fall back on impersonal economic and social forces leading to democratic change. The Turkish public expectation and subsequent failure of President Clinton to raise human rights concerns with Mrs. Çiller on a visit in 1995 drew much attention in the Turkish press and for a time at least hurt American credibility. President Clinton's very popular speech to the Turkish parliament in 1999 was what the *New York Times* called a "nudge" on human rights issues. Most presidential subordinates tend to feel that the most useful thing U.S. government officials can do is express, largely in private, as friends and as credibly as they can, the political implications for U.S.-Turkish relations of Turkish domestic policies. They are content to fall back on the belief that in the end only Turks can solve their persistent internal difficulties, and that political and economic change in Turkey supported by constant exhortation by Turkey's friends is moving the country in the right direction.

THE PERSONAL AND BUREAUCRATIC ELEMENTS IN U.S. POLICYMAKING

Despite the vast changes in the post–cold war world, particularly in Turkey's neighborhood, in Turkey's domestic difficulties, and in American domestic politics, U.S. policy has remained reasonably consistent and highly positive toward Turkey. Policymakers look for ways to strengthen Turkey, to deepen the American connection, and (with important exceptions such as Greek-Turkish issues) to help its external efforts. That has been true of Republican and Democratic administrations, although there are always arguments about the efficacy and farsightedness of any administration's policies.

Partisan proclivities notwithstanding, most senior policymakers, although generally interested and usually generous in rhetoric, do not spend much time on Turkey unless things are going badly or the United States needs something, as in the Gulf War, or there is a crucial moment such as in December 1999, when Turkey was admitted to EU candidacy. It is then that Turkey gets some very high-level attention, indeed much like many other foreign policy issues. In the Pentagon, however, and to some extent the intelligence community, Turkey gets both attention and support. While there have been frequent frustrations over day-to-day operational base issues in Turkey, the links between the two military establishments have remained strong. This does not necessarily translate into influence on nonmilitary matters. Efforts to use the presumed cachet of senior American military leaders with their Turkish counterparts on such issues as Cyprus have gotten nowhere.

Policymaking and implementation on most Turkish issues are a variable matter. At times these have been largely handled in Washington at relatively lower levels like the office director for southeast Europe in the Department of State's European bureau, such as during much of my tenure in Ankara as ambassador (1989–91). After Iraq's invasion of Kuwait, President Bush and Secretary of State James A. Baker became the managers of our Turkish policy. At other times strong officials at the assistant secretary level have dominated setting and implementing policy. Richard Perle played an important policy role in the 1980s from his position as assistant secretary of defense for international security affairs. In the Clinton administration, Assistant Secretary of State for European Affairs Richard Holbrooke, followed in that position by Marc Grossman, also a former ambassador to Turkey (1994–97), were initiators and implementers of significant policy measures.

Turkey is one of the handful of countries where the U.S. ambassador can exert real and continued influence in Washington. In great part this arises from the complexity and unfamiliarity of Turkish problems coupled with the lack of general knowledge about the country at high policy levels and the absence of high-level personal relationships; language also can sometimes be a problem inhibiting high-level

Washington-Ankara direct discussion. Much obviously depends on the character and drive of the ambassador and the issues in play.

The role of the U.S. president is also variable. He can be brought in to see a visiting Turkish prime minister or president or to smooth out abrasions or to call or send a personal message on an important subject. But presidents do not usually get engaged unless there is a war or a serious flap or they get interested in solving the Cyprus problem. Bill Clinton, however, became a major personal presence in Turkey by his visit in November 1999. His speech to the Turkish people was a stunning success and added significantly, at least for the moment, to American prestige in Turkey.

President Özal was the only Turkish leader who has had a real personal bond with an American president. It was of course the Gulf War that brought Bush and Özal together. The two respected each other's qualities and views and over time grew fond of each other. They talked on the telephone, I believe, more than fifty times between August 1990 and July 1991, perhaps as much or more as Bush talked with any other foreign leader by phone in any comparable period. Özal particularly liked the day he placed a call to Bush and watched him on CNN tell the White House press that he had to leave to take a call from the Turkish president. Bush invited Özal to stay with him at Camp David over a weekend in 1991—an infrequent presidential gesture to foreign leaders.

PROGRESS AND PROSPECTS

The circumstances under which the Bush-Özal phone calls began is revealing of the often fortuitous nature of U.S.-Turkish relations and how far they have come in the past decade. Unbeknownst to Turkey, the U.S. government had negotiated a new defense cooperation agreement (DECA) with Greece in June 1990. When it became publicly known in June, the Turkish government, particularly the Foreign Ministry, became enraged, seeing in some of its provisions a bias toward Greece and a threat to Turkey. These fears were unwarranted, but the episode—on the heels of the congressional resolution on Armenian genocide with its perceived lack of Bush administration support for Turkey—generated great anger in the Turkish media, guided by the bureaucracy. Secretary of Defense Dick Cheney happened to be visiting Turkey at the time, and he was treated with something approaching scorn and incredible bluntness, an unusual display by the invariably hospitable Turks. It was the low point of my two years as ambassador. (To demonstrate official displeasure most senior Turkish officials boycotted the annual Fourth of July reception.) I asked Cheney on returning home to urge Bush to call Özal to see what might be done to calm relations. That call took place a short time before Iraq's invasion of Kuwait: Bush asked Özal if it would help if he made a statement making it clear that there was nothing in the Greek DECA that was meant against Turkey. Özal said it would, and that call cleared the air; it probably helped accelerate Özal's decision quickly to close the Turkish pipeline after Saddam invaded Kuwait a short while later.

The major new ingredient in U.S. policymaking toward Turkey over the past ten years has been the more complex management and greater attention required because of the increasingly ramified nature of the U.S.-Turkish relationship and Turkey's new influence across a number of regions. There is now far more to discuss between the two countries than NATO or Greek-Turkish tensions, or base rights, and that is likely to grow over time. Turkey brings much more to the table than ever before, and its interests cannot be shunted aside. While fostering stable, independent states in Central Asia and the Caucasus may not be so compelling a mutual interest as the former Russian threat, the task is important and difficult to achieve. It affects how both the United States and Turkey deal with Russia and with each other. These new issues have led to a more active Turkish-American dialogue, to a search for more avenues of cooperation, and, in the case of pipelines and Caspian energy, to new ventures in cooperation. Economic relations have deepened but are still limited. Turks have liked the public attention associated with the Department of Commerce's pronouncing Turkey one of the ten big emerging markets, but that reality is some way off and requires considerable Turkish reform and high, sustained rates of growth. The economic dialogue has been more often than not filled with contentious issues such as textile quotas and antidumping complaints.

President Clinton's visit was the third presidential visit to Turkey in the postwar period, but his address to the Turkish parliament in November 1999 was a first and punctuated a decade's development in U.S.-Turkish relations. Clinton wove a tapestry combining an elaboration of Turkey's importance in the world and its even greater future promise in a way that touched the people of Turkey. He also indirectly prodded his Turkish listeners on their human rights lapses but offered them here as well a vision of what their country could become. It was in Ankara, if not in Washington, a deeply emotional moment in the Turkish saga of affection and disappointment with the United States in the latter half of the twentieth century. The president's ensuing visit to earthquake victims in their makeshift camps also endeared him to the Turkish public, contrasted favorably in the media with the absence or formality of senior Turkish officials. One Turkish journalist told me, "Clinton could have been elected president of Turkey."

The management of policy toward Turkey during the Clinton administration significantly contributed to that moment. The U.S. government focused on the strategic aspects of relations and on maintaining Turkish internal stability, weaving its way through domestic ethnic thickets and Turkey's own domestic troubles. It basically did not try to interfere with Turkey's approach to Kurdish problems or the politics of religion while using the rhetoric of democracy and human rights to limit the political costs incurred in the United States and to encourage Turkey in the right direction. It helped get Turkey through a difficult period of weak governments. It spent inordinate effort on the Cyprus issue but exported it to another century. This may convey too plain and serene a view of policymaking. Indeed, there continue to be many bureaucratic clashes, particularly over the U.S. response to human rights abuse, such as between the human rights bureau of the State Department and the regional political offices.[10]

In seeking ways to support Turkey the United States pursued major diplomatic issues that Turkey believed critical and needed help with. Some, it was felt, could constructively change Turkey. Most notably, the U.S. government in 1995 gave Turkey enormous diplomatic support in winning the European Parliament's approval of the customs union with Turkey and for Turkey's successful effort in 1999 to become a candidate for EU membership. It also gave important public support to Turkey's large incursion into northern Iraq in 1995 in pursuit of the PKK and has relentlessly promoted the ongoing initiative to build the Baku-Ceyhan pipeline.

These efforts have cost the United States little. The United States is, of course, not a member of the EU and has no vote. All it could do was to lobby, cajole, constantly raise the Turkish issue, and call EU leaders at critical times. And all this it did up to the finale at the Helsinki summit in December 1999, including calls by President Clinton. If Turkey were entering into some sort of agreement of which the United States was a part, such a protracted effort would have been tempered by serious domestic political and economic scrutiny. The only cost to the United States was a certain European annoyance, perhaps anger at times. The importance of American persistence to the final outcome in Helsinki is hard to judge—many American officials not surprisingly think it helped significantly. Others would rate the downfall of Helmut Kohl as the central factor in the European change of heart. The Turks certainly appreciated the American effort, and that may be most important for this discussion.

Similarly, the American approach to Turkey's first large-scale incursion into northern Iraq in 1995 and U.S. promotion of the Baku-Ceyhan pipeline had few financial costs. The United States won Turkey's great gratitude over the Iraqi invasion because it took the opposite approach to most of Europe and did not leave the Turks isolated. In the case of the Baku-Ceyhan pipeline, the U.S. government has argued for multiple pipelines on the basis of avoiding dependence on Russia and Iran and has enthusiastically sold the proposed project to the relevant new states of the former Soviet Union, while it has endlessly jawboned the oil companies to do what they have not wanted to do. Here again we tried to make one of Turkey's most devout wishes come to pass, one that the United States in fact did much to stimulate as a way of demonstrating support for Turkey. The final word on this effort is not yet in.

But it was different on the financial front. When Turkey sought help to alleviate the post–Gulf War recession, the foreign exchange crisis of 1994, or the earthquake of 1999, the U.S. government was quick to express concern but provided little assistance or financial help. The government gave minuscule financial help, far less than many other countries, for earthquake relief. Turkish leaders would often come to Washington with visions of sugar plums, but the best they got was a meal at the White House and a small increase in textile quotas or some surplus military equipment. The United States government also was quick to offer numerous bilateral consultative organs. But since no friendly leader likes to go home empty-handed, both sides usually proclaimed every visit a success. American officialdom would no doubt like to help Turkey in its economic travails, but Washington has not been willing to expend any serious political capital to find monies for Turkey. Turkey did not, of course, make it politically easy for the U.S. government to get it financial support. Moreover, the Turkish economy had grown so much that the sums the U.S. government might produce became less important. Turkey got by without American financial help. But American officials rarely made the case that Turkey did not need assistance. In any event future financial assistance to Turkey will have to come from the EU or the international financial institutions.

There was another reason why sustained American diplomatic support for Turkish objectives became more important than money. The Turks have had few friends in the world, certainly not their neighbors, and they have not received much sympathy from many of their NATO allies. Indeed, the country often has felt isolated and from time to time has been gripped by collective paranoia. EU rejection of Turkey's candidacy in 1997 was painful. It was tremendous support domestically for Turkey's government to have the most powerful country in the world as its best, at times seemingly only, friend. Having the United States on their side counted even more for secular nationalist leaders such as the present prime minister, Bülent Ecevit, who was often highly critical of U.S. policy out of office and in office sometimes remains so.

And the Future

But halcyon periods in relations between widely different states with somewhat differing agendas are difficult to sustain even if the states are friendly and allied. Turkey is in the midst of rapid internal change, while its external environment is unstable and can change dramatically in ways that we cannot predict or at times comprehend. The strategic underpinnings of the U.S.-Turkish relationship are not likely to be undermined, certainly for the next decade, unless Turkey's basic orientation toward the West were somehow to change. Indeed, the area's continuing instability should serve to cement those underpinnings. Turkey's three southern and eastern neighbors—Iran, Iraq, and Syria—also can be expected to change, perhaps radically, in the next decade. Military cooperation will remain a principal element in the thinking of policymakers in both allies, and Turkey will need the United States to deal with concerns over possible weapons of mass destruction in the hands of unfriendly neighbors. It is more on domestic and diplomatic issues than on basic security ones that the uncertainties—old and new—are presently greatest:

◆   Turkey has enormous potential, but its internal problems have prevented sustained, rapid growth and complicated relations with friends and allies. Many believe—or more accurately hope—that the EU accession process will permit Turkish governments now to do what previous governments could not do: to carry out often unpleasant and politically difficult tasks like reducing public sector borrowing and getting rid of restrictions on free speech. If Turkey can get on the road to sustained, high levels of growth, it will significantly increase its influence over a wide and difficult area of the world, have greater scope and confidence for diplomatic initiative, and change the quality of its relations with the United States and Europe. That would indeed create a new geopolitical situation. Clearly, however, for some time to come, Turkey's management of its political Islam and Kurdish issues will remain an important part of the U.S. policy dilemma.

◆ Turkey's integration into Europe in one way or another will probably be the single most important external factor shaping Turkey's foreign and domestic policies. At this point it is not clear how far and how quickly EU integration will go. Much depends on a continuing Turkish consensus to reform and on improvement in relations with Greece. But the accession process, if and as it moves along, will not only force internal reform in Turkey, it also will change policy perceptions in both the United States and Turkey and ultimately complicate their dealings as Turkey looks increasingly to its new European partners and meeting EU requirements for admission. New Turkish bureaucratic institutions are being set up to guide the EU accession process, and they could well become engines for slow, subtle change in existing U.S.-Turkish relations. Conceivably, for example, arms purchases could begin to shift away from U.S. sources. Given their vastly greater security confidence in the United States, however, the Turks—like the British—will try to maintain a special security relationship with the United States.

◆ The new states of the Caucasus and Central Asia are in parlous shape and are likely to remain so for a long time to come. The combination of stagnant economies; income inequalities; ethnic, religious, and other internal problems; and authoritarian leaders will breed continuing instability. Nevertheless, these countries have become important interests of both the United States and Turkey and a major consideration in their policies toward Russia. Efforts by Washington and Ankara to foster independent states in the area that are relatively unconstrained by Russia will continue to run into major problems and severely complicate both countries' dealings with Moscow, which has the means to undermine or create serious difficulties for such states as Georgia or Azerbaijan or Kazakhstan. Turkey seems to be pursuing a high-intensity role in the area that is at present inconsistent with its capabilities. Domestic political pressures pull it in that direction; Chechnya, for example, is a much more public issue in Turkey than in the United States because of a large Chechen population. But Turkey also has developed a major economic stake in Russia and depends on it for much of its energy and substantial exports. Managing this complex of relationships with their high nationalist resonance in Turkey and longstanding Russian-Turkish animosities will test both Turkish and American policymakers and could become highly contentious. The proposed Baku-Ceyhan pipeline is an important aspect of this larger issue, one in which politics has dominated over economics. Failure to build it after so much hoopla could significantly affect the tenor of U.S.-Turkish relations.

- Iraq remains an intractable problem. Efforts to promote a strong internal opposition to Saddam Hussein, difficult enough, falter also because of Turkish opposition. What happens to Iraq if and when Saddam departs the scene is a dangerous uncertainty. A democratic, decentralized, but united Iraq is a nice construct—but its likelihood is dubious. Another dictatorial regime is more likely to be needed to keep Iraq together. What worries many in Turkey and in the Middle East is that the end of Saddam will lead to chaos in Iraq, and the country will simply split or end up a loose, de facto confederation of sorts. If that were to happen and the Iraqi Kurds, who have gotten used to running their own show, were to try to establish a new entity in northern Iraq, it would starkly reopen the complex and sensitive Kurdish issue for the whole region and for U.S.-Turkish relations. There is another, much different uncertainty: that Saddam will emerge with weapons of mass destruction bent on regional domination.

- The continued influence of ethnic lobbies on U.S. Turkish policy will depend mostly on whether there is serious movement toward resolution of at least one major Greek-Turkish issue. If the improved atmosphere in Greek-Turkish relations generated by the Turkish earthquake and the constructive approach of two foreign ministers, İsmail Cem and George Papandreou, does not go beyond rhetoric and second-order meetings, U.S. policy is likely to continue to be constrained on specific Greek-Turkish issues by domestic ethnic lobbies. Barring a breakthrough this year, much diplomatic and political attention will have to remain focused on the Cyprus issue.

The United States and Turkey are headed for a more complex relationship, largely cooperative but with some old and new contentious issues. Much depends on Turkish internal developments and what happens to Turkey's EU candidacy. The uncertainties are bigger if only because Turkey could change significantly over the next decade and because it touches on so many areas of the new world in important ways. American policymakers are clearly going to have to focus more on Turkey, continue to secure the basic relationship, meticulously sort out U.S. interests on specific issues, and be inventive in dealing with occasional clashing perspectives.

CHAPTER SEVEN

THE UNITED STATES, TURKEY, AND GREECE— THREE'S A CROWD

M. JAMES WILKINSON

For much of the past fifty years, Greek-Turkish squabbling and its whiff of impending crisis has dogged U.S. efforts to foster regional stability and the further integration of Turkey into Europe. As recently as 1998 there was talk of military confrontation on Cyprus, and not long before that, in 1996, Greeks and Turks nearly started shooting at each other in the Aegean.

A new day may have dawned, with promising détente initiatives under way as the millennium turns. Ankara and Athens are concluding cooperative agreements, UN-sponsored Cyprus talks are again in process, and Turkey is on the track to EU membership.

Can this drive toward Greek-Turkish rapprochement last? Or is it doomed like the 1988 Özal-Papandreou "spirit of Davos" to die away and be followed by another round of hostile clashes? Is war between Greeks and Turks still conceivable? What are the underlying problems, why have they not been resolved, and what will it take to settle them? What can and should Washington do?

This chapter assesses the Greek connection to U.S.-Turkish policy and its implications for Washington policymakers.

TURKEY AND GREECE—
CROSSROADS OF AMERICAN INTERESTS

America's strategic interests have long required a Greek dimension in Washington's approach to Turkey and vice versa. President Truman paired the two countries at the outset of U.S. engagement in southeastern Europe when he propounded his famous doctrine. "It is only necessary to glance at a map," Truman said to Congress on March 12, 1947, "to realize that the survival and integrity of the Greek nation are of grave importance in a much wider situation. If Greece should fall . . . the effect on its neighbor, Turkey, would be immediate and serious." A half-century later, Greece is no longer in danger of falling, but what happens in one still reverberates in the other and on into the hinterlands of the Balkans, Europe, the Middle East, and Central Asia.

Problems between Greece and Turkey began to plague Washington when their bitter ethnic rivalry reemerged in the 1950s under the pressures of preparing Cyprus for independence from Britain. The Greek nexus underlay the two imbroglios that still haunt U.S.-Turkish relations: President Johnson's threatening letter, which prevented Turkish military intervention in Cyprus in 1964, and the arms embargo imposed by Congress after U.S. failure to stop the Turkish military intervention that split Cyprus a decade later.

In the latter case, the United States paid dearly for miscalculations and inattention. Henry Kissinger in his memoirs refers to the Cyprus warfare as an "ethnic conflict on a remote island," with protagonists who ignore outsiders' concerns and fight like gladiators to death or exhaustion.[1] He calls Cyprus "the forerunner of ethnic conflict," somehow, one must assume, a magnitude different from the India-Pakistan or Arab-Israeli struggles a decade before Cyprus. In the circumstances of 1974, he contends, the best that Washington could do was to protect the critical U.S. interest of the day, the integrity of the NATO alliance, which he did.

Dr. Kissinger would no doubt scoff at alternative analyses. But if, in the years leading up to 1974, Washington had not been so politely respectful toward the incompetent dictatorship of the colonels in Athens, the United States would surely have been better positioned to deal with the junta's loony coup plan against Cypriot president Makarios. If Kissinger himself had paid more attention to what he calls the "prescient" memorandum put forward by the State Department's Cyprus desk officer in May 1974 (two months before the Turkish invasion), he might have found a way as Johnson did to interrupt the Greek-Turkish march to disaster.

Kissinger demeans Johnson for having burdened NATO with the legacy of the (in)famous 1964 letter, but his own contrasting inaction in 1974 arguably bequeathed the worse incubus. In the process he incurred the enduring wrath of *both* protagonists—Turks are still galled by the embargo, while Greeks still resent Washington's acceptance of the colonels and bitterly fault its handling of the Cyprus fiasco.

AFTER THE COLD WAR—PLUS ÇA CHANGE

In the U.S. strategic calculus of the post–cold war world, Turkey has become considerably more important than Greece. Turkey's larger size and greater economic potential, its unique connections to both Central Asia and the Middle East, the ongoing U.S. concern with Iraq, the flow of Caspian oil and gas out to markets through Turkey, and the Turkish factor in the future of Russia all buttress this appraisal. True enough, but it does not follow that Washington should therefore choose Turkey's side or pay less attention to Greece when it comes to regional and Greek-Turkish affairs.

For starters, Mr. Truman's "glance at the map" is still instructive—whether one's eye runs east-west from the Middle East to Europe or north-south from the Black Sea to the Mediterranean, the central intersection is formed by the combination of Greece *and* Turkey. In the Balkans, for example, Greece and its territory made pivotal contributions to NATO military actions (notwithstanding hitches due to strong Greek popular disapproval of alliance policies). Greece is of course a full member of the EU and of NATO and has important communications and logistics facilities, notably the NATO naval base at Souda on Crete. Retaining Greece and Turkey in the same NATO house, however quarrelsome they may be, preserves a greater capability than either can offer on its own.

National security considerations aside, America's Greek lobby ensures through its congressional clout that no U.S. administration can deal with Turkey unless it deals with Greece. Greek-American organizations are straightforward in their objectives. A 1999 policy paper endorsed by the largest such entity, the American Hellenic Educational Progressive Association, declared, "The U.S. should recognize and state that the main impediment to progress on the region's problems lies with Turkey."[2] Governments in Athens encourage such overt and unqualified backing for Greek foreign policy.

Greek lobby partisans would assert that the positions they espouse stand on their merits. After all, it is not just Greeks who have qualms about the Turkish human rights record or who decry the continued presence of Turkish troops in Cyprus. The lobbyists also would argue, not without some justification, that they have to speak up when the State Department and the Pentagon play down Turkey's shortcomings to curry favor with Ankara in the interest of military sales or access for U.S. military operations against Iraq.

Be that as it may, the influence of the Greek lobby has created a dynamic of its own. Responding to the concerns of Greek-American constituents, Congress has manipulated arms sales, administrations have undertaken diplomatic initiatives as much for the sake of show as in expectation of progress, and official policy discussion has been kept within the bounds of a certain political correctness. These convolutions make it difficult to debate the issues objectively, assess the U.S. interest, and articulate the balance America should be seeking in its relations with Greece and Turkey.

It is not so much the Greek-Turk quarrels as the spillover effects that concern the United States. Greek-Turkish contention complicates U.S. relations with Turkey and over the long run could adversely affect U.S. access to the region. Unable to resolve the disputes, the United States has had to rely on containment and damage control—an uncertain course that has dealt with symptoms but left the malady in place. It would clearly be better for the United States to see the problems solved. Easier said than done!

THE CORE DISPUTES—
CURABLE DISORDERS OR BALKAN CANCERS?

Most Americans know that Greeks and Turks have been fighting off and on for a thousand years or so—from well before the fall of Constantinople in 1453 through the Greek war of independence in the nineteenth century to the Turkish reconquest of Asia Minor in 1922. They battled on Cyprus in 1974, displacing much of the populace and splitting the island into two antagonistic parts. They have almost come to blows over rights in the Aegean on three occasions in the past three decades.

While popular attitudes in both communities are influenced by images from the Byzantine and Ottoman Empires, the contemporary disputes on Cyprus and in the Aegean arose from developments that followed World War II. The issues involved are neither unique to the Balkans nor a priori unresolvable.

CYPRUS AND THE DILEMMAS OF POWER SHARING

Cyprus presents a classic problem of crafting arrangements to accommodate within a limited space two distrustful ethno-religious groups— in this case the Greek Orthodox majority, now slightly more than 650,000 people, and the Turkish Muslim minority, numbering about 200,000. From a Western perspective, the ideal would be a single country with power democratically shared between the communities. The British hoped they had succeeded on this model in 1960 when they granted independence under a constitution with complex mechanisms to balance the rights and benefits of both groups. Britain, Greece, and Turkey signed on as guarantor powers.

Cohabitation on the island was short-lived. Its unraveling from the breakdown of the constitutional mechanism in 1963 to the partition of 1974 has been amply documented elsewhere, although there is by no means agreement on facts or interpretations. Turks say Greeks sought total domination, while Greeks assert the unworkability of the constitution was the fundamental cause for the collapse of the bicommunal government. In November 1963, the Greek Cypriots demanded basic changes in the independence accords, and violence broke out when the Turkish Cypriots refused. British and U.S. observers at the time generally blamed Greek extremists and Cypriot government complicity for the brutal attacks on the outnumbered Turkish Cypriots that followed. In 1964, the UN Security Council dispatched a peacekeeping force; thirty-six years later it is still on the job.

For ten years thereafter, the two communities lived a tense, ghettoized coexistence, with sporadic outbreaks of violence, most notably in 1967. Right-wing Greeks seeking union (*enosis*) of the island with Greece kindled the war in 1974 when they launched an armed coup against Makarios. While American and European diplomacy floundered, Ankara sent in troops who seized the northern end of the island as a safe haven for Turkish Cypriots.

Turks see their military intervention of 1974 as an essential act, legal under the 1960 treaties, to save the lives of compatriots. Greeks consider the Turkish invasion unjustified and the continued occupation of about 38 percent of the country by Turkish troops a gross violation of international law. Each side may be more than half right, although to say this aloud makes you either anti-Turk or anti-Greek in their eyes.

The Greek view enjoys broad sympathy in the West and among nonaligned countries. This is true in part because time has blurred the background. Unless you are a Turk, it can be hard to believe that the Greeks and Greek Cypriots involved in the events of 1963–64 or 1974, much less today's citizenry, would want to massacre Turks or push them off the island. Perhaps more to the point is that the Turks appear intransigent, with their continued reliance on armed force to protect the Turkish Cypriots and the absence of any plan for troop withdrawal. This goes against the grain of widespread desires for non-military settlement of such disputes. Turks are frustrated to find themselves so often on the losing end of UN votes or nonaligned movement resolutions, but chalk it up to the misperceptions of foreigners who do not understand the consequences of a "premature" troop drawdown.

The decade of strife through the 1960s and the subsequent military intervention enormously complicated the difficulty of constructing a unified state. Trust between the two communities was destroyed. New and difficult issues were thrown on the table: how to decide future control of, and compensation for, territory and properties that changed hands; how to define and regulate a new concept of "bizonality"; how to put in place security arrangements giving the Turkish Cypriots enough confidence to permit withdrawal of their Turkish military protectors; how to deal with immigrants resettled from Turkey; how to resolve the cases of individuals missing in action; and so on.

After the debacle, leaders of the Cypriot ethnic communities agreed in two declarations—in 1977 and again in 1979—to work toward a unified, "bizonal" and "bicommunal" state. Negotiations followed on this basis under a UN aegis, and in 1992—after fifteen years in the bargaining trenches—UN diplomacy seemed close to pay dirt. Secretary-General Boutros Boutros-Ghali, aided by aggressive U.S. arm-twisting, had put together a "set of ideas" with a hundred paragraphs addressing every major aspect of a solution in outline.

Greek Cypriot president George Vassiliou accepted the set of ideas in late 1992 as a basis for proceeding. His Turkish Cypriot interlocutor,

Rauf Denktash, initially demurred and was soundly criticized by an unusually direct UN Security Council resolution. The most serious Turkish Cypriot objection involved an appended map providing for the return to Greek control of Morphou, a town where many Turkish refugees had settled into housing taken from Greeks in 1974.

The UN set of ideas might have been a negotiating anvil against which the Turks could have been hammered for intransigence, but the Greek Cypriots reversed course when national elections in March 1993 displaced Vassiliou. Major sticking points for the new president, Glafkos Clerides, included a provision that would give the Turkish community a strong hand in any accession of Cyprus to the EU. Denktash, who has kept his office, later asserted "basic agreement" with ninety-one of the hundred paragraphs, although by most indications he too was quite willing to let the set of ideas die a diplomatic death.

For our purposes, the point is that the outline of a Cyprus solution on the basis previously agreed by the two sides was within reach. It appeared in each side's interest to make the few remaining concessions necessary for closure—if not to resolve all issues, at least to make a substantive forward leap. When first the Turks and then the Greeks backed away from the set of ideas, a rational analyst would have been tempted to conclude that neither really wanted the bicommunal, bizonal power-sharing federation that had so long been the loudly proclaimed goal of both—except on maximal terms.

UN TRAIN DERAILED

Stymied, the UN backpedaled to emphasize confidence-building measures (CBMs). Proposals, most already on the table to complement the set of ideas, blended new and old notions, such as the reopening of the Nicosia airport and the return to Greek Cypriot owners of Varosha, a minisuburb on the edge of Famagusta, which had been seized in 1974 but thereafter left generally unused owing to international exhortations. The CBM "packages," however, were all rejected for one reason or another, and the atmosphere continued to worsen.

In August 1996, two unarmed Greeks were killed by Turkish defenders when they crossed the dividing line on Cyprus in the course of emotional demonstrations. Videos of the merciless killings inflamed Greek public opinion. A Turkish sentry was later shot dead at his post. The UN-sponsored bicommunal peace process went comatose.

The EU Luxembourg summit of December 1997 took the last vestiges of life from the UN talks for the succeeding two years. The EU not only dropped Turkey from active candidacy but also confirmed that the accession process would start for Cyprus even though no mechanism had been worked out for Turkish Cypriot participation. Denktash refused henceforth to take part in any UN negotiations unless given co-equal status with Clerides.

Making matters worse, the Luxembourg decisions provided the goad (Greeks would say excuse) for the Turkish side to drop the objective of a bizonal, bicommunal state in favor of a solution based on continued division of the communities.

Leaders in both Ankara and Turkish Nicosia explicitly changed official policy to adopt "confederation." Governmental statements have been short on detail, but the idea in essence is acceptance of two independent states, which could be joined as a confederation subject to mutual agreement. One news report presaging the shift indicated the Turks would leave the creation of any two-state association "to time" and focus initial negotiations on security, border demarcation, and land claims issues.[3]

Ankara's policy switch on Cyprus enjoyed wide acceptance. Turks across a broad spectrum were offended by the Luxembourg "slap in the face" and frustrated by a perceived lack of Western concern for their interests vis-à-vis the Greeks. Denktash and his supporting conservative majority in Turkish Cyprus had long plumped for "equal status" and must have welcomed the chance to make the jump. Objections from the more conciliatory Turkish Cypriot opposition were muted by the prevailing nationalist sentiment.

The Greeks, the UN, the United States, and almost everybody else remains committed to the goal of reunifying Cyprus into a pluralistic democracy. The crux of this stance is the preservation of the Republic of Cyprus as a political entity and the rejection of the secession accomplished in 1974 by force (whether one ascribes guilt to the Greek coupists or the Turkish military or both). The Greeks who constitute the internationally recognized Government of Cyprus claim sole representation for all of Cyprus, to maintain the legal principles underlying their legitimacy, even though on the ground there is a completely separate Turkish Cypriot administration running the northern third of the island. Mr. Denktash, with his demands for coequal status and his focus on the practical reality of his independent fiefdom, has tried to dismiss the Greek and Western position as injustice wrapped in legalistic fiction.

The contest presents variations of themes at issue in the case of China and Taiwan and, in an earlier time, the two Germanies.

The practical argument can be made in any case that after twenty-five years of failing to mix oil and water, alternatives merit more serious consideration. Indeed, Greek news media in early 2000 bandied about rumors that advisers close to Prime Minister Costas Simitis favored a new look at confederation. Even in Greek Cyprus, there has been talk of looking at the "Swiss model." In the background there are some who quietly wonder whether the inevitable costs of absorbing the far poorer Turkish side would be worth the benefits of reunification (in 1997 Greek Cyprus GDP stood at about $13,000; that of Turkish Cyprus at $3,600).[4]

THE AEGEAN AND THE DILEMMAS OF RESOURCE SHARING

Greek-Turkish disputes over the Aegean Sea appear more amenable to settlement than the Cyprus tangle. The airspace questions, for example, seem hardly so vital as to warrant the periodic confrontations that occur between armed and ready military aircraft. Greece in 1931 declared a ten-mile national airspace zone around its islands. The same islands, however, have six-mile territorial waters (declared in 1936), and Turkey, like the United States, objects, based on the international convention that air and nautical territorial boundaries should coincide. Also, the Flight Information Region (FIR) for civil aviation was fixed by international agreement to give Greek controllers responsibility for air traffic over most of the Aegean. Turkey has accepted this but insists it need not file flight plans for official (that is, Turkish military) planes flying into the Athens FIR. Athens demands such notification.

In point of fact these airspace contests are modest entries on a broader agenda—the future use of vast areas of the Aegean. What is so perverse is not so much ethnic or religious considerations as the accidents of geography and history that have put Greek-inhabited islands close to Turkish-inhabited coasts. This did not appear of great import in 1923 when the boundary lines drawn by the Treaty of Lausanne left most of the water between the islands and stretching back across to the Greek mainland as international space, free for use by the ships and planes of Turks, Greeks, and anyone else.

Circumstances changed drastically after World War II with the explosion of air and sea transport, advances in military technology, and the development of offshore drilling for oil and gas. The Aegean's "in-between" spaces from ocean floor to flight ceiling have taken on much greater significance and value. But there is no simple way to divide them without either enclaving the Greek islands, which is unacceptable to Greece, or giving Greece a lion's share of the sea bottom and sovereignty over cross-Aegean sea routes, which is unacceptable to Turkey.

The pivotal points are rights to the continental shelf (with its potential oil and gas deposits) and extension of Greek territorial seas to the now almost universal twelve-mile limit. With or without the thorns of ethnic contention, these two issues would present great difficulties since they involve control over important resources in a unique setting with unclear legal precedents.

Greece charges that Turkey wants to change the status quo by challenging existing Greek sovereign rights. For Athens, all boundaries except the continental shelf have been adequately fixed by existing treaties and established practice. On the continental shelf, Athens proposes recourse to the International Court of Justice (ICJ) in The Hague. As for territorial waters, Greece asserts that the Law of the Sea (LOS) Convention unequivocally gives it the right to extend maritime boundaries around its Aegean islands to the now standard twelve miles. Greece reserves this right even though Athens has no current plan to invoke it (thus in effect not confronting Turkey's declarations that such a move would be cause for war).

Turkey insists it is the one defending the status quo as established by the bedrock 1923 Treaty of Lausanne, which it contends bequeathed an overall balance of benefit for the two countries in the Aegean. From this standpoint, every issue is interrelated, and Turkey proposes bilateral discussions on the whole as a necessary prelude to settling individual parts, whether by mutual agreement or referral to third parties such as the ICJ.

Experts and scholars have suggested there could be Solomonic resolutions for these Aegean air and sea disputes. Not all maritime boundary wrangles in the world have been solved—the Spratlys, for example—but a number, of great complexity, have been successfully addressed—from the Torres to the Bering Straits, from the Outer Banks to the Gulf of Thailand.

The outcome of any arbitration is very unpredictable since the force of law and precedent in the Aegean case is far from 100 percent clear. The comprehensive 1982 LOS Convention, for example, would seem to favor the Greek position, as it accords considerable weight to islands for determining both continental shelf and surface boundaries. However, the convention also has a specific provision for alternative approaches in cases of special circumstance, such as the Aegean. Turkey's reservations about recourse to the ICJ or another arbitration body may have much to do with its failure during LOS negotiations to gain more understanding of its concerns, as well as with domestic perceptions that European entities are biased in favor of Christian Greece.

What Do Greeks and Turks Really Want?

Stepping back to view the sweep of events since 1974, an outsider may well ask how sincere either community is in pursuit of settlement. Two and a half decades of nonprogress suggest that underneath the rhetoric and negotiating probes, Greeks or Turks or both have been maneuvering to avoid any concession—holding out for unrealistic maximum gains as the price of agreement.

On Cyprus, for example, many would think the Greek side could settle on generous terms and still expect within a few years to dominate the island completely, thanks to the larger Greek population and its preponderance of wealth. Once the barriers were down, the economic differential would allow the hard-charging Greek Cypriot economy to move into control of investment, business, and employment throughout any Turkish Cypriot zone-to-be. And even if land transfers were strictly regulated, as foreseen in UN talks, Greek money would no doubt soon find ways to dominate resources held by cash-poor Turkish Cypriots. In sum, the argument goes, Greeks for a decade have been ideally placed to win back by economic means what they lost in military battle—with interest.

And why has Athens been so hesitant over the years to sit down at the table with Ankara to talk over Aegean differences? To skeptics, the Greek approach has overtones of artificial legalisms to avoid peaceful chat with a neighbor about whether or not shared backyard fences are in the right place. And if the Greeks wanted to resolve bilateral issues through the ICJ, why do they refuse to let the Aegean island militarization issue go to The Hague?

Similar arguments can be made about Turkish actions. In Cyprus, the Denktash equal-status strategy smacks of a drive for total autonomy that makes his 1977 and 1979 agreements on unification duplicitous in retrospect and his call for confederation a ruse. As for Ankara,

the government there had long professed earnest support for UN negotiations, but it did not rein in the cantankerous Turkish Cypriot leader when
he defied the UN Security Council on the set of ideas. Given Denktash's
political skills, this may well have been a case of the tail wagging the
dog—but the dog seemed more willing to be wagged than it let on.

Moreover, if the Turks wanted to solve their border disputes with
Greece, why have they been so unwilling to make use of third-party
arbitration? If not the ICJ, then why not some other appropriate tri-
bunal? Although Ankara argues that all the issues are interrelated, any
arbitration panel would be bound to consider all the elements of the
Turkish position, whether or not recourse was preceded by bilateral
dialogue. If your neighbor does not want to talk about the backyard
fence, why not just take your complaint to the appropriate authority?

Implicit in the foregoing questions is a Western diplomatic conviction that enlightened nations can either negotiate directly or use
arbitration mechanisms to resolve disputes fairly and equitably. If a
solution cannot be achieved in good time, the self-evident alternative
is to "agree to disagree," devise a temporary or transition regime, and
get on with civilized relations.

Both Greeks and Turks would proclaim agreement with the West
on the need for peaceful solutions and hotly defend their own good
intentions. Perhaps it is their perspectives on how nations act in the real
world that differ. In their own case, each has seen the other as an unrea-
sonable, obstinate, ideologically committed opponent. For both, therefore, it has been necessary to keep up political pressure and maintain
military preparedness. Seeking advantage in this circumstance, governments in Ankara and Athens have pursued an edgy strategic competition.

Escalating the Pressure—an "Aegean Curtain"?

On the surface, bilateral relations between Greece and Turkey are emi-
nently correct. International rules of commerce and transport apply, the
two participate in almost every multilateral organization, and they have
generally cooperated in regional affairs, such as Black Sea area development initiatives and the West's collective actions in the Balkans. In
the UN and other political bodies, their competition for support, for
instance on Cyprus, has been within norms for table-thumping disagreements between members.

Despite the apparent normalcy of relations, the fact is that until now the poor climate and the practices of both governments have discouraged private sector contacts. News media and demagogues have all too often promoted negative stereotypes and reinforced a kind of "glass curtain" across the Aegean. Consequently, bilateral trade, cultural and educational exchange, and travel and tourism have all been very meager between the two relative to their size, economies, and proximity.

The Greeks have sought to exploit their "comparative advantage" of EU membership by linking Turkish participation in the EU to specific Greek concerns over Cyprus and bilateral borders. Professor Theodore Couloumbis, at times an adviser to the Greek Foreign Ministry, describes the Greek stance as a "strategy of conditional rewards."[5] For the Turks, such a formulation equates to obstructionism, pure and simple. They know Greece by no means controls EU policy, but the Greeks help catalyze the whole and in some matters have a veto power. Greek "nays" have hit the Turks in the pocketbook by blocking implementation of the EU's "fourth financial protocol" framework for aid to Turkey, including a five-year program for more than a billion ECU in grants and loans agreed by the EU as part of the 1995 customs union agreement. And Greece has sought (unsuccessfully) to elicit EU guarantees for defense of its borders with Turkey.

Turkey, lacking any comparable family support group, looks more to self-reliance and its own military capabilities for the ultimate defense of its interests. Turkish governments have said that any action by Athens to extend Greek territorial waters to the world norm of twelve miles around Aegean islands would be a casus belli. Likewise, they have been insistent on a continued military presence in Cyprus. (Not that only Turks rattle the scimitar—Greek ministers have said that any aggressive action by Turkey against Greek-held Cyprus would be a casus belli.)

CROSS-AEGEAN ARMS RACE

It is in this sphere of national security that the governments have pursued their strategic contest with a vigor and pervasiveness suggestive at times of the Soviet-American cold war. The two military establishments maintain substantial forces squared off across their common borders. Both have major modernization programs under way, projecting expenditures costing billions of dollars. Each assesses the threat from the other as a clear and present danger.

Greece, since 1974, has focused its defense squarely on Turkey. This policy is backed by a strong political consensus across the board. The "joint defense doctrine" of 1994 formally weaves Cyprus into the Greek security posture. Both the Greek and Greek Cypriot governments are committed to improve cooperation and common training as long as Turkey maintains its occupation force on the island.

For Turkey, the military threat from Greece might seem minor compared to its own defense capacity. Not necessarily so—many Turks, including senior military officers in briefings for Western visitors, contend that Greeks still harbor ambitions to recover lands once ruled by the Hellenic Byzantine empire (in Greek, the phrase *megali idea* embodies this irredentist concept, which has not been given credence by the Greek political mainstream for many years).

The realistic danger for Turkey, in fact, is not so much a Greek military attack on Turkey as a unilateral Greek declaration to expand territorial seas in the Aegean or a move against the Turkish minority on Cyprus. The concern in Ankara is that unless any such Greek action is deterred (or immediately reversed, by force if need be), a situation could arise in which the United States and its European allies might enforce a cease-fire in place, leaving a Greek fait accompli impossible to overturn via negotiations.

Greek forces are arrayed on Aegean islands close to Turkey, in particular on Limnos, near the entry to the Dardanelles. Ankara charges that many of the deployments violate treaty provisions requiring demilitarization of certain islands. Greece rejects these assertions and in any case cites overriding self-defense requirements.

Turkey for its part established the "Army of the Aegean" on its western coast, avowing it to be purely defensive in character, although Greeks allege it has an offensive orientation with special force units and landing craft. Turkish air force planes regularly fly without Greek permission into airspace claimed by Greece or supervised by Greek air controllers. (The United States has conducted similar flights to assert rights in the airspace around Greek islands and other disputed corridors such as the Gulf of Sidra, although no U.S. incursions in the Aegean have been publicized for some years, and they may have been suspended.) Greece protests such Turkish flights and scrambles its own fighters to meet them.

In 1988, during a period of warming relations, Greece and Turkey formally agreed to avoid provocative military maneuvers and to suspend Aegean military exercises during the July-August tourist season.

Implementation of the two Yilmaz-Papoulias accords (named after the two signatory foreign ministers) has, however, been spotty.

When the political sun is shining, the military situation seems quite manageable—expensive, to be sure, but manageable. When the atmosphere cools or an incident pushes temperatures toward the boiling point, however, the presence of substantial forces on both sides means the risk of confrontation can quickly soar with accidental or deliberate airspace incursions, mock dogfights, warship bumping, arms competition, and impassioned rhetoric.

How Dangerous Are the Confrontations?

Hypothetical war scenarios are easy to construct. Fueled by ill-guided appeals to nationalism, an incident could escalate, leading to decisions made in the heat of the moment to launch punitive attacks. Turkey has the larger forces, giving it the capability to seize most or all of Cyprus, grab an Aegean island, or lunge into northeastern Greece across the land border. Greece, though outmanned and outgunned, has substantial military strength and modern equipment—enough to make a Turkish thrust costly or itself mount punishing strikes.

A military clash appeared imminent in 1996, when warships confronted each other over a disputed pair of Aegean rocks. And, as late as April 30, 1998, a *New York Times* headline proclaimed, "New Rumblings in Cyprus Raise Specter of War," referring to the projected deployment in Cyprus of S-300 missiles purchased by the Greek Cypriots from Russia.

A brief look at the two cases illuminates the potential for conflict and the indispensable crisis management role played by the United States and key European partners.

1996: IMIA/KARDAK IN THE AEGEAN. A small Turkish cargo ship went aground in late December 1995 less than four miles off the Turkish coast on an uninhabited rocky islet group, called Imia by the Greeks and Kardak by the Turks. A few days later, citing Greek sovereignty, a Greek ship towed the freighter into a Turkish port for repairs. The two foreign ministries thereafter exchanged information, holding to differing positions on the rocks' sovereignty but refraining from making confrontational demands or going public.

Nearly a month afterward, the story leaked in Athens. The local Greek mayor sailed out and raised a Greek flag over the islets. Next,

Turkish news reporters scouting the scene from a helicopter hoisted a Turkish flag in place of the Greek one. Media in each country took up the issue, in several cases with exaggerated, jingoistic coverage. Both governments dispatched warships, and the Turks landed a detachment of marines on one of the rocks. Military conflict threatened: the Greeks could not permit Turkish forces to remain in what they believed were Greek territorial waters, and the Turks could not withdraw without appearing to concede the point. Tension escalated rapidly.

Washington moved to defuse the crisis. President Clinton placed calls to urge a peaceful outcome, and Ambassador Richard Holbrooke began intense mediation. Both Ankara and Athens faced strong public pressures to hold the line—Athens was perhaps in the more difficult position, as the Imia/Kardak rocks lie on the Greek side of the generally accepted maritime boundary. Holbrooke—on the phone throughout the crucial night—successfully brokered withdrawals and a return to the status quo ante.

Western press coverage treated the matter as a dodged bullet, with the Americans getting credit for intervening to save the day. It was that to be sure, but Ankara's subsequent defense of its Imia/Kardak position became a much wider challenge to Greek sovereignty over small islets along the maritime border, as well as to the border itself.

The issue could well have died away. There had been no serious incidents before the accidental grounding, and most maps, including some Turkish ones, have shown the Imia/Kardak rocks on the Greek side of the accepted maritime boundary. A Turkish-Italian document from 1932 specifically lists Kardak as belonging at the time to the Italians, which means sovereignty would have transferred from Italy to Greece after World War II under terms of the 1947 Treaty of Paris.

The Turkish government, however, asserted that this Italo-Turkish protocol had never entered into force and that the rocks themselves had been "registered" by the onshore Turkish province of Mugla. Insider talk around Ankara at the time said top officials in the Turkish Foreign Ministry and the navy had fostered this legalistic case over the objections of many on their own staffs, and Prime Minister Çiller adopted the aggressive stance for her own political reasons. Leaked information about a cable from the Turkish ambassador in Rome, upholding the 1932 document, gave credibility to the notion that political expediency had carried the day.

In the period that followed, the Turkish government did not just refuse to concede on Imia/Kardak but also insisted there are "gray zones" in the Aegean and numerous small islets or rocks (Prime Minister Çiller said, "approximately 1,000") where sovereignty is unclear despite Greek claims. Ankara did not provide specifics, but neither did it abandon the position, which garnered broad public credence in Turkey.

This aftermath steeled Greek public opinion enormously. The Turkish government was seen to have embarked on a new and more aggressive course, threatening to redraw boundaries throughout the Aegean at Greece's expense—with the use of force if Ankara thought it could succeed in doing so. In Greek eyes, Turkish designs on Greek territory had been confirmed beyond a shadow of doubt.

1997–98: THE S-300 IN CYPRUS.

In January 1997, the Cypriot government revealed it had contracted with Russia to purchase S-300 missiles, an anti-aircraft system similar to the American Patriot missile of Gulf War fame. Cypriot officials cited self-defense—protection against Turkish warplanes, which can use bases on the mainland to strike anywhere on Cyprus on short notice. A small airbase also was established near Paphos in western Cyprus to take Greek fighter planes to operate with the missiles.

The Turks reacted vigorously. They denounced the missile buy as unwarranted escalation, denied there was any threat from Turkish planes, and described the S-300 as jeopardizing not only Turkish Cypriots but the security of Turkey itself. Ankara said it would "not tolerate" deployment, and the general staff was directed to take "additional military measures." The warning of a Turkish surgical strike was unmistakable. Washington decried both the deployment and the threat of military action in response. Most European governments took a similar stance.

President Clerides postponed implementation twice in 1998 and in December of that year announced a decision taken in consultation with Athens to cancel the deployment outright—the missiles were instead to be sent to Crete. The Clerides government, which backed down despite strong domestic calls to stay the course, cited intense pressure from the United States and Europeans and possible adverse effects on Cyprus's application for EU membership. Although statements from Athens were carefully phrased to maintain the credibility of the "joint defense doctrine," the Greeks had come around to opposing deployment presumably because it would have been nearly impossible to defend effectively against Turkish military action.

The pervasive politico-military rivalry between Greek and Turkish security establishments also lay at the heart of the Öcalan affair, which in early 1999 pushed bilateral relations near to the breaking point.

"THE ENEMY OF MY ENEMY . . ."

For years almost all Greeks, in and out of government, have been openly sympathetic to the cause of Kurdish insurgents in Turkey. A Greek parliamentarian had photo ops with PKK leader Abdullah Öcalan, lesser PKK figures circulate freely in and through Greece, Kurds distribute PKK propaganda pamphlets at the main intersections in Athens, and a large refugee camp not far from Athens has been a gathering place for Kurds. The Greek government defends its nonmilitary assistance to Kurds as stemming from its human rights concerns, on par with a host of other Europeans, in particular the Dutch.

Most Turks, especially those in the security forces, have been convinced that the Greek government (along with others, notably Syria) gave military training and supplies to the PKK, as part of its effort to offset Turkey's military superiority. Ankara often accused Athens, although before 1999 the evidence was circumstantial or relied on potentially suspect defectors. Athens regularly denied the charge.

In February 1999, Öcalan was captured by a Turkish commando group upon his leaving Greek embassy premises in Nairobi, Kenya. Turks were outraged to learn not only that Turkey's "public enemy no. 1" had spent a few days secretly in Greece with the Greek government's knowledge but also that Greek officials had clandestinely spirited him out of Athens, smuggled him into Kenya with a Cypriot passport, and given him sanctuary in the Greek embassy in Nairobi. Moreover, under Turkish interrogation, Öcalan asserted that PKK forces had received significant aid from Greece.

The Öcalan episode handed Turks a "smoking gun." Official denials became less plausible, although many moderate Greeks ascribed the incident to "cowboys" and "superpatriots" acting outside governmental channels. Whether or not the Greek government had earlier been pulling strings behind the scenes, the plotting by Greek ministers to help Öcalan escape Turkey's clutches amounted to a de facto embrace of the PKK.

Prime Minister Simitis got little credit from the Turks when Öcalan complained that the Simitis government did not give him the support he expected. And in fact the capture was made possible when the Greek government forced Öcalan to leave the embassy. No matter—for Turks, there was no longer any doubt about Greek intentions, official or otherwise.

Several observations on this Greek-Turkish strategic rivalry seem in order:

♦ When threatened by conflict, the Greek and Turkish governments have been unable or unwilling to deal directly with each other. It has fallen to Americans or Europeans to undertake critical mediation.

♦ Turkish and Greek public opinion, especially when egged on by extremist media, has supported nationalistic actions in a crisis, even if the consequence could be war.

♦ Nonetheless, when the chips were down, leaders in Ankara, Athens, and Nicosia decided in favor of peaceful resolution, recognizing that another bilateral war is not in either side's national interest.

♦ In the final analysis, however, a peaceful outcome to an incident involving military confrontation is not ensured. Miscalculations could result in escalation.

♦ The bilateral military competition has taken on a life of its own, with vested interests in large defense budgets and politically driven threat perceptions.

♦ Governmental defense policies have reinforced negative stereotypes and impeded consideration of alternative approaches.

It has been a bleak picture but not totally unrelieved. Greeks and Turks have always felt a measure of discomfort with traditional policies and the unpromising future they portend. This in turn has helped open occasional windows of opportunity for change.

THE POLITICS OF BILATERAL DÉTENTE—
THE RISE AND FALL OF THE "SPIRIT OF DAVOS"

In the months after a perilous brush with war over Aegean oil-drilling rights in March 1987, prime ministers Turgut Özal and Andreas Papandreou weighed the need for a more stable Greek-Turkish relationship. In early 1988, the two met at a World Economic Forum gathering in Davos, Switzerland, and set a détente process in motion, dubbed the "spirit of Davos." After a good start, it faltered and eventually expired in the mid-1990s.

The fathers of today's reconciliation bid—the foreign ministers, İsmail Cem and George Papandreou (son of Andreas)—have not sought to draw parallels with Davos, but there are many similarities. The obstacles in the path of the current effort are evident from a look at the earlier endeavor and the sequence of events that brought about its demise.

The 1988 Özal-Papandreou undertakings concentrated initially on bilateral issues, despite domestic criticism of Papandreou for giving short shrift to Cyprus. The major concrete manifestations included a bilateral commission of leading businessmen to promote commerce and agreements to reduce tensions between military forces. A number of positive spin-offs followed in the private sector.

Before long, however, national politics slowed the pace. In April 1990 elections, Constantine Mitsotakis replaced Papandreou as prime minister. Özal moved from prime minister to president in 1989 as his political position in Turkey started to erode. When, in consultation with President Bush after the Gulf War, Özal put forth an imaginative proposal for a four-way meeting with representatives of Greece, Turkey, and the two communities on Cyprus, the new Turkish prime minister, Mesut Yilmaz, declined to proceed. On the Greek side, Mitsotakis had agreed to participate but also wanted the UN Security Council to take part. Since the Americans nixed this, the no from Yilmaz saved Mitsotakis from a difficult spot.

In a joint effort to recover momentum, Mitsotakis and Suleiman Demirel met in January 1992, not long after the latter had ascended (again) to the Turkish prime ministership. Their foreign ministers, Hikmet Cetin and Michael Papaconstantinou, set up crisis management hot lines, drafted agreements on economic cooperation, and promoted exchanges. Mitsotakis staved off domestic pressure for linkages to Cyprus, helped by the parallel quickening of UN talks on Cyprus through 1992 and the evolution of the set of ideas discussed earlier.

THE DEMISE OF DAVOS

Then a cycle of negation and reversal set in. By March 1993, the UN's set of ideas had been rejected by both sides. In October of the same year Andreas Papandreou returned to power in Greece in a more negative mood toward Turkey. Although he renewed contacts with Ankara, he also joined with President Clerides in November to announce the new joint defense doctrine, which launched closer military cooperation directed specifically against Turkey.

By 1994, the spirit of Davos had been relegated to the back burner. Governments weakened by internal divisions were unable to sustain détente. The bilateral military CBMs fell into disuse. The UN was scrambling to keep bicommunal talks afloat. In 1995 there was a spate of harsh rhetoric about Aegean rights, and in June the Turkish parliament noisily authorized the government to take military action if need be to prevent extension of Greek territorial waters. Then came the Imia/Kardak incident at the beginning of 1996.

With the atmosphere still charged from Imia/Kardak, in March 1996 the new Turkish prime minister, Mesut Yilmaz, announced an "Aegean peace plan," calling for comprehensive talks without preconditions and for agreements on bilateral cooperation and military CBMs. The key new element was an explicit expression of willingness to consider other mechanisms, that is, mediation or arbitration by a third party such as the ICJ to resolve disputes if solutions could not be reached through bilateral negotiation.

A month later, on a visit to Washington, Prime Minister Simitis, who had replaced Andreas Papandreou only a few days before the Imia/Kardak crisis, took the occasion to put forth what he called a "step-by-step" approach to improve Greek-Turkish bilateral relations. He proposed referring the Imia/Kardak and continental shelf issues to the ICJ and resuming a bilateral dialogue on a number of specific outstanding issues. The "step-by-step" phraseology was new and with some mutual give could have been a bridge to the Turkish position.

But the two prime minsters were talking past each other. Athens declined to make a serious test of the Yilmaz initiative, and Ankara dismissed the Simitis formulations. Insecure at home, the two leaders could not get the ball rolling the way their predecessors had at Davos.

Western Prodding and the Luxembourg "Euroshock" for Turkey

American and European diplomats attempted to resuscitate dialogue and confidence-building measures, including revival of the Davos military CBMs and new conflict avoidance measures such as "no-fly" zones over Cyprus. The Dutch presidency of the EU persuaded Ankara and Athens to appoint a "wise men" panel of two members each to identify specific topics for bilateral talks. The project lapsed when Turks demanded a comprehensive agenda, and Greeks insisted that subjects be severely circumscribed.

Ambassador Holbrooke, taking up the cudgels in June 1997 as U.S. special presidential envoy for Cyprus, shifted the Western diplomatic machine into high gear to coax Cyprus negotiations from their low points of 1996. Leaders of the two Cypriot sides were induced to participate in talks under the UN secretary-general's aegis in Troutbeck, New York, in July, and a month later they met a second time in Switzerland. The United States then brokered a meeting on security issues in September 1997 and a sit-down with Holbrooke in November. The flurry of meetings produced no tangible results.

On the margins of a July NATO meeting in Madrid, Americans nudged Prime Minister Simitis and President Demirel into agreement on an eight-point declaration styled "a convergence of views on a basis for promoting better relations." Ballyhooed as a serious new beginning, the document did include potentially significant commitments, in effect trading off Greek agreement to refrain from unilateral acts (such as extension of territorial waters) for Turkish agreement to refrain from use of force or threat of force (as happened in the Imia/Kardak incident). There was, however, no follow-on mechanism; neither side seemed to take the document as a basis for action, and the "spirit of Madrid" began almost at once to evaporate.

Undaunted, U.S. diplomats strove to regenerate momentum with a package deal to be concluded on the sidelines of the UN General Assembly sessions in September 1997. The Americans proposed that Turkey agree to take Imia/Kardak to the ICJ in return for Greek willingness to unblock EU moneys promised to Turkey. The Greeks were said to have agreed and the Turks to have declined at the last minute. In apparent frustration, blunt-talking Foreign Minister Theodoros Pangalos made outrageously denigrating references to Turks in a newspaper interview, and relations ebbed further.

EU-Turkish relations also worsened markedly through 1997. A much tougher EU approach to Turkish membership emerged, encouraged by Greece but stemming primarily from the German government's efforts to exploit anti-immigrant feelings back home in anticipation of national elections. On Cyprus, Brussels pressed ahead with the idea that promoting the island's accession could usefully pressure the two communities toward reunification. A dubious proposition at best—one analyst observed, "the idea that the carrot of EU membership would lead [Turkish Cypriots] to give up the protection of mainland Turkey and live again as a vulnerable minority on the island was always either naive or disingenuous."[6]

Matters came to a head in December 1997 in Luxembourg, when the European Council approved not only Cyprus but also ten Central and East European countries for membership negotiations, and in the same breath left Turkey conspicuously absent from the candidate list. Relegation to the back of the bus was a shocking affront for Ankara, notwithstanding the Council's explicit confirmation of Turkey's eligibility in principle and avowals of a positive long-term strategy to build a better relationship with Turkey. One especially offensive aspect for Turks was the linkage of Turkish membership prospects to progress on Cyprus.

Ankara retaliated selectively. It vowed to continue economic cooperation but promptly suspended all political dialogue and joined with the Turkish Cypriots to counterattack on the issue of Cyprus as described above by suspending UN negotiations and later by abandoning the bizonal, bicommunal approach in favor of separation and confederation.

There was little Washington could do in the short run. After a last-ditch visit to Nicosia in May of 1998 and inconclusive private sector meetings with all four parties represented, Holbrooke gave up on Cyprus for the time being. The S-300 contretemps kept Greek-Turkish tensions high through the second half of 1998 and, even though resolved in December, produced recriminations all around. The Öcalan revelations in early 1999 marked rock bottom.

A postmortem look at the rise and fall of détente through the 1990s helps to understand better the dynamics of détente in 2000:

◆   The scare of March 1987 facilitated the Özal-Papandreou peace initiative. Once an immediate crisis passes, Turks and Greeks alike prefer to see their leaders talking about talking rather than talking about fighting.

◆   The general benefits of détente so often extolled by foreign pundits
    do not carry comparable weight with Greeks or Turks. Economic
    gains from trade, tourism, investment, and cooperation on regional
    development, as well as defense budget savings, regional envi-
    ronmental improvements, and cultural exchange, are all "good
    things" and breathed life for a time into the spirit of Davos but
    could not keep it animated over the long haul.

◆   However the parties start, sooner or later Cyprus has to be taken
    up; it can be put off only as long as there are other perceptible
    gains for the Greek side.

◆   Western promotion of talks has little lasting impact in the face of
    domestic divisions. And jump starts without a good substantive
    foundation not only create a false appearance of progress but can
    aggravate ill will when they falter.

◆   Relations with the EU have become an ever more critical deter-
    minant, especially for Turkey.

Most of these considerations are relevant to any assessment of
prospects for the improvement of Greek-Turkish relations that got
under way as the dust from Öcalan's arrest began to settle. External factors, however, have given the latest détente a character quite different
from the spirit of Davos and the stillborn ventures of 1996.

INTO THE NEXT CENTURY—
FRESH STARTS AND EARTHQUAKES

The new millennium of Greek-Turkish relations began early—in mid-
1999. In the wake of the Öcalan affair, Mr. Ecevit won an impressive
election victory and Mr. Simitis fired outspoken Foreign Minister
Pangalos, replacing him with the lower-key George Papandreou. In
June, the Eureopean Council in Cologne revealed a marked positive
shift toward Turkey. Germany's chancellor, Gerhard Schroeder,
reversed the negativism of the predecessor he had defeated in elections, while the British and French also pressed hard for a more constructive tack. No substantive decisions were taken in Cologne, but

the signals were clear that the next summit in Helsinki would give Turkey a new deal.

The winds of change in the EU and the strengthening of governments in Athens and Ankara created new possibilities. Foreign ministers Cem and Papandreou met in New York at the end of June and announced a process of bilateral talks. Both sides gave a little to get to the table. Both also took pains to keep expectations low but expressed determination to carry through in a sincere and serious way. Cyprus and core Aegean issues were not to be taken up until . . . well, later.

Papandreou gave a surprising fillip to the turn of events soon thereafter when he supported the appeal of Greece's three Muslim parliamentarians that Greek citizens with non-Greek ethnic backgrounds be allowed to identify themselves by ethnicity, for example, as Turks or Macedonians. (Greece holds to the 1923 Treaty of Lausanne provisions that recognize only religious, not ethnic, minorities.) Papandreou's public comment favoring individual rights drew fewer denunciations at home than most would have expected, while one Turkish paper headlined, "Bravo, George!" His politically courageous stand helped open up public debate.

On August 17, a dreadful earthquake struck Turkey, killing more than seventeen thousand people. Conventional assumptions about Greek-Turkish relations were upended when the Greek people poured out assistance and compassion in response to the disaster. Turks expressed appreciation with exceptional warmth. It seemed as if the two peoples suddenly began communicating through popular empathy, without need for governments or media.

The atmosphere of Greek-Turkish relations was transformed overnight. The unselfish public reaction in both countries was widely interpreted as a message from ordinary people—that the governments should stop denouncing each other and find ways to live together as neighbors. As if to reinforce the point, three weeks later an earthquake struck Athens, less severe but devastating nonetheless, with about 150 people killed. Turks immediately responded with rescue teams and much goodwill.

The impact on substantive politics was quick. EU preparations were under way for its December 1999 European Council summit in Helsinki, and Turkey was high on the agenda. The quake shifted Brussels debate from *whether* the Turkish candidacy would be elevated to *how* this should be done, from *whether* to loosen the purse strings for Turkey to *which* channel should be used for generous fund transfers.

The Helsinki summit proved the critical upturn to offset the 1997 Luxembourg downturn. Despite ambiguities in the Presidency Conclusions (the official decision document discussed later in this chapter), Ankara was pleased with the results, and the budding détente with Athens received a booster shot in both arms. The Greek government openly backed Turkish EU membership in principle, although emphasizing particular conditions favorable to Greek objectives.

Ministers Cem and Papandreou moved to speed up cooperation. Each traveled to the other's capital; Papandreou's official visit to Ankara in January was the first by a Greek foreign minister since 1962. The two concluded cooperative agreements on such topics as promoting investment, environment, combating organized crime and terrorism, and tourism. Agricultural ministers signed their own agreement; military units participated together in NATO maneuvers for the first time since 1974; train schedules have been expanded; local officials visited each other; businessmen connected; cultural events were programmed; journalists arranged exchanges—even Greek-Americans and Turkish-Americans joined in symbolic cheering. All in all, an extraordinary turnaround given the parlous state of relations less than a year earlier.

The détente process is addressed to the fundamental need for building trust and creating positive incentives. The formal agreements and the governments' encouragement should enable a significant expansion of beneficial business, exchange, and understanding. But rhetoric is not always followed by action. The Davos experience heightens concerns that these activities will not reach critical mass in time, and that there has to be some early gesture on Cyprus or the Aegean to sustain overall progress.

Everyone agrees that the problem of crossing the divide to take up the substance of the core disputes will be a difficult crunch point. In the initial rounds, the road forked as the Turks advanced suggestions made previously by the United States for military CBMs and a mixed diplomatic-military commission, while the Greeks dusted off the earlier EU-sponsored "wise men" forum.

The path ahead to a Cyprus settlement is still the most problematic. The Turks initially showed no inclination to give on confederation, and Denktash continued to insist on equal status before any face-to-face meetings with Clerides. The UN proximity talks (meaning the two Cypriot leaders do not meet directly but deal through a UN intermediary) produced little of substance in the first two rounds. In the third UN round, scheduled to begin July 5 in Geneva, the pressures will mount rapidly for some meaningful step.

What Is Really Different?

Three major factors stand out from the extraordinary events of 1999: the earthquakes, the unanticipated skill and tenacity of the two governments, and the momentous impact of the Helsinki EU turnabout. The Öcalan affair was an important catalyst but, one hopes, more a function of the past and less a determinant of the future.

The 1999 earthquakes did not, of course, change substance, but the positive effect on atmospherics and public attitudes appears set to last for some time. The public's empathy undermined the appeal of extremist stereotyping and buttressed the political viability of the détente process. The boost, however, could fade rapidly if events conspire to channel popular opinion into the notion that the people "over there" are good and it is the government that is bad. (This is a view of America not unknown in Turkey—and widely held in Greece, where it was newly reinforced by U.S. bombing of Serbs in NATO's Kosovo campaign.)

Although pundits in both Greece and Turkey ascribed the 1999 opening in varying degrees to the "pressure" of Western friends, the lion's share of credit has to go to the prime and foreign ministers of the two governments. On the Greek side, it is probably fair to say that Mr. Simitis from the beginning of his term in 1996 sought to improve relations with Turkey and astutely managed events to take advantage of the opportunity arising after Öcalan. Mr. Ecevit, a veteran hawk on Greece, falls perhaps more in the mold of "Nixon to China," which, however, is not to take anything away from the boldness of the stance he assumed when his public was still highly inflamed by the Öcalan revelations. Ministers Cem and Papandreou appear to have the good chemistry that facilitates meaningful communication even when agreement is not possible.

But it is the EU that may well hold the ultimate key to success. Its economic resources and political import could bring changes of enormous magnitude. It is a much more effective carrot than stick for Turkey—the prospect of EU membership has the substantive weight that can tip the scales of Turkish calculations. Greece also is vulnerable to EU pressure: it simply cannot afford to lose majority EU backing in its contests with Turkey.

The future of relations between the EU and Turkey is far from predetermined. A great deal hinges on what happens with the Cyprus and the Aegean disputes—both were given new, if somewhat ambiguous, dimensions at Helsinki. The EU's Presidency Conclusions underlined that "a political settlement will facilitate the accession of Cyprus" but added in the same breath that it was not a precondition. This formulation and its acceptance by Ankara clearly angered Denktash, who had hoped for direct linkage, in line with his position that accession is unacceptable (and illegal) unless Turkish Cypriots agree to the terms for Cyprus and Turkey becomes an EU member. Ankara went out of its way to assuage him.

The Helsinki conclusions did not name the Aegean, but it was clearly there between the lines of language calling on candidates (that is, Turkey) to resolve "border disputes and other related issues" and, failing to achieve this within a reasonable time, "to bring the dispute [to the ICJ]." The European Council stated it will review the situation at the latest by the end of 2004, "in particular concerning the repercussions on the accession process and in order to promote their settlement through the ICJ." The pressure on Turkey to accept ICJ recourse is unmistakable, although the artful drafting reserves considerable EU flexibility.

No one expects smooth sailing ahead for Turkey on EU seas. Human rights and economic concerns may have been muted by the earthquake but have not gone away, and much depends on change in Turkey itself. Elections in big member states could once again tip the balance in EU councils. And the time bomb of Cyprus accession continues to tick.

Also, the Greeks have retained their options in EU councils, notwithstanding their more forthcoming position on Turkish membership. Greece can still impose linkages on future funding for Turkey and work for explicit candidate milestones that Turkey must pass. These kinds of bureaucratic maneuvers could once again come to the fore, with sharply adverse consequences for bilateral cooperation.

The most likely hurdles ahead for Greek-Turkish détente are those on domestic fronts, especially on the Greek side. As early as mid-January there were signals from traditional ethno-nationalist factions in Greece and Greek Cyprus that they may be lying low for now but could yet awaken the reactions that ultimately sank the spirit of Davos. The Cypriot speaker of the house, hawkish former president Spyros Kyprianou, for example, angrily accused Clerides and Simitis of selling out Cyprus in the run-up to Helsinki by not insisting on linkage to Turkish candidacy decisions. In Athens, hard-liners within Simitis's PASOK party, including former foreign minister Pangalos, criticized the government for giving away something for nothing in the January exchange of ministerial visits. In any case, Simitis won a narrow victory in national elections on April 9, 2000, and thereby gained more time than Andreas Papandreou had after Davos to pursue his détente policies.

Prime Minister Ecevit was not under the gun of early elections, but he will not necessarily have an easy time orchestrating the détente issues at home or in Turkish Cyprus. Mr. Denktash, who won re-election in 2000 after a surprisingly tough fight in the first round, has been an effective campaigner for his cause in mainland Turkey and could demand more from the Greeks than Ankara would be able to deliver. Finally, an unexpected incident or misunderstanding could upset applecarts in either country, although a positive climate makes crisis management easier for governments and lowers odds that an episode will spin out of control.

TAKING STOCK

A State Department desk officer drafting the introduction to a Washington policy review might have summed up the situation in the spring of 2000 as follows:

- The détente process begun in mid-1999 is reasonably well grounded, thanks to the EU, the leadership of both countries, and the earthquakes.

- Continuation of the process will depend in the next phase on factors largely outside the reach of U.S. influence, namely, Greek and Turkish domestic politics and the evolution of EU-Turkish relations.

- The EU has great potential to stimulate more positive change, but it must develop the Helsinki decisions into a clearer vision of its relationship with Turkey and resolve the impasse on Cyprus membership. Turkey must accelerate its social and political modernization.

- Greeks and Turks will have difficulty moving on to the minefields of Aegean and Cyprus issues, given the historical resentments, opportunism, and fractiousness that figure so large on their domestic political stages. American leadership could be crucial.

CONCLUSIONS: WHAT DOES IT ALL MEAN FOR THE UNITED STATES?

A U.S. presidential visit to Athens and Ankara is almost by definition a seminal event. President Clinton's November 1999 journey presented a rare opportunity to exert U.S. influence, and the White House let it be known that Cyprus and Greek-Turkish reconciliation were high on his agenda. By the end of the day, however, neither stop yielded much of import in Greek-Turkish affairs.

On the eve of his arrival in Turkey, Mr. Clinton was able to claim credit for getting Denktash to back down and participate in proximity talks at the UN. This was a positive achievement but, as a practical matter, would have happened in any case. The UN negotiations were scheduled to start in New York just before the EU summit in Helsinki—the Turks could not afford to appear unreasonably intransigent in those circumstances.

In Athens anti-Clinton demonstrations forced curtailment of his itinerary and dominated media coverage. It was not a good environment for U.S. efforts to influence Greek thinking on Cyprus or Turkey. The president did give a slight new spin to U.S. policy in his expression of support for recourse to the ICJ on Aegean disputes, but this was later glossed over when the Turks related it to their own position, which does not rule out such mediation *after* bilateral talks.

In general, the Clinton administration's record on relations with Greece and Turkey deserves high marks. U.S. progress with Turkey and Turkey's progress with the EU materially advanced America's primary security interests in the region. Through some long, dark periods, the United States played the principal role in ensuring that conflict would be avoided, in particular when Imia/Kardak nearly spun out of control. And a quiet effort led by the United States succeeded after years of patient work in reestablishing NATO command and control mechanisms suspended since 1974.

U.S. relations with Greece are in fact quite good, in particular at the level of governments. On the ground, Greece has been an important cog in NATO Balkan operations and remains a key U.S. partner for regional development. The leftist-led protests against the president during his visit were more bark than bite.

PROMETHEUS BOUND

When one judges the administration in terms of its self-proclaimed priority task to advance Greek-Turkish reconciliation, however, the grades are not so high. Washington has put itself forth as the premier honest broker, it has used special envoys as its primary weapons, and it has focused principally on kick-starting negotiations. This high-visibility activism has mollified Congress at home but has had little lasting positive effect in the field.

Throwing emissaries at the problems has not achieved a great deal. Although the addition of a statesman with high rank and access is generally a plus for any negotiation, more than brains, charm, and connections are required to move Greeks and Turks who are supremely confident of their own rectitude and bargaining abilities. The Clinton administration tried unsuccessfully to demonstrate the contrary in 1994 by layering a new special presidential emissary on top of the existing special Cyprus coordinator, and then in 1997 by giving the post to Ambassador Holbrooke, fresh from his Dayton success. With nothing new to put on the table, however, the stepped-up U.S. diplomatic hustle over the past few years was mostly running in place.

The relative ineffectiveness of the world's only superpower in this specific peacemaking enterprise stems in large measure from the U.S. political considerations discussed by Ambassador Abramowitz in Chapter Six and noted at the beginning of this chapter. Greeks know the administration is bound to lean toward Turkey because of American strategic interests. Turks know Congress in a crunch is bound to support Greece because of Greek-American political influence.

Disconnects with the EU also have undermined the U.S. position. Washington and Brussels consult constantly, but their perspectives on Turkey have often differed. The EU actions on Turkish and Cypriot membership issues from 1995 to 1998 turned U.S. presidential envoys into paper tigers and vitiated the UN negotiating process.

Lastly, the administration's domestic political need to present itself as a global leader, as well as to stave off Congress, has led it to focus energies on visible, short-term gains—the kick-start tactics mentioned earlier. This at times has been counterproductive, as in the confusion over the Cyprus no-fly zone and the acrimonious September 1997 contretemps in New York.

None of this is to say the United States should hold back or that Washington's presence is unwanted. A strong American hand may be more important for Turkey, especially while still on the crest of the friendship mirrored by the president's visit, but Greece as well sees American approval as a sine qua non if any serious agreement is to be put in place and endure.

PLAY IT AGAIN, UNCLE SAM!

In the circumstances of early 2000, the primary U.S. objective seemed self-evident: to keep the Cem-Papandreou process going. Finding the most effective U.S. role is not a trivial problem. Pushing too hard or tilting in the wrong direction at the wrong time could be harmful.

Realistically speaking, the United States cannot be the driving force it has been, for example, in the Middle East peace process. Administrations are unlikely either to escape domestic political constraints or come up with major financial contributions to encourage settlements. If things go badly, the White House could find itself hard-pressed to minimize potential damage from self-serving congressional interventions such as the July 1999 House rider, passed unanimously, that unabashedly embraced the Greek position on Aegean maritime boundaries.

One place where Washington can hazard a bolder role is on defense and security issues. In military matters and in NATO councils, the United States is the unchallenged number one. It can and should take the lead to address those parts of the core problems that involve international security by taking measures such as these:

◆ Propounding a transition regime for Cyprus that for a specified period would protect the security of all citizens against internal disorder or outside attack and permit the drawdown of all or most foreign troops.

◆ Devising a way, preferably with NATO involvement, to unambiguously fix the existing maritime borders in the Aegean, including the question of sovereignty over rocks or islets, and achieve international acceptance thereof.

♦ Suggesting arrangements for territorial seas in the Aegean that would come to grips with the issue of twelve-mile limits. Until this matter is resolved by either doing something or explicitly agreeing to do nothing, the Aegean will not be secure.

♦ Promoting a tangible easing of the Greek-Turkish military rivalry.

But the touchstone of Greek-Turkish reconciliation remains Cyprus. There is still much to be said for trying again to put the island back together under the once-agreed bicommunal, bizonal federation formula. The 1992 UN set of ideas, as argued earlier, is the closest approximation to this vision of the future and is a reasonable place to start over. Regrettably, both sides are off on other tracks as of early 2000, and shoehorning them into these particular negotiating chairs against their will has not worked in the past.

To stand still on Cyprus, however, is to go backward. At this point it makes most sense to construct a more civilized form of coexistence that would give wider opportunities to both sides of the island and buy time to foster reconciliation between the two communities, but would not prejudice the details of any ultimate settlement. The Greeks would have to give up their effort to isolate the Turkish Cypriots, and the Turkish Cypriots would have to forgo their attempt to become a recognized state with coequal status to the republic. These are major concessions (although not necessarily irreversible). The alternative of continuing the present standoff will sabotage Greek-Turkish détente and enshrine a division of sterile cold war character—profitless for both sides, fraught with unpredictable forks in the road, and offering only the remotest possibility of victory for either community.

The United States, working with the EU, should advance a plan for a transitional regime in Cyprus covering the following elements:

♦ Resumption of direct negotiations under UN aegis on (a) as comprehensive an agenda as can be agreed without at this time prejudicing the goal expressed in Security Council resolutions of reunifying Cyprus into a single, pluralistic democracy subject to the final agreement of both sides, and (b) implementation of CBM packages already on the UN table, including at a minimum return of Varosha and opening of the Nicosia airport

♦   Phasing out the embargo against Turkish Cyprus and facilitating the movement of goods and people between the two zones using documentation (for example, UN paperwork) that would not imply international recognition of any permanent sovereignty separate from the Republic of Cyprus

♦   Establishment of one or more bilateral commissions on Cyprus to promote cooperation on matters such as bilateral commerce and investment; the environment, energy, and transport networks; and cultural and educational exchange

♦   Strengthening the UN Force in Cyprus (UNFICYP), perhaps with the addition of NATO and EU components to monitor better security along the dividing line and permit reduction of the Turkish military force

♦   Establishment of a neutral commission to study issues of property return and compensation, drawing on such precedents as the U.S. handling of Americans' claims against the former East Germany, to minimize individual proceedings (suspending the European Court examination of property cases pending a comprehensive solution)

♦   If necessary to assure continued progress, organizing a strengthened commission to resolve the remaining cases of persons missing since 1974, with the engagement of the American Defense Department offices working on MIA cases from Vietnam and prior wars

U.S. diplomacy until now has been unable or unwilling to explore alternatives to the entrenched UN formulations for Cyprus, even as it has watched the two communities march inexorably down their two widely diverging courses since 1992. Keeping Greek-Turkish détente on track when it approaches the Cyprus crossroads will require hard choices, compromise, and creativity. Washington should prepare itself for new departures.

CHAPTER EIGHT

U.S. POLICY TOWARD TURKEY
PROGRESS AND PROBLEMS

ALAN MAKOVSKY

"Full support from America!" the celebratory headline screamed in inch-high, boldface Turkish on the front page of *Sabah,* Turkey's largest-circulation newspaper of the day. Now, almost a decade later, the words are unremarkable. For nearly ten years, the United States seemingly has been giving Turkey "full support" on numerous issues deemed crucial by Turkish authorities, whether membership in the European Union, proposed energy pipelines from the Caspian Sea, support for besieged Bosnians, or, most important, opposition to the separatist Workers Party of Kurdistan, better known by its Kurdish initials PKK.

But on the day it appeared, April 2, 1992, that headline was indeed unusual, and, in retrospect, it can be said to symbolize a turning point and a new era in U.S.-Turkish relations. Although most Turks in early

I would like to thank the Smith-Richardson Foundation of Westport, Connecticut, for generous support to The Washington Institute for Near East Policy that has allowed me to study in depth various aspects of Turkish foreign policy, including U.S.-Turkish relations.

1992 recognized the United States as their preeminent ally and source of arms, surprisingly few saw Washington as a friend. The reasons for skepticism were largely historical, a residue of Turkish resentment over the 1964 "Johnson letter," which warned that NATO might forsake Turkey if it invaded Cyprus, and the 1975–78 congressionally imposed arms embargo, a response to Turkey's 1974 armed intervention in that island nation. Turkish attitudes were reinforced in subsequent years by various U.S. actions, mainly initiated in the U.S. Congress: indexing of Turkish aid to Greek aid, efforts to link Turkish aid to progress on Cyprus, and repeated attempts to memorialize the 1915–16 "Armenian genocide." On all of these issues, Greek-American and Armenian-American lobbies seemed to dominate the debate, convincing Turks that the cards were stacked against them in Washington.

For several years after the embargo—at least until the mid-1980s—the Turkish government used the word *ally* but almost never the word *friend* to describe the United States in its public diplomacy. Meanwhile, the Turkish press rarely showed anything other than skepticism and disapproval regarding Washington's policies toward Turkey and the surrounding region. An informal, only slightly tongue-in-cheek remark made to me in the late 1980s by a Turkish correspondent in the United States illustrated this attitude. "Covering Washington is easy," he said. "The story-line is that America is trying to undermine Turkey. All I have to do is supply the details."

In spring 1992, distrust of the United States seemed, if anything, to have intensified. The previous year Turkey had agreed to let U.S. bombers use Turkish air force bases to attack Iraq during the Gulf War. This decision, made by President Turgut Özal, had gone against the grain of popular feeling, the reflexes of most Turkish foreign- and security-policy decisionmakers, and decades of tradition that dictated that Turkey should not involve itself in Middle Eastern disputes. Moreover, after the war, U.S., British, and French warplanes stationed at Incirlik Air Base in southern Turkey enforced a "no-fly zone" in northern Iraq in order to protect Iraqi Kurds from air assault by Saddam Hussein's forces. Buoyed by the allied intervention, Iraqi Kurds drove Saddam's ground forces out of most of northern Iraq and set up an autonomous administration.

Much of the Turkish public came to see the United States as abetting Kurdish independence in northern Iraq and facilitating PKK use of that region as a staging ground. Some Turks even believed the United States wanted to establish a Kurdish state in southeast Turkey. In January 1992, just two months before the *Sabah* headline, newspapers claimed that a U.S. helicopter ostensibly on a humanitarian food-supply mission in northern Iraq had instead delivered food to a PKK camp on the Turkish side of the border.

With the PKK insurgency acquiring steady force, in March 1992 southeastern Turkey exploded in riots on the politically tinged Kurdish holiday of Nowruz. Caught by surprise, security forces reacted harshly, hundreds of casualties ensued, and international television caught ugly footage of Turkish repression of the riots. West European governments bitterly criticized Turkey. Germany, Turkey's number-two source of arms and aid, suspended arms sales to Turkey in response to apparent Turkish use of armed personnel carriers against the rioters. Virtually alone among Turkey's allies, the United States claimed to see the matter more or less the way Turkey did: as a reasonable and understandable response intended to preserve order and territorial integrity in the face of terrorism.

The *Sabah* headline applauding the U.S. response foreshadowed trends that would characterize much of the rest of the decade in U.S.-Turkish relations: increasing U.S. political support for Turkey's fight against the PKK, in large part as a trade-off for Turkey's acquiescence in U.S. policies toward Iraq; a growing tendency in Washington, uniquely among Turkey's NATO allies, to accommodate Ankara's point of view on many regional issues; and an overall warming of bilateral relations, fostered on Turkey's side by its alienation from Europe.

This chapter reviews the evolution of U.S.-Turkish relations in the post–cold war, post–Gulf War era, following on from the discussion of the period of the Gulf War and its immediate aftermath in Chapter Six. It considers some of the uncertainties facing those relations, discusses potential problem areas and opportunities in bilateral ties, and concludes with reflections on U.S. efforts to influence Turkey's regional and domestic policies.

BILATERAL RELATIONS IN THE 1990S: FROM ANGST TO EXUBERANCE

The end of the cold war robbed Turkey's long, formerly vulnerable borders with the Soviet Union and the Warsaw Pact of most of their strategic importance. Ankara initially feared this development would eliminate Turkey's importance to the United States and the West, leaving it bereft of security assistance and, possibly, security links to the West.

By the latter half of the 1990s, however, those fears had been put to rest. In addition to remaining a key member of NATO and serving as a base for enforcement of the no-fly zone in northern Iraq, Turkey has come to play an important role in numerous U.S. regional initiatives and strategies as

- An ideological counterweight to fundamentalist Iran

- A forceful, antiseparatist advocate of Bosnia and Kosovo and a participant in Balkan peacekeeping

- A pro-Western influence and non-Russian line of communication for Georgia and the Turkic states of the former Soviet Union

- An alternative to Russia and Iran as an outlet for Caspian Sea energy resources

- A buffer against potential Russian aggression toward the Turkish Straits and the Middle East

- A pacesetter in Muslim world normalization with Israel

- A strong supporter of the Israeli-Palestinian peace process that has won the trust of both sides

- A rare example of democracy (albeit flawed) in the Muslim world

An anti-Western or neutral Turkey could not fulfill most of those roles. Indeed, Turkey's very existence as a pro-Western state, interrupting lines of communication for fundamentalists, terrorists, and proliferators of weapons of mass destruction—and limiting Russia's reach into the Middle East—contributes substantially to U.S. interests.

Turkey affects other U.S. interests as well. It is crucial to settlement of the Cyprus dispute and, by definition, resolution of its own disputes with Greece—both of which are fundamental to stability in the eastern Mediterranean and within NATO.

That Turkey is a factor in such a wide array of potential problem areas gives it a higher-profile presence in U.S. policy than it had even during the cold war. In his November 15, 1999, address to the Turkish parliament, President Clinton said unqualifiedly that "in the post–cold war era, our [that is, U.S.-Turkish] partnership has become even more important [than before]."

Current U.S. interest in post–cold war Turkey has not been the product of a steady upward curve. During the first two years of the Clinton administration, Turkey was viewed by many U.S. policymakers as a declining asset. It was valued for hosting Operation Provide Comfort (OPC)—the aforementioned operation to enforce a no-fly zone in northern Iraq—but many at that time assumed the Saddam Hussein regime would soon fall, rendering OPC obsolete. The United States generally demurred on Turkey's security concerns about post-Communist Russia and was unresponsive to Turkey's importuning for a stronger NATO policy on behalf of Bosnia. Initial hopes that Turkey would prove to be an influential force in the Turkic states of the former Soviet Union were disappointed, owing mainly to lack of Turkish resources. Turkey also became an object of frequent U.S. criticism for its Kurdish policies during the early Clinton years.

It was in the mid-1990s that the ramified U.S.-Turkish strategic relationship of today began to evolve. It did so under the influence of American and Turkish responses to changed international circumstances, accompanied by new personalities on the U.S. side. The brutality of Russia's 1994–96 war against Chechnya and the continued prominence of nationalist and Communist voices among Russian politicians sobered U.S. policymakers about the prospects for Russia's smooth, rapid integration into the Western family of nations. Turkey once again loomed large as a buffer against possible Russian expansion toward the Straits or the Middle East and as a pole of pro-Western, non-Russian influence for the Turkic states of the former Soviet Union. Meanwhile, Washington stepped up its involvement in regional affairs, of which the Clinton administration initially had been chary. U.S. support for Bosnia, however belated, more closely aligned Washington's policy with Ankara's and raised American moral stature in Turkey. In 1995, U.S. support for construction of a pipeline from Azerbaijan to Turkey as a western outlet for Caspian Sea oil—one of Ankara's pet projects—further enhanced Washington's standing in Turkish eyes.

Turkey made its own policy adjustments. It softened a bit its hostility to Moscow with Russia's emergence as a major Turkish trading partner. Particularly after Saddam Hussein threatened to invade Kuwait once again in autumn 1994, Ankara came to accept that U.S. efforts to contain Saddam would not soon ease. In parallel, Turkey's increasingly close ties with Israel increased its stock with many U.S. policymakers.

Many of these changes coincided with—and some were partly the fruit of—the tenures of Richard Holbrooke as assistant secretary of state for European affairs and Marc Grossman as U.S. ambassador in Ankara, which began in late 1994. Holbrooke, a highly influential administration official, was a champion of Turkey's strategic importance and of robust U.S.-Turkish relations. Only Richard Perle, a similarly influential assistant secretary of defense during the Reagan administration, had previously exerted such strong influence in favor of U.S. strategic bonds with Turkey. As for Grossman, he was an experienced Turkey hand when he took up the reins in Ankara, having served there over three years as deputy chief of mission (1989–92), including one year as chargé d'affaires. He, too, was known to be an ardent supporter of U.S.-Turkish strategic links.

Holbrooke and Grossman energized U.S. foreign policy on Turkey's behalf. Under their stewardship in 1994–95, the United States embraced the Baku-Ceyhan oil pipeline initiative favored by Turkey, helped engineer Turkey's successful effort to achieve a customs union with the EU, and firmly established a sympathetic view of Turkey's fight against PKK "terrorism" as part of the U.S. policy canon. The notion of the United States as "Turkey's best friend" in the international arena began to take hold in Ankara in this era.[1]

As assistant secretary, Holbrooke consistently referred to Turkey as a "front-line state." Highlighting its importance before a congressional committee in March 1995, Holbrooke asserted that Turkey "stands at the crossroads of almost every issue of importance to the U.S. on the Eurasian continent"—a phrase that subsequently became virtually a battle cry for advocates of strong U.S.-Turkish ties.

But bilateral relations hit choppy waters again in mid-1996, when a coalition government headed by longtime Islamist leader Necmettin Erbakan came to power in Turkey. Erbakan had a history of anti-U.S., anti-Western, anti-Israel, and anti-Semitic rhetoric. In opposition, he had denounced Turkey's membership in NATO and its bid for EU membership. He argued that Turkey should ally itself with the Islamic world and take the lead in forming what he called an "Islamic NATO" and "Islamic common market." He scorned Turkey's traditional Western elite as poseurs, mere "imitators" of a Western tradition not their own.

The United States recognized that Erbakan was no friend but was not sure just what to expect from him and his government. Washington and Erbakan initially made tentative gestures toward one another, but relations never hit a smooth stride. Trips to Iran and Libya early in his term raised U.S. concerns that Erbakan might be just as bad as feared. For the most part, Washington conducted its foreign policy business with the Foreign Ministry and, more openly than at any time since the 1980–83 military government, with the Turkish armed forces. Bilateral relations were not derailed—Turkish generals and diplomats saw to that—but they stagnated, mired in uncertainty. Nonetheless, with Erbakan in office and Turkey caught up in a secularist-Islamist Kulturkampf, it became difficult for Washington to promote bilateral ties or to hold to its traditional view of Turkey as a bastion of secularism and stability.

As the military led an extraordinary campaign to force Erbakan from office, the United States watched the struggle mainly from the sidelines, confining itself to Delphic remarks of support for a "secular, democratic" Turkey[2]—a formulation that left many wondering whether the United States cared more about secularism, which the military claimed to be defending, or democracy, in whose name Erbakan sought to defend his office. In fact, Washington cared mainly about Turkey's pro-Western orientation, but it did not want democratic procedure disregarded either. In Erbakan's waning days, as rumors of an impending coup swept Ankara, Secretary of State Madeleine Albright cautioned that any change of government must be "within a democratic context with no extra-constitutional approach."[3] The U.S. government was relieved when the beleaguered Erbakan resigned and a secularist coalition under Mesut Yilmaz took power. Since Erbakan's departure, U.S.-Turkish relations have become closer than ever, particularly invigorated by U.S. backing for Turkey's ultimately successful bid for EU candidacy. Nevertheless, the Erbakan era left an uncomfortable legacy of questions about the durability of Turkey's traditional pro-Western orientation and about its internal stability, including the role of its military and the nature of its democracy.

Despite its growing strategic importance, Turkey has not been able to erase U.S. concerns about its human rights performance. Human rights abuses have impeded arms sales and undermined goodwill. Also, because of the Kurdish issue and the prominent political and policy roles played by the military, as well as other democratization and human rights problems, few Americans see Turkey as a nation that fully shares their values. In his November 1999 speech to the Turkish parliament, Clinton cautioned, "The future we want to build together begins with Turkish progress in deepening democracy at home."

Few doubt that Turkish progress in human rights would boost bilateral links. Still, Washington's priority is to preserve and build on the strategic partnership that had evolved by the end of the 1990s.

LOOKING TOWARD THE FUTURE: UNCERTAINTIES

The vast improvement in U.S.-Turkish relations since the mid-1990s is rooted mainly in Turkey's role in containing Iraq and in the near-unwavering backing the United States has given Ankara on a trio of issues: the PKK, the EU, and Baku-Ceyhan. As the twentieth century drew to a close, U.S. standing in Ankara was at its highest point in decades as a result of Clinton's November 1999 visit and the long U.S. campaign for EU endorsement of Turkey's membership candidacy, which was finally achieved in December 1999.

By the end of the 1990s, the U.S.-Turkish alliance had successfully completed a transition from a single-issue cold war paradigm to cooperation based on a multitude of issues. If bilateral ties were a cast-iron receptacle during the cold war, in the post–cold war era they have become a basket of many tightly woven strands. Both containers can bear the necessary weight of bilateral ties, but the latter is inherently more vulnerable and prone to fraying.

Notwithstanding the bilateral gains of the 1990s, any number of possible developments could threaten the structure of the post–cold war U.S.-Turkish relationship. For example, the issues through which the United States consistently demonstrated its support for Turkey in the 1990s may soon disappear from the agenda—in at least two cases, for the "right" reasons. With rebel leader Abdullah Öcalan in jail and fighting in abeyance, the PKK is a diminishing threat. Turkey's achievement of EU candidacy ironically may push Turkey closer to Western Europe at Washington's expense. At any rate, the United States will no longer be able to champion EU-Turkish relations as decidedly as it did when the relatively clear-cut issue of candidacy was still outstanding. The next stages in EU-Turkish relations will be more complicated. If the third of the trio of U.S. support issues, the Baku-Ceyhan pipeline project, proves uneconomic or infeasible—in early 2000, its status was uncertain—some Turks might see its demise as a U.S. failure. That might raise questions in Turkey about the value of U.S. support and the need to accommodate Washington's policy concerns. Collapse of the project also might decrease Turkey's strategic importance for Washington.

Second, Turkey—now more powerful, prosperous, and self-confident than ever—may be tempted to behave more independently in its region, implementing policies at odds with U.S. interests. Perhaps foreshadowing this prospect were Turkey's threats against Syria in autumn 1998, which resulted in Öcalan's expulsion from Damascus. Ankara's posture in this instance clearly made Washington uneasy.

Third, Bülent Ecevit—who throughout his long political career promoted a foreign policy focused on "the region" rather than on the United States or Europe—could revert to form. As prime minister, he has been a pleasant surprise to Washington. His strong support for U.S.-Turkish ties may be simply a recognition of Turkish foreign policy realities, but it runs counter to his historical record. Nevertheless, at times he shows flashes of the "old Ecevit." As deputy prime minister in 1998, angered that the United States brokered an Iraqi Kurdish agreement without consulting Ankara, he announced that Turkey was raising its relations with Iraq to ambassadorial level. In 1999, within weeks of President Clinton's well-received speech at the Turkish parliament, Ecevit surprisingly called for an easing of sanctions against Iraq and signed an agreement with Russia strengthening Turkey's commitment to a trans–Black Sea gas pipeline project opposed by Washington. In the Turkish system, it is difficult in any case for a prime minister to change foreign policy on his personal whim. The military and the Foreign Ministry tend to keep him on track, as Erbakan, for example, discovered. Having staked so much on relations with the United States during his prime ministry, it is unlikely Ecevit would now want to undermine them, but the possibility of future misunderstandings cannot be discounted.

There are other plausible developments that might weaken or challenge U.S.-Turkish strategic harmony over time:

◆ Deep deterioration in the quality of Turkish democracy—whether as a result of new restrictions on freedom of speech, a serious crackdown on the Kurds, or a military coup—well might limit the ability of the United States to sustain close security ties and to plead Turkey's case to the Europeans.

◆ A return to power of the Islamists, which would raise internal and bilateral security questions and once again bring sharply into focus doubts about the durability of Turkey's pro-Western alignment.

- Warfare or renewed tensions with Greece or on Cyprus, eventualities all likely to arouse formidable pro-Greek sentiment in Congress and possibly spark calls for restrictions on security ties with Turkey.

- Emergence of a Kurdish state in post-Saddam northern Iraq or a Turkish occupation of northern Iraq following implosion of the Baghdad regime. The former would anger the Turks, who would probably blame the United States. The latter, depending on circumstance, would be likely to upset the United States.

- A decline of U.S. interest in some of the regions surrounding Turkey.

As is the case with the apparent decline of the PKK as a fighting force, even good news can have an aspect problematic for bilateral U.S.-Turkish relations. A change for the better in Turkey's security environment—including the emergence of pro-Western regimes in Baghdad and Tehran or stability in Russia and the Balkans, or some combination of these developments—ironically might decrease Turkey's geostrategic importance to the United States.

Washington cannot easily deter or even much influence most of these scenarios. It should, in fact, encourage the "good news" prospects of Turkish integration with the EU, stability in southeastern Turkey, and stabilization of Turkey's security environment, all of which would serve larger U.S. interests. Probably the best way for deterring, or weathering, any future bilateral strains is to capitalize on current favorable trends to build the strongest possible structure of U.S.-Turkish relations.

PROBLEMS AND RECOMMENDATIONS

U.S.-Turkish bilateral relations are founded on security ties—arms sales, military cooperation, NATO membership—and a common, pro-Western strategic outlook. Beneath this common outlook, however, lurk several areas of U.S.-Turkish divergence. Only rarely conveyed in official statements these days, Turkish dissent from, even resentment of, U.S. policies occasionally emerges from surprising quarters. In 1996, a

Turkish Foreign Ministry official acknowledged that his country does not see eye to eye with the United States on many regional issues because each has its own distinct interests. A more senior colleague said Turkey has no desire to be America's subcontractor on regional issues.[4] More recently, in November 1999, the Turkish military issued a document called "Current Issues," which contained a strong attack on U.S. foreign policy motives.[5] Turkey worries about the security implications of U.S. policies designed to contain and possibly topple Saddam, isolate Iran, preempt a major Turkish-Russian natural gas deal, promote Syrian-Israeli peace, deprive the Turkish Cypriot–declared state of international recognition while backing EU membership for the Greek Cypriot–controlled Republic of Cyprus, and nudge the Turkish system toward adoption of U.S. norms of democratic governance.

The following section reviews nine important areas of U.S.-Turkish strategic relations, focusing mainly on existing or looming policy problems confronting Washington. The areas covered here are Iraq; Iran; Israel; the Middle East peace process; Russia, the Caucasus, Central Asia, and Caspian Sea energy; Europe; Greek-Turkish relations and Cyprus; human rights (including arms sales); and Islam and Islamism. Several—Iraq, Russia, Greek-Turkish relations, human rights, and political Islam—carry the potential to create intense bilateral problems. Thus, the order of presentation is meant to enhance readability and logical flow rather than suggest a hierarchy of importance. A brief set of general policy recommendations follows the nine discussion areas.

This list does not exhaust the U.S.-Turkish bilateral agenda. Rather, it represents an attempt to highlight some of the most important Turkey-related decisions that U.S. policymakers may face during the next five to ten years. Nearly half of these are related to the Middle East, the most unstable and threatening of Turkey's neighboring regions. Not included are vital areas of policy where a firm U.S.-Turkish consensus exists or where U.S. policy is well established and unthreatened by competing or impending policy demands—for example, Turkey's continued membership in NATO or its role in the Balkans. Treatment of the issues focuses on U.S. rather than Turkish perspectives.

Turkey's strategic location dictates that its importance to the United States is often a function of U.S. objectives in Turkey's neighboring regions. For purposes of the discussion here, continuity in U.S. policy goals and priorities regarding Turkey's neighbors will be taken as a constant. Thus, it will be assumed that Washington will continue to give primacy to relations with Western Europe, promote the Middle

East peace process, seek to isolate the Islamic Republic of Iran and contain or overthrow Saddam Hussein, and encourage Russia's integration into the Western family of nations.

Turkey is pivotal to the preservation or attainment of most U.S. regional policy goals, and a productive relationship with Turkey is therefore in the United States' strategic interest. Taken as a whole, the goal of the recommendations in this chapter is to create a stronger Turkey as well as one responsive to U.S. interests and more closely tied politically, economically, and militarily to the West.

IRAQ

No problem of the past decade has created more tension in U.S.-Turkish relations than Iraq, and no problem currently carries more potential for damage to those relations. At the same time, Turkey's domestically controversial support for Operation Northern Watch (ONW), as Operation Provide Comfort (OPC) was renamed in 1996, ironically has been an important binding element in bilateral relations, giving Turkey a crucial role in Washington's high-priority Iraq policy and helping launch the notion that Turkey is a regionally pivotal state.

OPC/ONW is unique in the annals of U.S.-Turkish relations. On no other issue has Turkish support for the United States been both so vital and, from the U.S. perspective, so uncertain. This combination of importance and unpredictability has occasioned an unprecedented U.S. responsiveness to Turkish concerns, particularly regarding the PKK. Washington's defense of Turkish actions in the March 1992 Nowruz riots provided the first glimmer of this phenomenon. U.S. support in the capture of Öcalan revealed it in full light.

Formally, Ankara and Washington agree on the outlines of Iraq policy. Both say that Baghdad should fulfill the terms of relevant UN Security Council resolutions, and both advocate maintenance of Iraq's territorial integrity. But the United States and Turkey differ in their priorities and, in some cases, their objectives regarding Iraq.

Turkey's three major policy goals in Iraq, in order of priority, are prevention of the emergence of a Kurdish state (or a robustly autonomous Kurdish entity), expulsion of the PKK from northern Iraq, and resumption of vigorous trade with Iraq, once one of Turkey's leading export markets.

Most Turkish policymakers have misgivings about Saddam Hussein, but they unequivocally favor any strong Iraqi central government, even one run by Saddam, over the prospect of state disintegration and Kurdish independence that might otherwise ensue. Turkey would like the Iraqi Kurds to negotiate with Saddam to achieve reintegration into Iraq; as long as they are outside Baghdad's control, however, Ankara would like to see their leaders, Massoud Barzani and Jalal Talabani, at peace but not united.

The United States, by contrast, seeks Saddam's collapse, does not want the Iraqi Kurds to negotiate with Saddam, and favors Iraqi Kurdish unity. Indeed, U.S. support for Iraq's territorial integrity more reflects deference to the wishes of its regional friends (primarily Turkey but also Arab states) than intrinsic U.S. interest; the United States certainly does not adhere to that position with Turkey's level of fierceness. Unlike Ankara, Washington would not oppose Kurdish autonomy within Iraq or a federated Iraq with a Kurdish component; in fact, it would probably favor some special status for the Kurds in post-Saddam Iraq.

From Ankara's viewpoint, current U.S. policies (not only U.S. objectives) are at odds with Turkish goals: U.S.-backed UN sanctions on Iraq prevent the resumption of Turkish commerce with a natural trading partner. Meanwhile, in Turkey's view, U.S.-led isolation of Saddam, implementation of a no-fly zone in northern Iraq, efforts to unite the northern Iraqi Kurds, and, more recently, support for the diaspora-based Iraqi opposition promote Kurdish separatism and the breakup of Iraq.

The reason for Turkey's determined opposition to Kurdish statehood in northern Iraq is obvious, though never acknowledged on the record: if Iraqi Kurds break away from Iraq, the separatist bug will further infect Turkey's own troubled Kurdish region across the border. Moreover, Turkish-Kurdish insurgents would have a cross-border haven from which to stage attacks.

Even Turkey's concern about Iraqi sanctions is closely related to its own Kurdish issue. The sanctions regime affects Turkey's overall economy but has its most direct impact on Turkey's Kurdish population in the southeast, contributing to impoverishment and radicalization.

Although the United States and Turkey try to maintain the appearance of unity, each side made a rare public acknowledgment of differences in late 1999. Whereas Turkey's priority is preserving Iraq's territorial integrity, the United States has other (unspecified)

priorities in northern Iraq, Foreign Minister İsmail Cem said in
September. He delicately suggested that U.S.-Turkish differences may
be due to the fact that the United States is a distant country with
global interests while Turkey is Iraq's neighbor.[6] In December, a
Clinton adviser acknowledged that Ankara and Washington "have
some differences of approach [in foreign policy], such as in Iraq."[7]

Bilateral differences regarding the Iraqi opposition would be particularly problematic if the U.S. administration were actively to support
an Iraqi armed insurgency or seek to enlist Turkey in overthrowing
Saddam—remote prospects for now owing to the weakness of the diaspora opposition. Ankara probably also would object to efforts to establish an Iraqi government-in-exile. In resisting such initiatives, however,
Turkey would find itself at odds not only with the administration but
with some of its most visible U.S. supporters, who include leading backers of the Iraqi opposition.

To encourage Turkey to back Baghdad's opponents, the United
States could consider a public pledge that Turkish economic and political interests will be taken into account in post-Saddam reconstruction
of Iraq and its internal political order, as well as public and private
assurances that the United States will actively oppose Iraqi Kurdish
independence and the breakup of Iraq. Washington also would have
to extract a similar pledge from the Iraqi opposition and its constituent
elements, including the Kurds. It is doubtful, however, that such a
package would convince the Turks, who could have no guarantee that
the United States and its friends would maintain control over the
process of regime change once it begins. Unless the opposition's success appears a certainty, Turkey will continue to shun any involvement with it.

Most U.S.-Turkish differences over Iraq are not easily bridged, but
they also need not be squarely faced until Saddam falls. Even should
the United States pursue a policy of active support for an antiregime
insurgency in Iraq, planned attacks could be focused on southern Iraq
(provided a neighboring state such as Kuwait or Saudi Arabia agrees)
rather than on the north and therefore would not require Turkish
acquiescence. Thus, for both Ankara and Washington, the status quo
is uncomfortable but manageable.

However, the United States should seek means to ameliorate
Turkish economic losses resulting from Iraqi sanctions. Ankara puts
its losses at $35 billion—perhaps an exaggeration, but it is clear that
Ankara's losses are considerable and that no country has suffered more

from Iraqi sanctions than Turkey. Washington opposes Turkey's bid for an Article 50 exemption from UN sanctions, fearing it would threaten the Iraqi sanctions regime and generally undermine the credibility of sanctions as a tool of UN diplomacy. Still, the United States might consider asking the Security Council to require Iraq to export additional quantities of oil to Turkey so that Baghdad can pay down its considerable prewar debt to the Turks, much as it pays off its Jordanian debt through oil exports.

Given the United States' own large trade volume with Canada and Mexico (which, together, accounted for 28 percent of all U.S. trade in 1998), Washington should appreciate the difficulty incurred when trade is sanctioned for nearly a decade with an economically important neighbor—particularly at a time when the United States also has asked Turkey to limit its energy relations with yet another neighbor, Iran.

IRAN

Much like the United States—perhaps in an even more immediate sense—secular Turkey sees the neighboring Islamic Republic of Iran as hostile and dangerous. Also like the United States, Turkey regards the emergence of President Khatami and his reform movement as a hopeful but not yet meaningful development.

For Turkey, Iran is an ideological rival and threat. Over the years, Turkish officials have several times accused Iran of interfering in Turkey's internal affairs, hosting and supporting the PKK, and training "fundamentalist terrorists" to carry out attacks on Turkish secularists. Turkish-Iranian relations, much like those between the United States and Iran, are likely to remain tense and brittle as long as the mullahs rule in Tehran.

Unlike the United States, however, Turkey is opposed to isolating Iran. Ankara especially wants good economic relations with Iran, which was one of Turkey's leading trading partners in the 1980s. Turkey was displeased by the Iran-Libya Sanctions Act (ILSA), passed by Congress in 1996, calling for sanctions on states or corporate entities that invest more than $20 million in the Iranian energy industry. Indeed, many Turks smoldered at the notion that Turkey once again, as in Iraq, was being asked to bear the economic brunt of what they saw as mainly a U.S. foreign policy problem.

Flowing from these differing outlooks is the only Iran-related irritant in U.S.-Turkish relations: projected Turkish imports of Iranian natural gas. Shortly after ILSA was signed into law, Prime Minister Erbakan visited Iran and signed an agreement to purchase $23 billion worth of Iranian gas through a pipeline that would traverse the Turkish-Iranian border. Although Erbakan was leader of Turkey's pro-Islamist party, it seems likely that, in this instance at least, he acted with the support of the Turkish establishment. U.S. unhappiness with the deal was palpable. Clinton reportedly wrote to President Süleyman Demirel asking that the arrangement not be implemented. Though energy starved, Turkey has indeed delayed implementation and convinced the Iranians to go along for now. Iranian gas shipments were to have begun in January 2000, but, as that date approached, Turkey announced that the pipeline on its side of the border was not yet ready, and Tehran agreed to delay delivery until July 2001.

Despite U.S. disapproval, Ankara has several incentives to go forward with the deal in 2001. First, Turkey badly needs new energy sources. Ankara claims it will need to import 52 billion cubic meters (BCM) of natural gas by 2010, a fivefold increase over its 1998 imports of 10.4 BCM. With such rapidly growing demand in Turkey, it is significant that Iranian gas could become accessible earlier than gas from other contemplated major sources in Russia, Turkmenistan, and Azerbaijan. The Iranians initially are to provide 3 BCM per year and eventually 10 BCM per year. Second, Turkey signed the contract with Iran on a "take-or-pay" basis, meaning that Turkey must pay even if it chooses not to accept the gas.

Third, Turkey considers its arrangement with Iran strictly as importing, not investment, whereas ILSA sanctions are activated only by "investment" in Iran's energy sector. The Turks point out that they will merely link up with an Iranian pipeline on the border, not build or otherwise fund the Iranian portion of the pipeline. (The United States reportedly has reserved judgment on whether the arrangement represents investment or trade.) Finally, under ILSA's terms, the U.S. president has the right to grant a national security waiver of sanctions, and President Clinton already has done so in the case of a French-Russian-Indonesian consortium. That makes it highly unlikely the administration would invoke ILSA sanctions against ally Turkey or its state pipeline company Botaş.

To avoid alienating Washington, Ankara may seek further to stall implementation of the agreement with Iran until U.S. sanctions are lifted (ILSA is scheduled to lapse in August 2001, pending renewal).

Aside from technical issues—such as whether Iran can complete its portion of the pipeline and supply the gas, matters that are in some doubt—three factors will determine whether Turkey goes through with the deal: the attitude of the United States, the amount of natural gas Turkey is able to secure from other sources, and the amount of money Turkey would be obliged to pay under the take-or-pay arrangement. (The payment schedule has not been made public.)

If the United States opts to impose sanctions on Turkey in 2001, it would have to decide whether to invoke them across the board or only on the involved Turkish Botaş. It also would have to decide how severe the sanctions should be. According to the ILSA legislation, the president must choose two of five possible types of sanctions. These include a ban on exports to the United States; no loans or credits from U.S. financial institutions; no sales to the U.S. government; no credit from the Export-Import Bank; and no serving (by financial institutions of the sanctioned entity) as a primary dealer of U.S. debt instruments.

Having made exceptions for others more clearly in violation of ILSA, Washington would be hard-pressed to justify penalizing Turkey, and it would be mistaken to do so. However, the United States does have an interest in discouraging Turkey from contributing substantially to Iranian economic development. High-level U.S. officials should consistently make clear to Ankara that Washington places high priority on limiting Iran's economic development so as to realize strategic objectives both sides share—the weakening of the clerical regime and restrictions on its ability to acquire weapons of mass destruction. Implementation of the gas deal should not trigger sanctions, but it would negatively affect the atmosphere of bilateral relations.

TURKISH-ISRAELI RELATIONS

One of the most significant Middle Eastern strategic developments of the past decade is the flowering of Turkish-Israeli relations. Although Israel and Turkey secretly engaged in intelligence cooperation for many years, they openly began to pursue close ties after the signing of the 1993 Israel-PLO Declaration of Principles, which freed Turkey to cooperate with Israel while maintaining its declared sympathies for the Palestinians.

Since that time, cooperation has blossomed at many levels. Most celebrated have been security relations, launched by a February 1996 "military cooperation and training agreement" that allows Israeli pilots to exercise in Turkish skies. Later that same year, the two nations finalized a $600 million deal for an Israeli upgrade of Turkish F-4 fighter jets as well as an agreement on defense industrial cooperation. In the civilian domain, 1996 witnessed the conclusion of a Turkish-Israeli free trade agreement. By 1999, surging nonmilitary trade volume approached $900 million, and Israel became Turkey's largest export market in the Middle East. From 200,000 to 300,000 Israeli tourists have been visiting Turkey every year since the mid-1990s.

Intently focused on the Middle East peace process at the time, the United States may have been less than ecstatic when Turkey and Israel signed their first military cooperation agreement in 1996 since it raised suspicions in Syrian and other Arab minds about Israeli regional intentions. Nevertheless, Washington has taken a supportive position toward the deepening attachment of its two friends—underscored by its participation in trilateral search-and-rescue exercises in 1998 and 1999—while letting Ankara and Jerusalem direct the pace.

For Washington, Turkish-Israeli relations present far more opportunities than problems. From the standpoint of U.S. interests, Turkish-Israeli cooperation serves as:

◆ a model of regional normalization between Israel and a Muslim-majority state;

◆ an opportunity for deeper trilateral cooperation, enhancing Israeli and Turkish security and increasing weapons interoperability for U.S. forces at times of regional crisis;

◆ a source of pressure on Syria's peace process policies;

◆ a potential means for the executive branch to bypass Congress in supporting Turkey (through presidential waivers on Israeli sales of arms that include U.S.-origin technology); and

◆ a potential nucleus for pulling other pro-U.S. states, such as Jordan, into a wider Middle Eastern regional security regime.

The main challenge for the United States will be to support development of Turkish-Israeli relations while seeking to ensure that those relations do not undermine other key regional objectives: Arab-Israeli peace and Greek-Turkish stability. For now, there do not appear to be any serious problems. After initial nervousness, Athens seems reconciled to Turkish-Israeli cooperation and has even taken tentative steps of its own to develop ties with Israel. As long as Greek-Turkish rapprochement continues, so also will Greek equanimity about Turkish-Israeli ties. Should the United States judge that deepening Turkish-Israeli relations are adding to Greek-Turkish instability, it might seek to discourage high-profile manifestations of Turkish-Israeli security cooperation, such as military exercises, and might be less inclined to grant presidential waivers for Israeli sales to Turkey of weapons incorporating U.S. technology.

Nor has peace process diplomacy been compromised by Turkish-Israeli ties. If anything, Syria's concern about that cooperation has probably encouraged it to reengage with Israel. Although states bordering Turkey that feel directly threatened—Syria, Iraq, and (non-Arab) Iran—have complained loudly about Turkish-Israeli ties, overall Arab reaction has been relatively muted (contrary to widespread belief), at least at the official level. Egypt was an early critic but has backed off.

The United States has every reason to encourage further development of Turkish-Israeli cooperation as long as its other regional interests are unaffected. The United States should continue participating in annual search-and-rescue exercises with Turkey and Israel as a sign of its support for Turkish-Israeli partnership. It also should encourage other regional states to participate in the exercises—particularly Jordan but also Gulf and Maghreb states, as well as Egypt and Greece. However, Washington should not increase its level of joint participation in Turkish-Israeli military activities if there is a prospect that that would alienate Syria from peacemaking with Israel or would raise concerns elsewhere in the region. It also should take care not to allow trilateral U.S.-Turkish-Israeli ties to overshadow the bilateral Turkish-Israeli relationship lest the latter lose its image of authenticity. The United States can more easily reap benefits if Turkish-Israeli relations do not carry a "made in the U.S.A." label. That way, Ankara and Jerusalem can support U.S. interests in the region, while Washington retains some deniability regarding their actions.

Turkish-Israeli cooperation also enhances Israel's legitimacy in the eyes of the Turkic states of the former Soviet Union, opening the prospect of new avenues of cooperation among states friendly to the United States. Washington should promote trilateral U.S.-Turkish-Israeli economic development projects in the Turkic states of the former Soviet Union, as it tepidly began to do in the mid-1990s. Such initiatives would enhance the attractiveness of both Turkey and Israel in the Turkic states while projecting a more pacific image of Turkish-Israeli relations in the region.

Ankara would clearly like to receive more public acclaim than it so far has from Washington for its bold diplomacy toward Israel. More U.S. official praise for Turkey's regionally pacesetting role in building multidimensional ties with Israel, as well as the constructive role it plays in Israeli-Palestinian relations, would help Turkey politically in U.S. public opinion and in Congress.

THE MIDDLE EAST PEACE PROCESS

Turkey has good relations with the Palestinians, and the Palestinian issue retains some political resonance in Turkey. Progress on the Israeli-Palestinian peace track would strengthen Israel's legitimacy regionally and in Turkish public opinion, thereby facilitating Turkey's pursuit of close relations with Israel. Thus, Ankara has every reason to hope for an Israeli-Palestinian peace settlement.

Turkey contributes a small military contingent to the Temporary International Presence in Hebron (TIPH), a monitoring apparatus established as part of the Israeli-Palestinian Hebron agreement of January 1997. Turkey is the only Muslim participant in TIPH, and its participation is a mark of the trust it enjoys with both Israel and the Palestinians. All TIPH participating states were approved both by Israel and the Palestinians. Turkey also was an active member of the multilateral peace process, particularly the arms control and regional security working group before that body deadlocked over Israeli-Egyptian disagreements in the mid-1990s.

The Syria track, however, raises a number of concerns in Ankara that could have an impact on U.S.-Turkish relations. First, Turkey does not want to be pressed to provide Syria with additional amounts of Euphrates water so that Jerusalem and Damascus can more easily solve their water disputes. To Ankara's displeasure, Syrians and Israelis did discuss Turkish water in their negotiations in 1995–96 without consulting Turkey beforehand.[8]

Second, Turkey does not want Syrian troops currently concentrated on the Golan Heights cease-fire line to be redeployed to the now lightly guarded Turkish border. It also would like to see restrictions on Syria's weapons-of-mass-destruction capabilities.

Third, Turkey wants Syria to end its support for anti-Turkish terrorist groups—especially the PKK and other leftist factions that enjoy safe haven in Syria—as a condition for removal from the U.S. list of state sponsors of terrorism. Removal from the list is widely believed to be a key Syrian objective in pursuing peace with Israel, which certainly will demand that Syria end its association with anti-Israel groups.

Fourth, Turkey does not want Syria to achieve the sort of favored relationship with the United States that Washington bestowed on Egypt and Jordan following their peace treaties with Israel. In particular, Turkey would object to U.S. military assistance to Syria.

Turkish concerns assumed new urgency with the resumption of Israeli-Syrian talks in December 1999. As much as achievement of Arab-Israeli peace is a long-standing and pressing priority for Washington, Ankara is not willing to sacrifice its own interests to help the United States secure that goal. Turks remain sensitive about U.S. failure to consult during the 1995–96 phase of Israeli-Syrian negotiations and, in general, about what Turkey perceives as Washington's relegation of Turkish interests to a priority considerably lower than that of Middle East peace. For Ankara, U.S. indifference is symbolized by the fact that President Clinton's first-term secretary of state, Warren Christopher, made nearly two dozen trips to Syria without once stopping in neighboring Turkey. Some also might note that the United States was represented by Secretary of State Madeleine Albright at Syrian president Hafiz al-Asad's funeral in June 2000, whereas Deputy Secretary of State Clifford Wharton led the U.S. delegation to the funeral of staunch ally Özal in April 1993.

Keeping in mind Turkish anxieties about the Syrian-Israeli peace track, the United States should provide Turkey with private, senior-level briefings after each round of negotiations. Washington should make certain no demands are made on Turkey without prior consultation with Ankara. The United States also should affirm that cessation of all forms of support to the PKK and other anti-Turkish terrorist groups is a prerequisite for Syria's removal from the state sponsors of terrorism list. Likewise, the United States should seek to ensure that other Turkish interests, such as the nature of a post-peace-agreement security regime, are taken into account in Syrian-Israeli diplomacy. It should consult with Turkey, as it undoubtedly will with Israel, regarding the nature of U.S.-Syria relations after the peace agreement. As reassurance for Ankara regarding redeployment of Syrian troops and warning to Damascus, Washington might consider urging NATO to issue a statement reaffirming its treaty obligation to defend Turkey against attack on any of its borders.

RUSSIAN-TURKISH RELATIONS

Washington's primary goal regarding Turkey and the former Soviet Union is to strengthen Turkey's role as a westward outlet for Central Asian and Caucasian states (for energy, trade, and human contact) without unduly upsetting Russia or Turkish-Russian stability. This serves a larger objective of enhancing former Soviet perimeter states' independence from Moscow and inclining them toward the West. A secondary U.S. goal, driven in great part by domestic politics, is to improve and normalize Turkish-Armenian relations.

On balance, current relations between traditional arch-foes Russia and Turkey constitute a post–cold war success story. Collapse of communism and termination of the NATO–Warsaw Pact confrontation have opened a new era in bilateral ties, marked by heavy Turkish investment in Russia, flourishing trade (at least before the 1998 Russian economic collapse), proposed energy deals, and even an occasional Russian military sale to Turkey. A significant pro-Russian lobby has gained a foothold in Turkey's influential business community and in former prime minister Mesut Yilmaz's Motherland Party (ANAP). One prominent Turkish scholar has referred to the state of Turkish-Russian relations as "virtual rapprochement."[9]

Nevertheless, fears of a "return to history" grip both sides—a history marked by the cold war and, earlier, by some dozen wars between Czarist Russia and the Ottoman Empire. Turkey's security establishment worries about a resurgence of Russian aggression, a possibility underscored by Russia's 1994–96 and 1999 wars on Chechnya, its efforts to bully Georgia and Azerbaijan, and its failure to limit its forces and materiel in the Caucasus in accordance with 1990 CFE treaty requirements. That agreement was modified in Russia's favor at the 1999 Istanbul summit of the Organization for Security and Cooperation in Europe, but Turks and others question whether Moscow will implement even the newer, easier-to-meet targets. Russian officials at times charge Turkey with pursuing an unnecessarily large naval buildup on the Black Sea and limiting freedom of navigation through the Straits via unilaterally imposed safety measures. In the mid-1990s, each side accused the other of aiding domestic separatist movements, that is, the Chechens and the PKK, and each remains wary on that score.[10] Turkey and Russia also are on opposite sides of the Armenia-Azerbaijan conflict. Turkey strongly backs Azerbaijan and provides it with limited military training; Russia reportedly provides arms to Armenia. Likewise in the Balkan conflicts, Turkey has backed the Muslims of Bosnia and Kosovo, while Russia has supported Orthodox Serbia.

Ankara's interest in creating a sphere of influence in the Turkic-language states of the former Soviet Union clashes directly with Moscow's attempts to preserve its prerogatives in what it calls its "near abroad." Part of this rivalry is reflected in Turkish-Russian competition for Caspian Sea energy pipeline routes.

Because the United States gives high priority to relations with both Russia and Turkey, Washington is often a factor in their own bilateral considerations. The United States has actively promoted the Baku-Ceyhan pipeline, which would carry Caspian Sea oil from Azerbaijan through Georgia to a Mediterranean terminal in Turkey. Transport of Caspian oil to the West is in itself an important strategic interest for the United States since it helps to diversify the West's energy sources and lessen somewhat its dependence on the Middle East. But the Baku-Ceyhan pipeline, in particular, would serve at least three aims: enhancing Turkey's regional importance, isolating Iran (by preventing it from being the outlet for Caspian Sea energy), and strengthening the independence of former Soviet states Azerbaijan and Georgia. Washington favors Turkey's efforts to gain influence in the Turkic-language states. Meanwhile, Moscow opposes Baku-Ceyhan precisely because it would loosen Azerbaijani and Georgian dependence on Russia and extend Turkey's influence in the region.

Washington's energetic diplomatic support for Baku-Ceyhan is probably the main reason that project remains a live option. But the United States says Baku-Ceyhan must be "commercially viable" and has promised only that Overseas Private Investment Corporation and Trade and Development Agency funds would be made available after the pipeline consortium secures financing. By refusing to make any serious financial commitments, the United States projects a somewhat equivocal attitude toward the pipeline project.

The United States also has eschewed security commitments to Azerbaijan and Georgia, the Caucasus states through which the pipeline would pass, which feel exposed to possible Russian destabilization.

Few would expect Washington to risk confrontation with Russia for the sake of those distant and fragile nations, but that prudence undercuts prospects for realization of Baku-Ceyhan as well as the credibility of President Clinton's claim that the region is "critical to the future of the entire world."[11]

Turkish-Russian relations raise key issues for U.S. policymakers: How can the United States support ally Turkey on regional issues without antagonizing nuclear power Russia? How far should the United States go in convincing Turkey to support the independence of Caucasian and Central Asian states and to seek to loosen their ties with Moscow?

These questions dovetail in the so-called Blue Stream project, which foresees an underwater pipeline in the Black Sea that would supply Russian gas directly to Turkey. The Blue Stream pipeline is to be built by the Italian firm ENI. Its technical feasibility is still uncertain. Blue Stream seemingly conflicts with a U.S.-backed project Ankara is simultaneously pursuing, the Trans-Caspian Pipeline (TCP), which would carry Turkmenistani gas to Turkey via the Caspian, Azerbaijan, and Georgia. TCP, to be built by a U.S. consortium, is designed like Baku-Ceyhan to bolster the independence of former Soviet states and enhance Turkey's strategic standing at the expense of Iran's and Russia's. Although Turkey says otherwise, most experts believe energy demand in Turkey at best justifies only one of the two pipelines in the near term. Further complicating the viability of TCP is the discovery of major natural gas deposits in Azerbaijan.

Russia already supplies the overwhelming majority of Turkey's natural gas via a pipeline that circumvents the Black Sea and enters Turkey from across the Bulgarian border. If Blue Stream is realized, Russia will guarantee itself a dominant share of the Turkish gas market for years to come.

Although it stops short of saying so, the United States opposes Blue Stream. That is natural, since the Black Sea project and the American project TCP are commercial rivals. Viewed strategically, the United States also fears that Turkey, if dependent on Russian gas, would become subject to Russian blackmail on regional issues such as Iran, Iraq, and the Balkans. Washington's concern puts it in the ironic position of seeming to care more about diversification of Turkey's energy sources than the Turks do themselves. But U.S. worries may be excessive. Turkey already relies heavily on Russian gas but does not take pro-Russian positions on regional issues. And Russia would not readily turn off the Blue Stream tap since Turkish payments would be a significant source of much-needed hard currency for Moscow.

In fact, it is not clear if U.S. unhappiness about Blue Stream mainly reflects support for U.S. commerce or actual concern about Turkish dependence on Russia. If the latter, it is at least somewhat at odds with the U.S. approach in countless other areas around the globe, such as the Middle East, where the United States praises economic interdependence as a way of reducing historical antagonisms. At the November 1999 Istanbul signing ceremony for the "Baku-Ceyhan and Trans-Caspian Gas Pipeline Protocol," President Clinton assured his audience that the pipelines would "prove how much more countries have to gain from economic and commercial bonds, rather than from political rivalries." That same rationale presumably should apply to relations between Turkey and Russia, which are seeking to overcome centuries of enmity. Turkish-Russian economic relations likewise presumably contribute toward "help[ing] Russia to complete its democratic revolution," which Clinton told the Turkish parliament should be a U.S.-Turkish objective.

Turkish officials say Blue Stream is appealing because it is geo-graphically more direct and politically simpler than TCP, which involves four countries and requires further negotiations with the always difficult Turkmenistanis. It would deliver gas sooner, provided it proves technically feasible.

Blue Stream also tracks with traditional Turkish strategic thinking regarding Russia. Respectful of Russia's size and power, Turkey has always been loath to antagonize Moscow and has often sought means to temper Turkish-Russian bilateral rivalry. As Ankara has confronted Russian interests in a number of important areas in the post–cold war years—through its campaign to secure the Baku-Ceyhan pipeline, its deep engagement with Azerbaijan, its efforts to achieve influence in the Caucasus and Central Asia, and its more assertive management of the Bosporus—it also has vigorously pursued bilateral economic cooper-ation, at least in part in order to pacify Moscow. Blue Stream fits into this pattern.

Turkish-Russian tranquility serves U.S. interests in a region where Washington favors stability. The United States does not, and should not, want Turkey to be needlessly provocative toward Russia,[12] and it should be accommodating of Turkish-Russian economic inter-dependence. That does not mean surrender to Russia's regional strate-gic goals, however. Washington should put more teeth into its support of the strategically important Baku-Ceyhan project—for example, by offering to back Turkish financial guarantees for pipeline construction. Further, to facilitate the loosening of Russia's grip on its former domains, the U.S. should support, in a low-profile manner, the spread of Turkey's pro-Western influence in the Turkic states by initiating joint U.S.-Turkish development projects in the region. A U.S. effort along these lines was undertaken in the early 1990s but faltered from lack of U.S. commitment and Turkish efficiency. It makes strategic sense, however, and should be given an energetic second chance.

The United States should consider as well initiating a trilateral dialogue with Turkey and Russia about regional issues. If both parties accepted—Moscow would be the more reticent—such a forum would be useful for promoting Russian-Turkish rapprochement and discussing the three states' overlapping, sometimes conflicting, regional interests, and as a means of formalizing U.S. interests in the region and redressing the Russian-Turkish regional power gap.

ARMENIA

U.S. interest in improving Turkish-Armenian ties focuses mainly on Washington's encouraging Ankara to open the land border with Armenia that it closed in response to Armenia's occupation of Azerbaijani territory. The Turkish-Armenian relationship is also freighted with historical memories of Armenian massacres by Ottoman Turks; Armenians insist the 1915–16 massacres were a "genocide," a term Turkey decidedly rejects.

Once the nub of Armenian-Azerbaijani conflict—the Nagorno-Karabakh dispute—is resolved, Ankara and Yerevan will likely pursue constructive relations. Turkey would probably open its land border now were it not for Azerbaijan's objections. In the mid-1990s, after Turkey indicated it was prepared to open a gate on its Armenian border, the Azerbaijani foreign minister publicly dressed down his visiting Turkish counterpart, warning that if the gate were opened, Azerbaijan would reconsider its choice of Baku-Ceyhan as the main export pipeline for its oil.

U.S. domestic politics endow Turkish-Armenian relations with a prominent place on the U.S.-Turkish agenda. As a result mainly of Armenian-American lobbying, the U.S. government encourages Turkey to make a gesture to help Armenia reduce its dependence on Russia. Moreover, improved Turkish-Armenian relations might lessen

Armenian-American opposition to U.S. support for Turkey. Washington's efforts do not reflect purely domestic politics; there is a strategic dimension as well. Right now Armenia's only outlets to the world are through Russia, Iran, and troubled Georgia. An open land border with Turkey would allow better access to and by the West. Nevertheless, resolution of this matter will probably have to await a solution to the Nagorno-Karabakh dispute.

Intrinsically and in fact, Turkey's relations with Armenia are not crucial to U.S.-Turkish bilateral relations. Improvement in the former, however, might remove an obstacle to the latter.

TURKEY AND EUROPE

Washington favors Turkey's fullest possible participation in Western institutions, primarily as a means to ensure that Turkey remains Western-oriented in foreign and security policies. In promoting Turkey's "anchoring to the West," the United States must reckon with two overlapping elements of Turkey's relations with Western Europe: the political and the strategic, as embodied in Turkey's ties with the European Union and European security structures, respectively.

Washington has won Turkish praise by vocally endorsing Turkey's European integration efforts. To a thunderous ovation, President Clinton told the Turkish parliament in November 1999 that "our vision of a Europe that is undivided, democratic, and at peace . . . will never be complete unless and until it embraces Turkey."

While Turks have long suspected the EU was holding them at arm's length because it is a "Christian club," the United States has consistently objected to religious criteria for Turkey's EU membership bid. In May 1997, Deputy Secretary of State Strobe Talbott urged the EU to "define itself as inclusively, expansively, and comprehensively as possible" and warned of future dangers "if we define the 'European-ness' of a village on the basis of whether its landmarks are church spires or minarets."

To the annoyance of some EU members, the United States has persistently pleaded Turkey's case, publicly and privately. Washington was probably an important factor in achieving two major milestones in EU-Turkish relations in the 1990s: the 1995 customs union agreement and the 1999 affirmation of Turkey's candidacy for membership. Some Europeans dispute this, but most Turks are convinced that Washington was crucial to the success of those efforts.

Turkey also enjoys U.S. support for its full participation in European security, whether through traditional structures such as NATO or nascent initiatives such as the European Security and Defense Identity (ESDI), an effort by the EU to develop the ability to carry out military operations without the direct participation of the United States. Turks are concerned that implementation of ESDI will result in a downgrading of NATO's importance and relegate Turkey, still a non-EU member, to second-class status in European security.

Mainly with Turkey in mind—in fact, there are other NATO states that are not part of the EU, such as Norway, Iceland, and the three newest members, Poland, Hungary, and the Czech Republic—the United States worked to shape the text of the March 1999 NATO fiftieth anniversary communiqué to say that non-EU-member NATO states would have the "fullest possible involvement" in ESDI-related operations.[13] Moreover, all such operations, which would draw on NATO equipment and command-and-control mechanisms, would be subject to NATO approval—giving Turkey, as a NATO member, a veto over them, at least in theory. But, in reality, decisions about such undertakings would probably have been made in consultations between the United States and the EU-member allies long before the stage was reached where Turkey would have any formal say. Security-minded Turks worry that they will be effectively excluded from ESDI operational planning and decisionmaking, leaving them fully dependent on the United States to guard their interests.

These concerns deepened when the EU surprisingly decided at its June 1999 summit that it should develop an autonomous defense capability fully independent of NATO's. To add to Turkey's displeasure, the EU also said it hoped ESDI developments would allow the EU to disband its current "security arm" grouping, the Western European Union (WEU), by the end of 2000.[14] The WEU is a weak organization but one that includes Turkey and other non-EU-member NATO states as active "associate members." EU states lack the means to carry out ESDI-based operations any time soon, but Turkey frets about the day when they achieve such capability. More generally, Turkey sees development of ESDI as a sign of its own marginalization in Europe.

Turkey has taken steps to try to secure full participation in ESDI—for example, by offering to provide a brigade to a 50,000-man rapid deployment force, envisioned to be operational by 2003. It is unclear if the EU will be receptive to Turkey's full participation in ESDI before it becomes an EU member; at this early stage, there are conflicting indications.[15]

Even were it to become an EU member—and, because of its size and military capacity, an important participant in all phases of ESDI operations—Turkey would probably have misgivings about ESDI, which it fears will weaken the U.S. link to European, and perhaps Turkey's own, defense. Given its unique and geographically varied vulnerabilities, Turkey's security outlook is more compatible with Washington's global view than with that of its European allies. The United States often takes up the cudgel for Turkey's legitimate security needs in the face of European indifference—whether regarding the PKK or renegotiation of limits on nearby Russian troops and materiel included in the 1990 Conventional Forces in Europe (CFE) Treaty. Turkey has come to count on this type of U.S. support and doubts that it would receive similar backing from its European allies, even if they are also fellow EU members.

The United States will need to remain actively involved in EU-Turkish relations, encouraging both sides to make progress toward Turkey's full EU membership and full ESDI participation. Membership in the EU would be Turkey's strongest possible "anchor" to the West. Meaningful progress toward membership also might contribute to res-olution, or easing, of the Cyprus problem and other Greek-Turkish disputes—longtime U.S. priorities. If Ankara comes to evaluate EU membership as a realistic possibility, it will have unprecedented incen-tive to compromise on those issues.

Inevitably, Turkey and the EU will encounter misunderstandings during the accession process. As long as the United States is closer to Turkey and to the EU than Turkey and the EU are to one another—a sit-uation likely to continue for some time—Washington will almost cer-tainly play a mediating role. The United States should not be deterred by EU complaints about U.S. interference in this regard. Given the broad scope of U.S. relations with the EU and its member states, Washington's importuning on behalf of Turkey is at most a minor irritant.

As in the EU context, the United States should press European allies to continue "anchoring Turkey to the West" as they proceed with ESDI. The EU has said that ESDI-based actions carried out with refer-ence to NATO will be open to non-EU-member NATO states but that EU states will decide case by case whether to include nonmember states in "autonomous" EU-led operations. Washington should lobby EU states to include Turkey in all aspects and stages of ESDI and, par-ticularly, to ensure that disbanding of the WEU does not diminish Turkey's involvement in European security.

Turkish integration with Western Europe is an appropriate goal for U.S. policy, but it may not be an unmixed blessing. If Turkish-European integration achieves momentum, the United States might lose some of the lucrative Turkish arms market to the Europeans. More broadly, Washington will have to reflect on the implications of closer Turkish-EU relations for its own regional policies. Close U.S.-Turkish relations of recent years are partly the result of Turkish alienation from Europe. A Turkey more closely associated with the EU's "common foreign and security policy" might drift more clearly into opposition to some U.S. policies, such as those regarding Iran or even the Israeli-Palestinian peace process. Nevertheless, the United States would benefit from the trade-off. Turkey's reliance on the American contribution to its overall security would likely mitigate any negative developments resulting from a closer EU-Turkish association, and EU membership would singularly solidify Turkey's Western orientation.

GREEK-TURKISH RELATIONS AND CYPRUS

For decades, congressional initiatives have linked U.S.-Turkish relations to progress in Greek-Turkish relations and the Cyprus dispute. The most famous example was the arms embargo Congress imposed following Turkey's military intervention in Cyprus in 1974. There are also more recent, if less dramatic, illustrations. After a Greek-Turkish near clash in the Aegean in early 1996, one senator managed to delay for nearly two years announced U.S. plans to transfer three frigates to Turkey.

Termination of foreign assistance to Greece and Turkey in fiscal year 1998 has had an ironically healthy impact on U.S.-Turkey relations. Congressional imposition of a ratio for aid to Greece and Turkey and efforts to impose Cyprus-related and other political conditions on Turkish aid are now relics of the past. However, linkage still has echoes, including in the executive branch, where congressional attitudes circumscribe policy development and shape priorities. A U.S. official contemplating an initiative toward Turkey that requires congressional approval first must sift through the filter of congressional attitudes toward Greek-Turkish relations and the Cyprus problem. The prominent place on the U.S.-Turkish agenda that Washington gives Greek-Turkish relations and the Cyprus problem irritates Ankara. Moreover, senior U.S. officials who consider visiting Turkey usually feel they must visit Greece as well, complicating and sometimes halting their plans.

This situation is primarily the result of domestic political consid-erations, but there is a substantive dimension as well. Resolution of Greek-Turkish problems and the Cyprus dispute, which threaten to destabilize the eastern Mediterranean and create havoc in NATO, is an important U.S. interest.

Although perturbed by the priority Washington accords these issues, Turkey generally welcomes U.S. involvement in Greek-Turkish relations. Ankara recognizes that hostilities are undesirable and that the United States is far more neutral than any other (presumably European) potential intermediary would be. Turkey likewise sees Washington as the most trustworthy among potential "honest brokers" of the Cyprus dispute, in a world that (from Ankara's perspective) unfairly insists on changes to the status quo in Cyprus.

During 1999 and early 2000, a budding Greek-Turkish rap-prochement seemed to lay the groundwork for meaningful progress toward Aegean stability. At U.S. urging—and abetted by "earthquake diplomacy"—Greece and Turkey began talks and signed agreements on cooperation in trade, tourism, and antiterrorism. In a startling turn-about, Greece supported Turkey's bid for EU candidacy.

The new, implicit willingness of Athens to decouple Greek-Turkish relations from the Cyprus problem—or, at least, to loosen the link—marks a significant policy departure. If it proves durable, it will have at least two potentially important implications for U.S. policy and U.S.-Turkish relations. One is that Turkey's problems with a pro-Greece congressional lobby in Washington may ease, which, in turn, would give U.S. policymakers greater latitude for pursuing U.S.-Turkish ties. Second, Washington would have greater scope to encourage and pur-sue solutions to Greek-Turkish problems, without necessarily having to await a settlement of the Cyprus problem. Cyprus apart, Greek-Turkish bilateral problems are knotty but appear amenable to diplomatic solution.

Regarding Cyprus, two overarching issues have implications for U.S.-Turkish relations—Cypriot accession to EU membership and a solution to the Cyprus problem itself. If the Greek Cypriot–controlled (and internationally recognized) Republic of Cyprus (ROC) becomes an EU member without the Turkish Cypriots and before the Cyprus problem is resolved, the result will almost certainly be trouble—Turkish anger and alienation from Europe, a sharpening of Greek-Turkish hostility, and, quite possibly, a permanently divided Cyprus. Perhaps a negative Turkish reaction would be tempered if Ankara itself were advancing rapidly toward membership but probably not much.

(Turkey's position is that Cyprus should not be admitted to the EU under any circumstances until Turkey itself is admitted.) Washington thus has an interest in opposing EU membership for the ROC before the Cyprus problem has been settled, and it should lobby EU states accordingly. Of course, such a policy—at least to the extent it is pursued openly—would incur strong opposition from the organized pro-Greece lobby and many Greek Americans, creating domestic political challenges for any U.S. administration.

As to the Cyprus problem itself, Washington will have to decide whether to continue to muddle through with the status quo, as it has now for more than a quarter-century, or to push more actively for a settlement. If Greek-Turkish rapprochement continues to develop independently of progress on Cyprus, the prospect of hostilities will diminish, and the status quo may become increasingly viable.

Breaking the Cyprus stalemate might require a fresh U.S. approach, such as advocacy of a solution that entails a very loose form of association enshrining near total physical separation of the two Cypriot communities. (A stable security regime and significant cession of territory by the Turkish Cypriots also would have to be part of the package.) The obstacles to achieving this type of solution would be daunting. The United States would have to win over not only the regional parties and their American backers but also the EU, whose own rules of association would seem to prohibit this type of separation (presuming Cyprus were to become an EU member).

The United States is unlikely ever to support permanent division of the island—either Turkish annexation of northern Cyprus or the two-state solution often advocated by Turkish and Turkish-Cypriot leaders—except in the unanticipated case that the Greek Cypriots also choose permanent division. Even permanent division by agreement of the parties would be a highly undesirable result from the U.S. point of view, particularly if the Greek Cypriots enter the EU and Turkey and the Turkish Cypriots do not since it probably would create long-term alienation of Turkey and the Turkish Cypriots from Western Europe and the EU.

The issues of the Cyprus problem and Cypriot membership in the EU are now intimately linked. Perhaps only a major prize like EU membership might induce the Greek Cypriots to accept a minimalist form of association with the Turkish Cypriots. If the EU were to embrace the notion of near separation for the Cypriot communities and make it a condition of (rather than a drawback to) EU membership, all parties might have enhanced incentive to achieve a permanent solution on the island.

In general, the lure of EU membership—if Ankara sees that goal as realistic—should make Turkey a more flexible negotiating partner regarding both Aegean issues and the Cyprus problem. Significant progress in both areas is probably a prerequisite for Turkish membership in the EU. Because of its security relationship with Ankara, among other factors, the United States likely would continue to lead diplomatic efforts to help resolve those issues, but the EU-membership incentive could provide Washington with a big assist in its work.

THE ROLE OF HUMAN RIGHTS: A PLACE FOR "MORALPOLITIK"?

The primary motivation for strong U.S.-Turkish relations is strategic, the primary glue the security relationship. Yet concern about human rights, like the Cyprus problem and Greek-Turkish disputes, is also a persistent and important theme in relations between Ankara and Washington. Every American involved with U.S.-Turkish relations, policymaker and layman alike, acknowledges that Turkey has troubling human rights shortcomings. The human rights situation in Turkey has restricted bilateral ties in the past and can seriously undermine them.

The core policy question for Washington is how to balance geostrategic and human rights concerns. Several factors complicate this equation. Yet, Turkey is a democracy, however flawed; it should not be equated with the many dictatorships and never-changing governments in its region. In the vast Islamic world Turkey has by far the most democratic tradition. On the other hand, Turkey is also a member of the Western community, and it aspires to be a member of the EU and to be seen as a fully Western country; thus, in effect, it is asking to be held to the highest possible standards. Beyond these considerations, Turkey has fought an ethnic Kurdish insurgency—now in abeyance—for the better part of two decades. This struggle, which became a lightning rod for human rights criticism of Turkey, reflected legitimate Kurdish grievances abut also an understandable Turkish insistence on maintaining its territorial integrity.

Also complicating U.S. human rights policy toward Turkey is the fact that, although Turkey acknowledges that it has human rights problems, the two nations often do not agree on what those problems are. Both agree that torture is an abuse and should be eradicated. But certain other practices—limitations on Kurdish linguistic and cultural freedom, restrictions on certain types of political expression, and the paramount role the military arrogates to itself in security policy and, often, internal politics—are seen by the United States as human rights restrictions but are supported as necessary or desirable policies by many Turks. These policies, unjustifiable to an American audience, are deeply embedded in the Turkish state structure and will not be changed easily (even with the incentive of EU membership).

Another complication is that many U.S.-based human rights groups focus on Turkey because they see U.S.-Turkey relations as a litmus test of the sincerity of Washington's global human rights policy. They reason that human rights criteria should be applied equally to friend and foe, and they say no U.S. ally has a more vexed record than Turkey. Typical of this view, and of the tone of argumentation, is a recent study of U.S. arms sales to Turkey issued jointly by two human rights organizations, the World Policy Institute and the Federation of American Scientists. Referring to NATO intervention in Kosovo, the authors write, "Perhaps the best test of the staying power of the 'new humanitarianism' is the U.S. relationship with Turkey, a NATO ally that has engaged in its own unique brand of internal 'ethnic cleansing' against its Kurdish population."[16]

Human rights–oriented critics see close U.S.-Turkish ties as a cynical triumph of American strategic interests over American values. Defenders of close ties say that the United States cannot afford to give up Turkey's strategic value for the sake of a human rights situation over which it has little direct influence, and that Turkey anyhow deserves credit as the most democratic state in the Islamic world. They also assert that, through close relations with Turkey, the United States can be more effective in encouraging human rights reform. Critics say they see little evidence that close ties have produced much reform.

The State Department's human rights report annually depicts a bleak scene for freedom in Turkey, but only rarely have U.S. officials publicly set out a view on the proper balance between geostrategic and human rights considerations in U.S.-Turkish relations. Two Clinton administration officials who have are Richard Holbrooke and Strobe Talbott. Visiting Turkey as assistant secretary of state for European affairs in 1995, Holbrooke seemed to offer a rare acknowledgment that human rights plays a secondary role in the formulation of U.S.

policy toward Turkey. Human rights are important, he was quoted as saying, but should not be allowed to "rupture" bilateral relations.[17] Asked about Holbrooke's formulation in 1998, Deputy Secretary of State Talbott took exception. He said it mistakenly suggests that bilateral relations are "an either/or choice. You either support a country's security policies, or you give priority to the promotion of human rights. . . . Countries which trammel the rights of their own citizens . . . end up paying a price not only in terms of political stability, but indeed the viability and stability of the state itself. So . . . when we talk . . . to some of our best friends in the world about their human rights practices, we try . . . to couch the argument very much in terms of *realpolitik,* as well as what might be called *moralpolitik.*"[18]

Human rights occasionally has an operational impact on U.S. policy, usually in the realm of arms sales—a highly emotional subject for Turkey. In the 1990s, Congress often used human rights abuses to insert itself into U.S.-Turkish relations. In 1998, for example, Turkey turned down some $40 million in economic assistance because of human rights conditions imposed by Congress. In 1995, Congress mandated that the executive branch investigate whether Turkey had used U.S.-supplied weapons against civilians in its anti-PKK campaign. A subsequent State Department report technically cleared the Turks, but only by a whisker. Issued in June 1995, the report acknowledged that U.S.-origin equipment had been used in operations "during which" abuses occurred—without specifically saying that the U.S.-origin materiel had been used in the actual abuses—and termed it "highly likely" that U.S.-origin equipment was used "in support of the evacuation and/or destruction of villages."[19]

With Congress looking over its shoulder, and with the often active intervention of executive branch officials as well, particularly from the State Department's Bureau of Democracy, Human Rights, and Labor, the administration has several times held up arms sales on its own initiative. In 1996, the United States delayed the transfer of ten AH-1W Super Cobra attack helicopters, ultimately leading Turkey to cancel the deal. The United States also has withheld approval of smaller items, such as pistols, sniper rifles, and communications equipment.[20] In 1997, the government gave U.S. firms permission to bid on a projected Turkish purchase of 145 attack helicopters but with no guarantee that a sale would actually be approved. Rather, it reportedly made clear, the United States would review Turkey's human rights performance and make the decision partly on that basis if a U.S. firm won the bid.

Human rights conditionality creates a dilemma for Turkey, particularly regarding arms sales. It offends Turkish pride—at least in the Turkish military and political establishment—and throws off Turkish security planning. In recent years, Turkish officials have often complained that the United States has become an unreliable source of arms. In the mid to late 1990s, they often accused Washington of imposing an "unstated arms embargo" on Turkey—even though a vigorous arms flow continued— because of U.S. reluctance to sell attack helicopters and the long-term delay in transfer of the frigates. On the other hand, Turkey has a strong preference for, and is in fact dependent on, U.S. military equipment, which constitutes some 80 percent of its military inventory. As this goes to press, more than two years after Ankara first raised the issue of a major purchase of attack helicopters, Turkey has not made a decision on which of three bids, including one from an American firm, to accept. It is widely believed Turkey has delayed making the decision until it feels confident that the U.S. administration and Congress will approve the sale.

Balancing strategic and moral concerns is a challenge that is likely to continue to trouble U.S. policy toward Turkey. But there are sound *strategic* reasons for patiently supporting and fostering further democratic evolution in Turkey, both near and long term. Greater democratization might increase stability in Turkey, as Talbott suggested, and would remove a primary impediment to security ties, including arms sales. According to *New York Times* correspondent Stephen Kinzer, "the great question" of U.S.-Turkish bilateral relations is "what can we [the United States] do to encourage Turkey to become the kind of country we can help without reservation."[21] It was perhaps in that spirit that President Clinton told the Turkish parliament, "The future we want to build together begins with Turkish progress in deepening democracy at home."

Turkish officials are likely to choose the approximate course for their nation based on their own judgment of what is best for their society, not on American advice or pressure. The Turkish regime understands the stresses that human rights issues cause to the quality of bilateral relations, but it reasons—with historical justification—that the United States will continue to give primacy to geostrategic considerations. In light of Turkey's geostrategic importance and its history of support for major U.S. foreign policies—Korea, the cold war, Iraq— Ankara deserves patience and the benefit of the doubt, although not a blind eye, on human rights issues.

The United States can contribute to improving human rights in Turkey while maintaining U.S. security interests, mainly through public diplomacy, by retaining human rights as a bilateral agenda item and by encouraging Ankara to pursue EU membership, which is Turkey's most powerful incentive for reform. The U.S. dialogue with Turkey on human rights should be regularized and conducted at a relatively authoritative level—for example, by the U.S. State Department's assistant secretary for human rights and the Turkish minister of state for human rights. (A structured dialogue of this sort might ensure that future Turkish governments continue to assign a ministerial-level human rights portfolio, a relatively recent practice.) At the same time, it should be conducted in a supportive and usually low-key manner.

In the dialogue, the United States should put the case for human rights reform in the context of Turkey's practical interests in relations with the West. The United States should make Turkey understand that it damages its standing in U.S. public opinion and Congress and binds the hands of its supporters by limiting freedom of expression and Kurdish cultural and linguistic rights. The United States might consider setting out a structure of political, diplomatic, and economic incentives for significant Turkish political reform. Washington, in effect, would be telling Ankara that, as it takes risks for reform, the United States will work to minimize those risks (a variation of what President Clinton told Israeli prime minister Yitzhak Rabin regarding the Middle East peace process in early 1993).

In public diplomacy, the United States should continue actively to affirm support for all freedom of expression that does not constitute a "clear and present danger" to public order, as well as for democratization and linguistic and cultural freedom. In trying to nurse progress in these areas, particularly regarding the Kurdish issue, U.S. officials need to be aware that their Turkish counterparts are often convinced that Americans have little understanding of what is best for their society. Many Turks are uneasy at the prospect of letting the ethnic genie out of the bottle. Once Kurdish linguistic freedom is fully granted, other ethnic groups, such as Arabs or Circassians, might demand similar rights, and many Turks sincerely question whether their nation can sustain such pluralism.

Tone is important in dealing with Turks and Turkey. A confrontational approach is likely to stiffen Turkish backs. Particularly in public, the United States should avoid sounding preachy. It is instructive that, in his speech to the Turkish parliament, President Clinton won Turkish praise for referring frankly to the U.S. experience with slavery.

The United States also can help promote democratization in Turkey through a practical measure: encouraging U.S. NGOs to maintain contact with Turkish NGOs, particularly those focused on human rights, democracy building, and social issues. This is already done to some extent via programs and funding from the National Endowment for Democracy, the National Democratic Institute, and the International Republican Institute. The notion of voluntary civic associations is relatively new in Turkey, but the number of NGOs grew steadily in the 1990s. This trend should be further energized by the August 1999 earthquake, which clearly demonstrated the value of voluntary associations to a wider Turkish audience.

Linkage of arms sales with human rights performance is one of the most contentious issues in U.S.-Turkish relations, as already noted. From a strategic standpoint, arms sales are important both intrinsically as a means of maximizing U.S. influence in Turkey and symbolically as a sign of U.S. support. Washington retains an important stake in U.S.-Turkish bilateral security relations and in a Turkish military that is strong, well equipped, and U.S.-influenced. The United States also has a large commercial stake in the Turkish arms market.

When arms sales are controversial for human rights–related reasons, the United States and Turkey—and, separately, the U.S. administration and the congressional leadership—should quietly discuss reasonable criteria for human rights improvements that, once met, would allow the administration to go forward with the sale and Congress to approve it. If Turkey chooses to make the purchase and meets the reasonable criteria, the United States should pledge that the sale will be defended in Congress by high-level officials, at least at the level of assistant secretary.

U.S. support of human rights improvement in Turkey should be consistent and firm. Turkey is not Pakistan, and it should be expected to adhere to Western standards. To be most effective, however, the United States should continue to package its criticism as that of a friend and ally. The United States also would be wise to focus on positive trends, since thoroughgoing or fundamental change is not likely to come easily or quickly, notwithstanding Turkey's EU candidacy.

ISLAM AND ISLAMISM

Because of the sensitivities of the Turkish secular elite, no issue in U.S.-Turkish relations is more delicate than Islam. U.S. policy touches upon Turkey and Islam in at least three ways: touting Turkey as a role model for or representative of the Islamic world, dealing with political Islam, and considering human rights issues raised by Turkey's internal policies toward religion.

U.S. public diplomacy about Turkey projects it as a secular, democratic, free market role model for the Islamic world, as well as an important representative of that world in its encounter with the West. According to President Clinton, "It is at Turkey where Europe and the Muslim world can meet in peace and harmony."[22] This is a theme played for Turkish and American audiences but with little substantive content. With the exception of a few limited programs undertaken in the Turkic states of the former Soviet Union in the early 1990s, the United States has never actively encouraged other Islamic states to look to Turkey for guidance on political and economic matters. Probably that is just as well. Outside the Turkic world, Turkey has little influence among Muslims. Arabs deeply resent Turkey for a perceived history of oppression during the Ottoman period. Religious Muslims in Iran and elsewhere are contemptuous of the uncompromising secularism of the Atatürk revolution. Most non-Turkic Muslims see Turkey as sui generis, unrepresentative of the Muslim world as a whole. They may monitor EU treatment of Turkey as a barometer of European attitudes toward Islam, but they do not look to Turkey to help with their relations with Europe.

Even the United States has an equivocal attitude toward some structural aspects of Turkish democracy—for example, the Turkish military's penchant for acting autonomously against Islamic fundamentalists and other perceived radicals. This role of the military as a fire wall might actually provide a useful model of transition to democracy for authoritarian, Muslim-majority regimes that fear democracy will lead to a fundamentalist takeover. Jordan has taken steps in that direction since the late 1980s, with the military-backed monarchy playing the role of guarantor and modulator of a limited democratic experiment. Because of its distinctly nondemocratic dimension, however, this type of "muscled democracy" is not something the United States would openly promote as a model.

Turkey itself traditionally does not claim any type of leadership role in the Islamic world or any special ability to represent Islam in its engagement with the West.[23] Members of Turkey's elite consider their state more Western and secular than the rest of the Islamic world.

Political Islam in Turkey raises several difficult issues for the United States, although fewer now than when Islamists were in power in 1996–97. In determining its approach, Washington takes into account several factors: its own views of Turkish Islamists, the views of Turkey's traditionally pro-Western secular establishment, U.S. democratic values, and U.S. strategic interests. There is considerable debate in Turkey and among U.S. government analysts as to whether Turkey's Islamists are moderates or radicals, democrats or closet *sharia*-ists, pro-Western or anti-Western. The issue is complicated by the fact that former Prime Minister Necmettin Erbakan's *Refah* (Welfare) Party was banned in 1998 and Erbakan himself has been suspended from politics until 2003. A de facto replacement party, the *Fazilet* (Virtue) Party, has tried to present a more moderate, more pro-Western face than did *Refah;* it even endorsed Turkish membership in the EU, which was anathema to Erbakan. However, a significant segment of the Turkish secular establishment, led by the military, believes *Fazilet* is merely dissimulating its real fundamentalist aims behind a facade of legally safe pro-Western, pro-democracy rhetoric.

When Erbakan was in power, U.S. decisions about how to deal with him had substantive consequences. With the Islamists out of power, issues related to *Fazilet* are more symbolic in nature, mainly about the extent and level of contact. For now, the United States seems to accord *Fazilet* the courtesies it would any European opposition party. Were *Fazilet* closed by the Turkish courts as *Refah* was—and it currently faces charges that could result in its closure—the United States would be critical.

The United States usually treads carefully in the sensitive realm of relations in Turkey between state and religion even when they raise human rights concerns. For example, the United States has avoided direct criticism of the Turkish state's military-driven, hard-nosed policies toward Islamism and Islamic practice. It has not taken a position, for example, on the so-called February 28 process, the military's Western working group, or the Higher Education Council's ban on women's wearing headscarves on university campuses (which, the Turkish establishment believes, reflects and promotes Islamism). Actually a form of state control of religion, Turkish-style secularism does differ from U.S.-style secularism. Some U.S. officials may be pleased the military plays the role of fire wall against fundamentalism—which helps to ensure Turkey's westward orientation—but most would prefer that the military played it in a less activist manner and with greater tolerance for manifestations of Islam and Islamism.

When the United States does venture into areas related to Islamism and Islam, its approach tends to be indirect. *Fazilet* leader Recai Kutan visited Washington in 1999 as his party faced possible court closure on charges of being an illegal stalking-horse ("successor party") for the banned *Refah*. His reception by the assistant secretary of state for European affairs—treatment normally accorded any major European opposition leader—seemed to indicate that the United States sees *Fazilet* as a legitimate part of the system and opposes its closure. It also suggested the United States welcomed and wanted to encourage *Fazilet*'s proclaimed moderation.

Without referring specifically to secularist-Islamist disputes, Clinton appeared to urge the Turkish parliament to support greater freedom of religious expression in speaking of his hope for "a future in which people are free to pursue their beliefs and proclaim their heritage." He philosophized, "When people can celebrate their culture and faith in ways that do not infringe upon the rights of others, moderates do not become extremists, and extremists do not become misguided heroes."

At times the United States has taken a more direct approach. In 1998, Deputy Secretary Talbott publicly took Turkey to task for judicial actions that year—closing *Refah,* banning Erbakan, and removing Istanbul's elected pro-Islamist mayor Tayyip Erdogan from office and banning him from politics. (The State Department also issued critical statements when those rulings were announced.) Talbott's hard-hitting remarks angered the Turkish establishment, and—perhaps mainly for that reason—his criticism was isolated and did not become a recurrent theme in U.S. public diplomacy toward and about Turkey.

U.S. reticence regarding state-versus-religion issues in Turkey makes sense. First of all, a strong Islamist movement, with its inevitable anti-Western themes, is contrary to U.S. interests in Turkey. Second, many pro-U.S. Turks, including liberals, are more sensitive about Islamism—and its potential to subvert the secular nature of the state—than about any other issue. (Since the Erbakan period, the military has ranked Islamism ahead of Kurdish separatism as the "number one" threat to the state.) Although many secularists favor more liberal attitudes—for instance, toward headscarves or even toward Erbakan's political participation—the more uncompromising secularist view associated with current state policy is widespread and extends well beyond the military. Third, the United States has relatively little credibility on these issues among Turkish secularists because it (obviously) lacks their experience of trying to institutionalize Western values in a Muslim-majority culture. Many Turkish secularists are convinced that Islam itself, unlike Christianity, presents intrinsic challenges to the healthy development of democracy and that its practice must be guided by the lay state.

The United States should keep Turkey's Islamist leaders at arm's length, even while defending their right to participate in the democratic process. Washington's ability to affect Turkish politics is limited, but U.S. approval is something most Turkish leaders seek. The United States should refrain from statements or actions that would redound to the benefit of Turkey's Islamist movement or appear to acquiesce in anti-secular, anti-Western goals. Although *Fazilet* projects a more pro-Western image than its proscribed predecessor, the United States should not be too quick to take it at its word. Erbakan, from behind the scenes, is the leading power in the party. Should it become clear over time that Erbakan and the radicals have been eclipsed and that pro-Western, pro-democracy moderates are ascendant in the party, the United States can warm its attitude accordingly. Meanwhile, despite all the handicaps the system has imposed on it, *Fazilet* and the Islamist movement retain a large, if distinctly minority, following. Their ultimate return to power—and an ensuing confrontation between Islamists and military-led secularists like that which occurred in 1997—cannot be ruled out.

STRENGTHENING TURKEY AND BILATERAL TIES:
GENERAL POLICY RECOMMENDATIONS

Because of Turkey's location and the strategic role it plays throughout the region, close bilateral ties are in the U.S. interest. Most important, Turkey is an island of relative stability in a tempestuous sea. Washington thus has good reason to favor its emergence as a regional military and economic power—a process well under way.[24] It is true that a more powerful Turkey is also one more capable of pursuing independent foreign policy initiatives, including some that may not be to Washington's liking. However, the United States can mitigate that possibility through a structure of close security and diplomatic ties.

The United States should establish a high-level commission, on the Gore-Chernomyrdin model, to spur bilateral relations and serve as a clearinghouse for the growing number of "multiagency" bilateral topics, including trade, energy, security, and regional issues, as well as human rights, Greece, and Cyprus. This would assure that high-level attention to Turkey is sustained, that U.S. and Turkish bilateral regional policies are coordinated, and that both Turkish interests and perennial U.S. concerns such as Cyprus and Greek-Turkish relations receive their senior-level due. The commission should meet in Washington at least once a year, ensuring an annual official visit by the Turkish prime minister. Turkey merits this level of attention based on its strategic importance and its domestic uncertainties.

Trips to Turkey should be a regular part of a U.S. president's itinerary, undertaken at least once in a four-year term. The Clinton trip, although initiated for the OSCE summit rather than for bilateral reasons, is a promising beginning. Regular visits of this kind would be a visible and reassuring sign of U.S. support in a highly personal culture, particularly for the many Turks long bothered by their difficulty in attracting visits from prominent U.S. officials. Presidential attention provides the United States some of its best opportunities for reinforcing bilateral bonds and influencing Ankara on a range of issues, including human rights. Turkey's enthusiastic response to President Clinton's trip demonstrates the potential of such visits to transform both the Turkish political landscape and U.S.-Turkish relations, provided presidential declarations are sustained by post-trip, senior-level involvement.

The United States and Turkey should initiate dialogues on counterproliferation and counterterrorism, given Turkey's borders with three terrorism sponsors and proliferators, Syria, Iraq, and Iran. U.S. officials also should invite Turkey to participate in the U.S. ballistic missile defense program. As matters stand, Ankara lacks meaningful missile and missile-defense capabilities to counter the threat from its neighbors.

Turkey's economy is now so large that any support the United States can realistically offer would have only a marginal effect. A marginal effect can nevertheless be a useful one. In that spirit, the United States should implement a package of measures to expand U.S.-Turkish economic ties and assist the Turkish economy in compensation for nine years of Iraqi sanctions. This package might include eased quotas on Turkish textiles and incentives to U.S. businesses to invest in Turkey, particularly in its Kurdish-majority southeast. Washington has a significant stake in the successful development of Turkey's southeast, both because of its impact on overall Turkish stability and because it is the area through which the Baku-Ceyhan pipeline would pass.

The United States also could explore the possibility of a free-trade agreement, as proposed in 1999 by Senator Daniel Moynihan. To stimulate indigenous Turkish economic development, the United States should condition any of these measures on continued Turkish progress in opening its economy, including privatization of the still oversized public sector.

One step the United States should not take is renewing foreign aid. Any U.S. aid package would have minimal impact on the Turkish economy and Turkey's ability to purchase military hardware. Its significance would be outweighed by problems created in U.S.-Turkish and Greek-Turkish relations as representatives in Congress seek to attach Cyprus- or human rights–related conditions to it.

CONCLUSION: USES AND LIMITS OF U.S. INFLUENCE ON TURKEY

Considering how important U.S. support is to Turkey, it is surprising that Washington rarely if ever succeeds in convincing Ankara to do its bidding on those issues that most trouble bilateral ties—Cyprus, Greek-Turkish relations, and human rights. The most famous U.S. effort to pressure Turkey to achieve a major diplomatic goal, the 1975–78 arms embargo, was a colossal failure. By playing on its geostrategic importance—shutting down U.S. bases on its soil—Turkey inflicted pain sufficient to convince the United States to end the embargo. For Washington, the lesson of the embargo was that it is difficult to pressure Turkey on issues of major national interest.

If anything, U.S. ability to press Turkey has probably diminished in recent years, particularly with Turkey's increased prosperity and the ending of foreign aid in 1998. Even before the aid program ended, levels of assistance were steadily shrinking in absolute terms and in economic impact. In 1983, for example, when the era of top-level U.S. assistance to Turkey began, formal aid (that is, military grants and loans and economic support funds) was $700 million—more than 1 percent of Turkey's $50 billion economy. When the aid program reached its peak in 1991 at $850 million (all but $100 million in straight grants), the total was little more than 0.5 percent of Turkey's $140 billion GNP. In the final year of the program, 1997, U.S. aid amounted to $197 million (including only $22 million in grants, the remainder in loans), less than

0.1 percent of Turkey's $200 billion economy—and less than one-tenth of its 1983 value to the Turkish economy.

Today, the major sources of U.S. leverage on Turkey are influence in the international financial institutions (IFIs)—the World Bank and the International Monetary Fund—weapons sales, and support for Turkish diplomatic goals. Together, these factors create marginal but sometimes meaningful influence, inclining Ankara to be supportive of U.S. policies when possible and nonconfrontational about those policies it dislikes. These factors mean little in terms of inducing Turkey to compromise on policies it deems crucial to its national interest, however.

U.S. influence in the IFIs is considerable. Turkey has often turned for help to the IFIs—twice in late 1999 alone. Following the August 1999 earthquake, Ankara secured $420 million in loans from the World Bank. In December 1999, it signed a $4 billion standby loan agreement with the IMF. In both of those instances, the United States is believed to have worked behind the scenes for the most generous allotment and terms possible within the bounds of what could be justified economically. Ankara has healthy respect for—and perhaps even exaggerates—the U.S. role within the IFIs.

Washington's major lever of influence is its security connection to Turkey, the most important aspect of which is Turkish access to U.S. military equipment and know-how. Some 80 percent of Turkey's military inventory consists of U.S.-origin equipment. Yet, as Ankara realizes, it is unlikely that the United States will again significantly curtail these sales for the purpose of forcing policy choices on Turkey, given how lucrative the Turkish arms market is, how miserably the 1975–78 arms embargo failed, and how much geostrategic importance and status Turkey has as a NATO ally. Turkish cognition of these factors limit the leverage Washington derives from arms sales. Occasionally, an arms sale may be rejected by Congress, but that will have little impact overall on Turkish policies; to the extent it does have an effect, it may be opposite to that intended.

In recent years, as the United States alone has stood by Turkey on issues of crucial importance to Turkish national interests—the PKK, the EU, and Baku-Ceyhan—more and more of the Turkish establishment has embraced the importance of close ties with Washington. Even Bülent Ecevit, Washington's longtime critic, now extols the value of U.S. support. Gratitude for Washington's backing has not compelled Turkey to make fundamental policy changes regarding Cyprus, Greek-Turkish relations, or human rights, however, and it will not. Aware that it is the junior partner in bilateral relations, Turkey is on guard not to be bullied. Ankara sees U.S. diplomatic support mainly as functions of Turkey's hosting Operation North Watch (ONW) and of a larger U.S. interest in Turkish stability and cooperation.

One potential lever of influence the United States generally has eschewed is consistent attention from the president and secretary of state. On that score, 1999 was an aberrational year. Demirel and Ecevit each visited Washington and met with Clinton, and Clinton, thanks to the OSCE summit, found his way to Turkey. However, no secretary of state has made a substantive visit to Turkey during the Clinton administration. Madeleine Albright was in Turkey twice in 1999—once on a symbolic visit to inspect earthquake damage, the other time accompanying Clinton to the OSCE summit. Warren Christopher ignored Turkish pleas for a stop in Ankara, despite nearly two dozen trips to neighboring Syria. An exception to the general pattern occurred during the 1990–91 Gulf crisis and war when President George Bush was in constant contact with Turkish president Turgut Özal and Secretary of State James Baker made several trips to Turkey—to positive effect for U.S. interests, as Turkey became a leading supporter of the United States' anti-Iraq effort.

Accumulated experience suggests that U.S. influence may, at most, help convince Turkey to make a concession it is already open to making. Resumption of Cyprus negotiations in December 1999 is a good example. For months, Rauf Denktash had insisted he would not resume talks unless the Greek Cypriots withdrew their candidacy for EU membership and "acknowledged" the existence of the Turkish Republic of Northern Cyprus. He reversed that position in the face of several external incentives given to Turkey. In meetings in Washington and Ankara, Clinton personally appealed to Ecevit for a resumption of Cyprus talks just as Turkey was negotiating a standby agreement with the IMF and receiving strong U.S. backing for its bid for EU candidacy. Most important, the EU, which was to decide on Turkey's candidacy at its December 1999 summit in Helsinki, was also urging Turkey to show flexibility on Cyprus. For all of this, Denktash came around, no doubt as a result of Ankara's importuning.

But the convening of Cyprus talks in early December 1999—just one week before the crucial EU summit—required no major concession of Turkish or Turkish Cypriot interests. No substantive changes in Turkey's or Denktash's approach to the Cyprus problem were demanded or offered. Denktash even refused to meet face to face with his Greek Cypriot counterpart Glafcos Clerides at the New York-based negotiations; instead, UN officials shuttled between rooms conducting "proximity talks." Also per Denktash's wishes, the exchange was publicly described as nonsubstantive and merely laying the groundwork for future rounds.

Despite their limited scope, the Cyprus talks met U.S. and EU minimum requirements. The Clinton administration was satisfied. The EU summit declared Turkey a candidate for membership, after which Denktash agreed to a second round of Cyprus talks early in 2000. And, with happy timing, the IMF and Turkey came to agreement on a standby loan. Without the influence of these factors, there would probably have been no Cyprus dialogue at all, but the price Turkey and Denktash paid, nonsubstantive proximity talks, was minimal.

Use of Incirlik Air Base for ONW, crucial to Washington's Iraq policy, fits into a similar pattern. Contrary to a common impression, Turkish willingness to host the operation serves larger Turkish interests and is not simply a concession to the United States. Certainly Turkish decisionmakers take into account the negative impact on bilateral ties that would result were Turkey to expel the operation. But Turkey also shares the U.S. goal of preventing another heavy flow of Iraqi Kurdish refugees toward its border, which could again include large numbers of PKK infiltrators or subject Turkey to international pressure and criticism if it chooses to block its border.

As an IFI decision on a Turkish application—or a U.S. decision on a Turkish arms sale request—draws close, Turkey is more likely to be responsive to U.S. requests. But Ankara is aware that U.S. support is the result not of American charitable impulses but of Washington's strategic interest in encouraging a Turkey that is stable and Western-aligned. Therefore, Turks do not feel they must compromise on basic national interests—Cyprus, Greece, human rights issues—in order to please the United States. And, as the arms embargo showed at a time when Turkey was weaker, poorer, and more dependent on the United States, Turks are willing to sacrifice for the sake of national interest and pride.

Turkey would make concessions on issues of vital national interest only if it were rewarded with a benefit of greater value that would otherwise be withheld, such as EU membership. The prospect of full EU membership—provided Turkey sees it as a real possibility and is serious about pursuing it—is now the strongest external incentive for changes in its traditional domestic and foreign policies.

As a result of its strong support for Turkey, the United States can usually count on Ankara's taking into account crucial U.S. interests. But Turkey is unlikely to compromise on its own perceived areas of fundamental national interest simply to show itself responsive to U.S. desires. Rather than leverage, the best assurance of Turkish support for U.S. policy initiatives—particularly in an era of growing Turkish power and prosperity—resides in Washington's persistent cultivation of a climate of genuine partnership, mutual interest, and respect. That will continue to be so, barring some dramatic shift in Turkey's fortunes or in the regional or international landscape.

| Notes

Chapter 2

1. See Feroz Ahmad, *The Making of Modern Turkey* (London and New York: Routledge, 1993); Hugh Poulton, *Top Hat, Grey Wolf and Crescent: Turkish Nationalism and the Turkish Republic* (New York: New York University Press, 1997); Nicole Pope and Hugh Pope, *Turkey Unveiled: A History of Modern Turkey* (New York: Overlook Press, 1997); and Erik J. Zürcher, *Turkey: A Modern History* (London and New York: Tauris, 1993).

2. For a detailed analysis of this aspect of Özal's character, see Heath W. Lowry, "Challenges to Turkish Democracy in the Decade of the Nineties," in W. Harris et al., *Challenges to Democracy in the Middle East* (Princeton, N.J.: Weiner, 1997), pp. 89–111.

3. See Heath W. Lowry, "Foreword," in Andrew Mango, *Turkey: The Challenge of a New Role* (Westport, Conn.: Praeger, 1994), p. viii.

4. Yılmaz Esmer, *Devrim, Evrim, Statüko: Türkiye'de Sosyal, Siyasal, Ekonomik Değerler* [Revolution, Evolution, Status Quo: Social, Political, and Economic Values in Turkey] (Istanbul: TESEV, 1999), p. 129.

5. International Monetary Fund, *Turkey: Recent Economic Developments and Selected Issues* (IMF Staff Country Report no. 97/110) (Washington, D.C.: International Monetary Fund, 1997), p. 9.

6. Esmer, *Devrim, Evrim, Statüko;* Yılmaz Esmer, "18 Nisan 1999 Seçimlerinin Analizi" [An Analysis of the April 18, 1999 Elections], a series of five lengthy articles that appeared in the İstanbul daily *Milliyet* between May 2 and 6, 1999.

7. Ibid.

8. Ibid.

9. "Erbakan ve Kaddafi'nin Hikayesi" [Erbakan and Qaddafi's Story], *Hürriyet,* January 23, 1998.

10. Heath W. Lowry, "How Turkish Leaders View America and the World," in P. Zelikow and R. Zoellick, eds., *America and the Muslim Middle East: Memos to a President* (Washington, D.C.: Aspen Institute, 1998), pp. 159–68; Heath W. Lowry, "Critical Strategic Choices in U.S. Policy toward Turkey," in Zelikow and Zoellick, *America and the Muslim Middle East,* pp. 179–91.

11. Sedat Ergin, "Paşa Konuştu" [The General Spoke], *Hürriyet,* March 18, 1999.

12. Lowry, "How Turkish Leaders View America and the World," p. 168.

13. Ibid., p. 163.

14. Sedat Ergin, "Askerden 12 Mesaj" [Twelve Messages from the Military], *Hürriyet,* September 4, 1999.

15. Esmer, *Devrim, Evrim, Statüko,* pp. 42–43.

16. Ibid., pp. 43–44.

17. Ibid., pp. 42–43.

18. Ibid., p. 79.

19. Şükrü Elekdağ, "AB ve Kürt sorunu" [The European Union and the Kurdish Question], *Milliyet,* May 24, 1999; Şükrü Elekdağ, "Büyük ve cesur düşünme" [Big and Brave Thinking], *Milliyet,* June 7, 1999; Şükrü Elekdağ, "Tabuları Yıkalım" [Let's Get Rid of Taboos], *Milliyet,* June 14, 1999; Şükrü Elekdağ, "Kimlik sorunu (1)" [The Identity Question (1)], *Milliyet,* June 21, 1999; Şükrü Elekdağ, "Kimlik sorunu (2)" [The Identity Question (2)], *Milliyet,* June 28, 1999; Şükrü Elekdağ, "PKK Apo'nun idamını neden istiyor" [Why Does the PKK Want Apo to Be Executed?], *Milliyet,* July 5, 1999.

20. Sedat Ergin, "Orduya Haksızlık" [Injustice to the Military], *Hürriyet,* September 5, 1999.

21. Anayasa Mahkemesi and Başkan Ahmet Necdet Sezer, "Anayasa Mahkemesi'nin 37. Kuruluş Günü Törenini Açış Konuşması" [A Speech on the Occasion of the Thirty-seventh Opening of the Constitutional Court], April 26, 1999, Ankara; Yargıtay Birinci Başkan and Doç. Dr. Sami Selçuk, "1999–2000 Adli Yılı Açış Konuşması" [A Speech on the Occasion of the Opening of the Judicial Year 1999–2000], September 6, 1999, Ankara.

CHAPTER 3

1. Arnold Toynbee and Kenneth Kirkwood, *Turkey* (London: Ernest Benn, 1926), p. 272.

2. For the best and most up-to-date books on Turkey's Kurdish challenge, see Henri J. Barkey and Graham E. Fuller, *Turkey's Kurdish Question* (Lanham, Md.: Carnegie/Rowman & Littlefield, 1998); Kemal Kirişci and Gareth M. Winrow, *The Kurdish Question and Turkey* (London: Frank Cass, 1997); and Michael M. Gunter, *The Kurds and the Future of Turkey* (New York: St. Martin's Press, 1997). For an authoritative study of the Kurds, see David McDowell, *A Modern History of the Kurds* (London: Tauris, 1996).

3. For a discussion of earlier missed opportunities for addressing the Kurdish issue in Turkey, see Philip Robins, "The Overlord State: Turkish Policy and the Kurdish Issue," *International Affairs* 69, no. 4 (1993): 657–76.

4. This distinctiveness is based on a combination of language, culture, and self-identity, and in these elements (though not in demography) the Kurds are analogous to the Welsh in Great Britain.

5. For a discussion of Kurdish demographics and a serious attempt to come up with a working figure for Turkey's Kurdish population, see Servet Mutlu, "Ethnic Kurds in Turkey: A Demographic Study," *International Journal of Middle Eastern Studies* 28 (1996): 517–41. Mutlu estimates the Kurdish population at 12.6 percent of the total in 1990, though this figure, based on successive censuses, may be an underestimate. With Kurdish demographic growth greatly exceeding the average for Turkey, using Mutlu's approach, the Kurds were probably around 15 percent of the population by 2000.

6. Barkey and Fuller, *Turkey's Kurdish Question,* pp. 67, 91.

7. Peter Alford Andrews, ed., *Ethnic Groups in the Republic of Turkey* (Wiesbaden: Reichert, 1989), p. 113.

8. The population of Adana grew by some 700,000 as a result of the violence and turmoil in the southeast and has been described as "a bomb waiting to go off." See Cengiz Çandar in *Sabah,* March 5, 1998.

9. Martin van Bruinessen, "The Ethnic Identity of the Kurds," in Andrews, *Ethnic Groups in the Republic of Turkey,* p. 620.

10. Mutlu estimates that about 20 percent of Kurds lived in western Turkey in 1965, this proportion having risen to about one-third by 1990. See Mutlu, "Ethnic Kurds in Turkey," pp. 532–33.

11. The *Independent,* March 16, 1993, noted that Öcalan had apparently dropped his demands for the creation of a separate Kurdish state.

12. Interview with *Turkish Daily News,* November 8, 1994.

13. In a particularly memorable phrase, Bülent Ecevit, currently prime minister, once said that "racially and ethnically, Turkey is as mixed as the American nation." Roundtable meeting at Chatham House, January 24, 1989.

14. In 1992 sources in Ankara were cited by Ismet Imset, a commentator on the Kurdish issue, as saying that the current insurgency represented the twenty-eighth Kurdish rebellion against the state.

15. For a discussion of economic interests and the perpetuation of civil wars see David Keen, *The Economic Functions of Civil Wars* (London: IISS Adelphi Paper no. 320, 1998).

16. *Turkish Probe* no. 96, September 23, 1994.

17. For insights into the role of ultranationalists in undertaking attacks on ASALA camps and personnel, see *Turkish Daily News,* November 23, 1996, and *Turkish Daily News,* January 28, 1997.

18. Human Rights Watch, *Weapons Transfers and Violations of the Laws of War in Turkey* (New York: Human Rights Watch, 1995), p. 52.

19. Interview with Jonathan Sugden, Human Rights Watch, London, July 7, 1999.

20. For an excellent discussion of the notion of strong and weak states with much relevance to Turkey, see Nazih Ayubi, *Overstating the Arab State* (London: Tauris, 1995).

21. Since 1993 and the banning of the PKK in Germany, elite opinion in Europe has been suspicious of the PKK. Nevertheless, the organization and its leader, Abdullah Öcalan, subsequently missed a historic opportunity to engage with European elites during Öcalan's three-month stay in Rome between October 1998 and January 1999.

22. *Guardian,* December 22, 1992.

23. Israel did this both through high-level statements distancing itself from the Turkish stance and through the adoption of certain measures such as limiting routine exercises near the Syrian border in order to reassure Damascus. See, for example, the statements of Prime Minister Benyamin Netanyahu and Defense Minister Yitzhak Mordechai quoted in AFP and AP reports respectively in *Jordan Times,* October 5, 1998.

24. For the best work on the origins of the PKK up to 1992, see Ismet G. Imset, *The PKK* (Ankara: Turkish Daily News Publications, 1992).

25. This is the first of a number of references to the Palestinians in this chapter. One reason for bringing up the topic is to explore some of the similarities between the Palestinians and the Kurds, which are illuminating for the purpose of analysis. Like all analogies, however, the parallel between the two cases should not be pursued too far. Indeed, there are a number of significant differences between the Palestinians and the Kurds of Turkey. These include the status of the Palestinian "occupied territories," the position of the Israeli army as an occupation force being fundamentally different from the status of the Turkish military in areas regarded as Kurdish in southeastern Turkey but still intrinsically part of the Turkish state, and also the nature of the PLO as an umbrella political organization that includes a number of ideologically differing constituent groups and hence must be considered to be more pluralist in its composition than is the PKK.

26. The seven expelled were Mahmut Alinak, Mehmet Ali Eren, Adnan Okman, Ismail Hakki Onal, Kenan Sonmez, Salih Sumer, and Ahmet Türk.

27. Hasan Cemal, *Sabah,* August 9, 1994.

28. This is an irony, as Öcalan does not come from a patrician family, while the PKK has often sought to subvert the established social order in the southeast.

29. AP report by Selcan Hacaoglu, May 31, 1999, which quoted Öcalan as saying, "For peace and brotherhood I am ready to serve the Turkish state, and I believe that for this end I must remain alive."

30. In renaming both organizations, the congress omitted the word "Kurdistan" from both names, thus, the Kurdistan National Liberation Front (ERNK) has become the Democratic People's Union. See "Our Extraordinary 7, Congress Is a New Beginning for Our Party and People," press communiqué of the PKK, February 9, 2000.

31. A model for such a disengagement might be Aryeh Deri, the leader of the ultraorthodox, Oriental Jewish party Shas in Israel. Deri was forced to relinquish his leadership of Shas as the price of the party's entry into the current coalition government led by Ehud Barak.

32. *International Herald Tribune,* January 19, 2000.

33. *International Herald Tribune,* March 31, 1992.

34. Çiller interviewed by Cengiz Çandar in *Sabah,* October 31, 1994, reprinted in *British Broadcasting Corporation/Summary of World Broadcasts/Eastern Europe,* November 4, 1994.

35. *Briefing* no. 1256, August 23, 1999.

36. For a discussion of its limitations with respect to the PKK, see *Briefing* no. 1255, August 16, 1999.

37. "Turkey: Earthquake Politics," *Oxford Analytica Daily Brief,* August 31, 1999.

38. Hamit Bozarslan, "Political Crisis and the Kurdish Issue in Turkey," in Robert Olson, ed., *The Kurdish Nationalist Movement in the 1990s* (Lexington: University Press of Kentucky, 1996), p. 142.

39. These figures were taken from a press conference by Akin Birdal of the Turkish Human Rights Association and reproduced in the *Turkish Daily News,* January 7, 1998.

40. The former MPs still imprisoned: Hatip Dicle (Diyarbakır); Orhan Dogan (Sirnak); Selim Sadak; Ahmet Türk (Mardin); Selim Yurttas and Leyla Zana (Diyarbakır). Two other deputies, Mahmut Alinak (Sirnak), an independent, and Serri Sakik (Mus) also were jailed at the same time but received lesser sentences and have since been released.

41. The six former MPs in de facto exile: Zubeyir Aydar (Siirt); Naif Gunes (Siirt); Remzi Kartal (Van); Mahmut Kilinc (Adiyaman); Nizamettin Toguc (Batman); and Ali Yigit (Mardin).

42. Elçi is a former CHP minister under Ecevit in the late 1970s, while Firat was first elected to parliament on a DYP slate.

43. For example, in December 1991 Inönü was quoted as saying: "'The Kurdish citizens' cultural identity must be recognized in full. That is, we must acknowledge the reality that some of our citizens are not Turks but Kurds who belong to the Republic of Turkey. This should not create a sensitivity. It is a nationalist phenomenon that exists in many states. So what is important is to recognize the cultural identity of the Kurds, who should enjoy all the rights available to Turkish citizens." Interview with *al-Hayat,* December 9, 1991, reprinted in *Foreign Broadcast Information Service,* December 17, 1991.

44. This was an important change in the national security policy document formally adopted by the National Security Council on October 31, 1997. See *Turkish Daily News,* November 6, 1997.

45. For an excellent discussion of the restrictions on the use of the Kurdish language in different fields, see Human Rights Watch, *Violations of Free Expression in Turkey* (New York: Human Rights Watch, 1999), pp. 88–110.

CHAPTER 4

1. For a comprehensive discussion of the import-substituting industrialization process in Turkey and the crisis of the late 1970s, see Henri Barkey, *The State and the Industrialization Crisis in Turkey* (Boulder, Colo.: Westview Press, 1990).

2. For detailed evidence concerning the size of adjustment assistance provided to Turkey during the early 1980s, see Colin Kirkpatrick and Ziya Öniş, "Turkey," in P. Mosley et al., eds., *Aid and Power*, Vol. 2. (London: Routledge, 1991), pp. 1–29.

3. On the characterization and examination of different facets of Turkish neoliberalism, see Tosun Arıcanlı and Dani Rodrik, eds., *The Political Economy of Turkey: Debt, Adjustment and Sustainability* (London: Macmillan, 1990); and Ziya Öniş, *State and Market: The Political Economy of Turkey in Comparative Perspective* (İstanbul: Boğaziçi University Press, 1998). Specifically on the dynamics of export expansion in the post-1980 period, see Robin Barlow and Fikret Şenses, "The Turkish Export Boom: Just Reward or Just Lucky?" *Journal of Development Economics* 48 (1995): 111–33.

4. On the Turkish privatization experience and its limitations see Merih Celasun and İsmail Arslan, "State-owned Enterprises and Privatization in Turkey: Policy, Performance and Reform Experience, 1985–1995," ERF Working Paper no. 9709, Economic Research Forum, Cairo, Egypt, 1997.

5. On the underlying reasons for the inability of policymakers to pursue the aggressive real devaluation policy of the early 1980s, see Tosun Arıcanlı and Dani Rodrik, "An Overview of Turkey's Experience with Economic Liberalization and Structural Adjustment," *World Development* 18, no. 10 (1990): 1343–50.

6. For detailed evidence on Turkey's foreign trade performance, see Undersecretariat of Foreign Trade, *Foreign Trade of Turkey, 1998,* July 1999. Concerning the limitations of Turkish export performance in terms of its ability to diversify exports, see Ismail Arslan and Merih Celasun, "Sustainability of Industrial Exporting in a Liberalizing Economy: The Turkish Experience," in Gerry K. Helleiner, ed., *Manufacturing for Export in the Developing World* (London: Routledge, 1995), pp. 131–66.

7. For a concise discussion of South Korea's and Taiwan's ability to combine an export boom with an investment boom, see Stephan Haggard, "Lessons from Successful Reforms: Korea and Taiwan," *Economic Reform Today* 1, no. 2 (1996); and Yılmaz Akyuz and Charles Gore, "The Investment-Profit Nexus in East Asian Industrialization," *UNCTAD Discussion Papers* no. 91 (October 1994).

8. Gini coefficient as a key indicator of income inequality has been estimated as 0.55 in 1963, 0.51 in 1973, and 0.50 in 1994, pointing toward persistently high income inequality. See Süleyman Özmucur, *Türkiye'de Gelir*

Dağılımı, Vergi Yükü ve Makroekonomik Göstergeler [Income Distrubtion, Tax Burden and Macroeconomic Indicators in Turkey] (İstanbul: Boğaziçi University Press and Devlet İstatistik Enstitüsü [State Institute of Statistics], 1996); *1994 Hanehalkı Gelir ve Tüketim Harcamaları. Anket Sonuçları ve Gelir Dağılımı* [Results of the Household Income and Expenditure Survey for 1994 and Income Distribution] (Ankara: Devlet İstatistik Enstitüsü, 1996).

9. For a documentation of similar tendencies in Latin America, see Graham Bird and Ann Helwege, "Can Neoliberalism Survive in Latin America?" *Millennium: Journal of International Studies* 26, no. 1 (1997): 31–56; and UNCTAD, *Trade and Development Report, 1999* (Geneva: United Nations Conference on Trade and Development, 1999).

10. For a comprehensive coverage of political dynamics involving the military interlude and the subsequent stage-by-stage return to democracy, see Metin Heper, ed., *The Strong State and Economic Interest Groups: The Post-1980 Turkish Experience* (Hawthorne, N.Y.: Walter de Gruyter, 1991). For another good discussion of the military interlude and the subsequent Motherland Party (ANAP) governments under Özal's leadership from a political economy perspective, see John Waterbury, "Export-led Growth and the Center-Right Coalition in Turkey," *Comparative Politics* 24, no. 2 (1992): 127–45.

11. For a comparison of the Turkish, Mexican, and Asian financial crises, see Ziya Öniş and Ahmet Faruk Aysan, "Neo-liberal Globalization, the Nation State, and Financial Crises in the Semi-Periphery: A Comparative Analysis," *Third World Quarterly* 30, no. 1 (2000): 119–39.

12. For a strong defense of the argument concerning the premature nature of capital account liberalization in Turkey, see Dani Rodrik, "Premature Liberalization, Incomplete Stabilization: The Özal Decade in Turkey," Center for Economic Policy Research Working Paper, no. 402, London, 1990.

13. On the consequences of financial globalization for the Turkish economy, see Faruk Selçuk, "A Brief Account of the Turkish Economy," in Libby Rittenberg, ed. *The Political Economy of Turkey in the Post-Soviet Era: Going West and Looking East?* (Westport Conn.: Praeger, 1998), pp. 17–36; and Nurhan Yentürk, "Short-term Capital Inflows and Their Impact on Macro-economic Structure: Turkey in the 1990s," *Developing Economies,* 37, no. 1 (1999): 89–113.

14. For a detailed documentation of the nature of fiscal disequilibrium in the Turkish economy and its relationship to the financial crisis of 1994, see Fatih Özatay, "The Lessons from the 1994 Crisis in Turkey: Public Debt (Mis) Management and Confidence Crisis," *Yapı Kredi Economic Review* 7 (1997): 21–38; and İzak Atiyas and Şerif Sayın, "A Political Economy Perspective on Turkish Budget Deficits," *Boğaziçi Journal* 12, no. 1 (1998): 55–79.

15. For a valuable contribution concerning the high degree of labor market flexibility in Turkey, see Fikret Şenses, "Labor Market Response to Structural

Adjustment and Institutional Pressures: The Turkish Case," *METU Studies in Development* 21, no. 3 (1994): 405–48.

16. The share of wages and salaries in total factor incomes appears to have dropped from 36.8 percent in 1992 and 35.1 percent in 1993 to 26.5 percent in 1994. See Özmucur, *Türkiye'de Gelir Dağılımı.*

17. The annual surveys undertaken by the Istanbul Chamber of Industry concerning the productivity performance and profitability of the five hundred largest industrial establishments in Turkey reveal a striking pattern. A progressively bigger share of total profits of the largest industrial corporations in recent years has been originating from "nonindustrial," namely financial, activities. Profits derived from "nonindustrial activities" or interest income have accounted for 51.7 percent of total profits of such companies in 1997 and for 87.7 percent in 1998. Clearly, the ability to lend to the public sector at high interest provides an important mechanism of flexibility for large industrial firms in the short run, but it is inefficient for the economy as a whole from a longer-term perspective. For evidence concerning this issue, see Istanbul Chamber of Industry, *Türkiye'nin 500 Büyük Sanayi Kuruluşu* [Turkey's 500 Largest Industrial Establishments] (İstanbul: İstanbul Sanayi Odası Yayını, 1999).

18. The unusually large gray or informal economy in Turkey by OECD standards is a reflection of cross-border smuggling and the vibrant drug trade as well as widespread tax evasion due to the inadequate tax collection capacity of the state. The tax reform of 1998 has been attempting to address these issues by reducing tax rates and expanding tax discipline. Estimates of the gray economy vary depending on definitions and coverage. However, typical estimates of the size of the gray economy appear to be in the region of 20–30 percent of GDP. For a good, concise discussion of the informal economy in Turkey, see United Nations, *Human Development Report: Turkey* (Ankara: United Nations Development Program, 1997). On the limitations of the Turkish tax system and the nature of the recent reform process, see James Chan-Lee, "Tax Reform in Turkey Since the 1980s," *Yapı Kredi Economic Review* 9, no. 1 (1998): 43–61.

19. For an elaboration of the argument concerning the limitations on Turkey's ability to manage its domestic debts given the small size of the capital market, see Hasan Ersel and Ercan Kumcu, "İstikrar Programı ve Kamu Dengesi," in *TÜSİAD Türkiye için Orta Vadeli İstikrar Politikaları* [Medium-term Stabilization Policies for Turkey] (İstanbul: TÜSİAD Yayınları, 1996), pp. 171–84.

20. For evidence concerning the serious increase in the deficits of social security institutions in Turkey in the second half of the 1990s and the underlying causes of this process, see Oktar Türel, "Restructuring the Public Sector in Post-1980 Turkey: An Assessment," METU Economic Research Center Working Papers in Economics no. 99/6, Middle East Technical University, Ankara, Turkey, 1999.

21. The Russian Federation has emerged as the fifth major market for Turkish exports in the second half of the 1990s, reaching a peak in 1997 with a share of 7.8 percent in total Turkish exports. The Russian Federation managed to retain its relative position in 1998. The share of the Russian market in Turkish exports, however, dropped to 5.0 percent during the same year. Prior to the Russian crisis, the number of Russian tourists reached a peak of one million per year, with a sharp decline thereafter. For evidence on these issues, see Undersecretariat of Foreign Trade, *Foreign Trade of Turkey, 1998,* July 1999.

22. For an elaboration of the argument by Ajay Chibber (the World Bank economist responsible for Turkey) that Turkey has adjusted better to external shocks than many other emerging markets in the latter part of the 1990s, see Ajay Chibber, "Emerging Markets: Is Turkey Different?" *İktisat, İşletme ve Finans* 14, no. 155 (1999): 22–32.

23. The human development index is a composite index developed by the United Nations, which attempts to measure performance with respect to several indicators including per capita income level, degree of relative income inequality, and capacity to alleviate absolute poverty. For a detailed elaboration and measurement of the index, see United Nations, *Human Development Report, 1999* (New York: Oxford University Press, 1999).

24. For a penetrating discussion concerning the importance of transparency for the efficient functioning of the Turkish economy in general, and for improvement of public sector performance in particular, see İzak Atiyas, "Governance, Transparency, and Economic Development," paper presented at the Boğazici University Center for European Studies conference titled "Turkey in the EU: A Question of Image or Governance?" Boğazici University, İstanbul, 1999.

25. An important issue that needs to be emphasized, however, is that the current coalition government rests on a precarious balance. DSP, the major partner in the coalition, is thoroughly dominated by its leader, Bülent Ecevit, who is an old man in the final stages of his career. Given that no serious contenders exist within the party for the prime ministerial position, a serious leadership vacuum in the post-Ecevit era is certainly a possibility. This, in turn, might be a source of political instability.

26. On the advantages provided by NAFTA to the Mexican reform process, see Pedro Aspe, *Economic Transformation: The Mexican Way* (Cambridge, Mass.: MIT Press, 1993).

27. For a valuable discussion of the customs union agreement with Europe from a broad historical perspective, see Canan Balkır, "The Customs Union and Beyond," in Rittenberg, *The Political Economy of Turkey in the Post-Soviet Era.*

28. For detailed analyses of the complex issues and interests surrounding "pipeline politics," see Gareth Winrow, "Pipeline Politics and Turkey: A New Great Game in Euroasia?" paper presented at the conference titled "Russia-China–Central

Asia: From Geo-politics to Geo-economics in Eurasia," organized by the Center for Euro-Asian Studies, Reading University, England, 1998; and Geoffrey Kemp, *Energy Superbowl: Strategic Politics and the Persian Gulf and Caspian Basins* (Washington, D.C.: Nixon Center for Peace and Freedom, 1997).

29. The information concerning Turkish-U.S. economic relations has been taken from the two recent reports published by Dış Ekonomik İlişkiler Konseyi [The Council on Foreign Economic Relations], "Turkish-U.S. Economic Relations" (İstanbul: Dış Ekonomik İlişkiler Konseyi, November 1998 and September 1999).

CHAPTER 5

1. John P. MacKenzie, review of Rodney A. Smolla, *Free Speech in an Open Society, New York Times Book Review,* July 26, 1992.

2. Publisher's synopsis, "Rodney A. Smolla's Free Speech in an Open Society," websites of Amazon.com and BN.com.

3. James A. Baker III, *The Politics of Diplomacy* (New York: Putnam, 1995), p. 282.

4. Ibid.

5. Reşat Kasaba, "Kemalist Certainties and Modern Ambiguities," in Sibel Bozdogan and Reşat Kasaba, eds., *Rethinking Modernity and National Identity in Turkey* (Seattle: University of Washington Press, 1997), p. 24.

6. For the full text of President Johnson's letter, see *Middle East Journal* (Summer 1996): 386–93.

7. Dankwart A. Rostow, *Turkey: A Forgotten Ally* (New York: Council on Foreign Relations), p. 95.

8. Metin Toker, *Demokrasimizin İsmet Paşalı Yıllari, 1944–1973* [The Years of Our Democracy with General Ismet (Inönü), 1944–1973] (Ankara: Bilgi Yayınevi, 1991), pp. 195, 211.

9. Çetin Yetkin, *Türkiye'de Askeri Darbeler ve Amerika* [The Military Coups in Turkey and America] (Ankara: Ümit Yayıncılık, 1995), p. 199.

10. Ibid., p. 200

11. İsmail Cem, *Tarih Açisindan 12 Mart* [March 12 from the Angle of History], 3rd ed. (Istanbul: Cem Yayinlari, 1980), p. 299.

12. Ibid., p. 300.

13. Cengiz Çandar, "Postmodern Darbe" [Postmodern Coup], *Sabah,* June 28, 1997.

14. Genelkurmay Başkanlığı, *Güncel Konular* [Main Issues] (Ankara: Genelkurmay Başkanlığı [General Staff Publishing House], 1999), pp. 10–11. See also Evren Değer, "TSK'ya göre ABD 'sabıkalı'" [According to the Turkish Armed Forces, the USA Is the Culprit], *Radikal,* November 23, 1999; Fehmi Koru, "Change, Little by Little," *Turkish Daily News,* November 25, 1999; Nazli

Ilıcak, "Türk Silahli Kuvvetleri'nin Broşürü" [The Turkish Armed Forces' Brochure], *Yeni Şafak,* December 1, 1999.

15. Richard Perle, "A Turkish Story: The First Annual Robert-Strausz-Hupe Lecture," *Foreign Policy Research Institute Wire* 7, no. 11 (September 1999): 3.

16. Sabri Yirmibeşoğlu, *Askeri ve Siyasi Anılarım* [My Military and Political Memoirs] (Istanbul: Nisan, 1999), p. 140.

17. General Kemal Yavuz (ret.), Durum [Situation] Programı, Kanal D (Turkish private TV channel), February 6, 1998.

18. Yirmibeşoğlu, *Askeri ve Siyasi Amlarım,* p. 54.

19. Ibid., p. 456.

20. Ibid., p. 139.

21. Harun Kazaz, "Turkey Fires a Policy Warning Flare in Washington Conference," *Turkish Daily News,* May 8, 1999.

22. Nur Batur, "Soysal'dan Çekiç Güç için Ilk Uyarı" [First Warning from Soysal for the Poised Hammer], *Milliyet,* September 12, 1994.

23. *Türkiye,* June 23, 1995.

24. *Milliyet,* August 27, 1992.

25. *Milliyet,* December 19, 1992.

26. Örsan Kunter Öymen, "Çekiç Güç Savaşa Götürür" [Poised Hammer Leads to War], *Milliyet,* July 18, 1991.

27. *Cumhuriyet,* March 31, 1995.

28. Baskin Oran, *Kalkık Horoz: Çekiç Güç ve Kürt Devleti* [Hammer Up: Poised Hammer and Kurdish State] (Ankara: Bilgi, 1996), p. 13.

29. Rostow, *Turkey: A Forgotten Ally,* p. 19.

30. Robert Litwak, "Rogue States and US Foreign Policy: Containment after Cold War" (unpublished manuscript), p. 162.

31. Strobe Talbott, "Turgut Özal Memorial Lecture: US-Turkish Relations in an Age of Interdependence," address to the Washington Institute for Near East Policy, Washington, D.C., October 14, 1998.

32. Perle, "A Turkish Story," pp. 2–3.

33. Remarks by the president in address to the Turkish Grand National Assembly, White House Office of the Press Secretary, November 15, 1999.

34. Remarks by the president at Quandt Lecture, Georgetown University, White House Office of the Press Secretary, November 8, 1999.

35. Press briefing by National Security Adviser Sandy Berger, White House Office of the Press Secretary, November 12, 1999.

CHAPTER 6

1. This account, as with other episodes I was involved in and describe in this chapter, is based on personal recollections supplemented by fragmentary notes and discussions with other U.S. officials who were involved in the events recounted.

2. These issues were discussed in four meetings between Secretary of State Baker and President Özal, and on a number of occasions between Özal and me, between August 1990 and January 1991.

3. I first heard the term in a luncheon speech by General Cevik Bir, then deputy chief of the Turkish General Staff, at a conference of the New Atlantic Initiative in Istanbul, May 3, 1998.

4. The figures for tourists come from the Ministry of Tourism, those of students in the United States from the Turkish embassy in Washington.

5. There are many American ethnic advocacy groups. Prominent Greek-American organizations include the National Coordinated Effort of Hellenes and the World Council of Hellenes Abroad. Prominent Armenian-American orgnanizations include the Armenian Assembly of America and the Armenian National Committee. Active among Jewish groups are the American Israel Public Affairs Committee and the American Jewish Committee.

6. Before the National Press Club, Washington, D.C., January 6, 2000.

7. Figures supplied by the Turkish embassy in Washington.

8. Many Americans both inside and outside the U.S. government resent the Turkish term, considering it an attack on American citizens of ethnic background and implying they should not be able to exercise their democratic rights to lobby their government.

9. These figures have been supplied by senior Turkish officials involved in the effort.

10. This document is invariably a subject of significant of bureaucratic dispute among and within Washington agencies; in recent years its tone has become more direct and tougher on Turkey's human rights performance.

CHAPTER 7

1. Henry Kissinger, *Years of Renewal* (New York: Simon & Schuster, 1999).

2. American Hellenic Educational Progressive Association, *1999 Greek American Policy Statements,* March 1, 1999, http://www.ahepa.org/policy/gaps.

3. Yusuf Kanli, "Federation Shelved, Turks Want Two-State Settlement on Cyprus," *Turkish Daily News,* January 18, 1998.

4. U.S. Department of State, "Background Notes: Cyprus, October 1998," October 1998.

5. Theodore Couloumbis, "Strategic Consensus in Greek Domestic and Foreign Policy since 1974," *Thesis: A Journal of Foreign Policy Issues,* no. 4 (Winter 1998), http://www.mfa.gov.tr. *Thesis* is a publication of the Ministry of Foreign Affairs, Athens. See also Theodore A. Couloumbis, *The United States, Greece, and Turkey* (New York: Praeger, 1983).

6. Philip H. Gordon, "Storms in the Med Blow towards Europe," *World Today,* February 1998.

CHAPTER 8

1. Holbrooke, who left his assistant secretary post early in 1996, later claimed that all this happened according to plan. "Soon after we [Grossman and Holbrooke] started our new jobs . . . we sat down to discuss what Turkey meant for us in the post-Cold War era," he said. "We developed a new concept . . . fully backed by the White House and Pentagon, that Turkey was the new front state [sic] for the West, and in that sense, she had taken up the role of Germany during the Cold War." Quoted from pp. 40–41 of Yasemin Congar, "The State of Turkish-American Dialogue," *Private View* 3, no. 7 (Spring 1999): 40–46.

2. See, for example, U.S. Department of State daily press briefing transcript, May 14, 1997.

3. Transcript of press remarks by Secretary Albright during visit by Foreign Minister Valdis Birkavs of Latvia, June 13, 1997, as released by the Office of the Spokesman, U.S. Department of State.

4. Quoted from p. 48 of Malik Mufti, "Daring and Caution in Turkish Foreign Policy," *Middle East Journal* 52, no. 1 (Winter 1998): 32–50.

5. See "'Current Issues' as Seen by the Turkish Military," *Mideast Mirror,* February 9, 2000. Under the title "Main Issues," this general staff document is discussed in detail elsewhere in this book, in chapter five.

6. "ABD'ye Kıbrıs Eleştirisi" [Cyprus Criticism Directed at the U.S.], *Cumhuriyet,* September 15, 1999.

7. "After the Summits—The Future of U.S.-Turkish Relations," speech delivered by Antony Blinken, special assistant to the president and senior director for European affairs at the National Security Council, at The Washington Institute for Near East Policy, Washington, D.C., December 2, 1999.

8. Uri Savir, *The Process: 1,100 Days that Changed the Middle East* (New York: Vintage Books, 1999), p. 279; and Itamar Rabinovich, *The Brink of Peace: The Israeli-Syrian Negotiations* (Princeton, N.J.: Princeton University Press, 1998), p. 223.

9. Duygu Bazoglu Sezer, "Post–Cold War Turkish-Russian Relations: From Adversity to 'Virtual Rapprochement,'" in Alan Makovsky and Sabri Sayari, eds., *Changing Dynamics in Turkish Foreign Policy* (Washington, D.C.: Washington Institute for Near East Policy, forthcoming 2000).

10. In 1996, a leading Turkish intelligence official startled his audience at a seminar in Washington by labeling Russia the "main source" of anti-Turkish terrorism, including the PKK. See "The Soref Symposium: Fighting Terror, Waging Peace: Twin Challenges for Democracies and Peacemakers, May 20–21, 1996," Washington Institute for Near East Policy, Washington, D.C., p. 32.

11. From remarks by President Clinton at the signing ceremony for the Baku-Ceyhan and Trans-Caspian Gas Pipeline Protocol, Istanbul, November 18, 1999.

12. Turkey's willingness to view Russia's 1999 assault on Chechnya as a Russian "internal" problem (despite much popular support for the Muslim Chechens among Turks) probably played well with the U.S. government. See Stephen Kinzer, "Turkey Faces a Quandary on Rebellions by Its Friends," *New York Times,* November 28, 1999.

13. See "Washington Summit Communique Issued by the Heads of State and Government Participating in the Meeting of the North Atlantic Council in Washington, D.C. on 24th April 1999," paragraph 9(d) in "The Reader's Guide to the NATO Summit in Washington: 23–25 April, 1999," p. 16, http://www.nato.int/ docu/home.htm.

14. See "Annex III: European Council Declaration on Strengthening the Common European Policy on Security and Defense," appended to "Presidency Conclusions: Cologne European Council, 3 and 4 June 1999," press release, Vienna, June 4, 1999—Nr. 150/99 (Presse), p. 28. It should be noted that the EU itself refers to its effort to develop autonomous defense capability as its "Common European Security and Defense Policy (CESDP)." The initiative within NATO is properly called "ESDI," and outsiders often refer to the EU-only initiative also as "ESDI." For the sake of simplicity, I (an outsider) refer here to both as "ESDI." Turkish concerns about ESDI and CESDP are similar.

15. See, for example, Douglas Barrie and Luke Hill, "Non-EU Members May Be Included in Military Fold," *Defense News,* February 28, 2000, p. 1; and Lale Sariibrahimoglu, "Europe Signals Democratization of Military as Condition for Full Integration into ESDI," *Turkish Daily News,* February 25, 2000 (Internet edition), http://www.turkishdailynews.com.

16. Tamar Gabelnick, William D. Hartung, and Jennifer Washburn, "Arming Repression: U.S. Arms Sales to Turkey during the Clinton Administration—A Joint Report of the World Policy Institute and the Federation of American Scientists," World Policy Institute, New York, October 1999, p. 1.

17. Richard Holbrooke, press conference, Ankara, February 21, 1995.

18. Strobe Talbott, "U.S.-Turkish Relations in an Age of Interdependence," Turgut Özal Memorial Lecture, delivered under the auspices of the Washington Institute for Near East Policy, Washington, D.C., October 14, 1998. (Full text can be found on the Internet at http://www.washingtoninstitute.org.)

19. "Report on Allegations of Human Rights Abuses by the Turkish Military and on the Situation in Cyprus," typescript prepared and issued by the State Department, "submitted in compliance with the congressional requirement as set forth in Public Law 103–306—August 23, 1994," p. 23.

20. Umit Enginsoy, "U.S. Rejection on Turkish Debt Could Complicate Arms Sales," *Defense News,* October 18, 1999.

21. Stephen Kinzer, "Between Strategic Interest and Democratic Imperative," *Private View* 3, no. 7 (Spring 1999): 48–54. Quote is from p. 49.

22. Remarks by the president at Quandt Lecture, Georgetown University, White House Office of the Press Secretary, November 8, 1999.

23. Turkey's decision to become a candidate for the secretary-generalship of the Islamic Conference Organization in mid-2000 was surprising and unprecendented. It also had little prospect of success. Given Turkey's distant hope of actually winning the job, Ankara most likely undertook the initiative as a statement on behalf of moderate Islam, demonstrating that it is unapologetic about its own approach to Islam and, if it is able to garner some votes (say from other Turkic states), as a show of some strength. If Turkey is starting to take it seriously, it would mark a significant policy departure.

24. See Alan Makovsky, "The New Activism in Turkish Foreign Policy," *SAIS Review* 19, no. 1 (Winter-Spring 1999): 88–119.

Index

About the Contributors

Morton Abramowitz is a senior fellow at The Century Foundation. He was assistant secretary of state for intelligence and research (1985–89) and ambassador to Turkey (1989–91). He also was president of the Carnegie Endowment for International Peace (1991–97). He is the author of numerous articles on a wide range of foreign policy issues.

Cengiz Çandar is a political columnist for the Turkish daily *Sabah* and has worked for other major Turkish newspapers and as a contributor to the Lebanese press. He was special adviser to President Turgut Özal of Turkey (1991–93) and is a founding member of the New Democracy Movement in Turkey. Formerly a public policy scholar at the Woodrow Wilson International Center in Washington, D.C., he is now a senior fellow at the U.S. Institute of Peace. He is the author of six books in Turkish, mainly on Middle East politics.

Heath W. Lowry is the Atatürk Professor of Ottoman and Modern Turkish Studies at Princeton University, where he was chair of the Department of Near East Studies (1994–97). An Ottoman historian by training, his interest in contemporary Turkey stems from his longtime residence in the country (thirteen years). He is the author of several books on Ottoman history and numerous articles on a wide range of topics dealing with all periods of Ottoman and Turkish history.

Alan Makovsky is a senior fellow at the Washington Institute for Near East Policy, Washington, D.C., where he specializes in Turkish and Middle Eastern affairs. A former State Department official, he is the author of numerous articles on contemporary Turkish politics and related U.S. policy issues.

ZIYA ÖNIŞ is a professor of international political economy at Koç University in Istanbul. He was previously a professor of economics and international affairs at Boğaziçi University, Istanbul. His primary fields of interest are comparative and international political economy and political economy of development, on which he has published numerous articles in different journals.

PHILIP ROBINS is a university lecturer in politics and a fellow of St. Antony's College, Oxford, where he has spent the past five years. Before that he was head of the Middle East program at the Royal Institute of International Affairs at Chatham House in London. He is the author of *Turkey and the Middle East* (Pinter/RIIA, 1991) and has just finished a book on Turkish foreign policy.

M. JAMES WILKINSON had an active role in U.S.-Greek-Turkish affairs as deputy assistant secretary of state for Europe and U.S. special Cyprus coordinator (1985–89). He also was engaged in Cyprus issues at the UN as deputy U.S. representative to the UN Security Council with the rank of ambassador (1989–90). He consulted (1996–98) for the Carnegie Commission on Preventing Deadly Conflict, which published his report on the area in June 1998.